Knowledge and Human Interests

KNOWLEDGE
AND HUMAN INTERESTS ,

by Jürgen Habermas

Translated by Jeremy J. Shapiro

Beacon Press   Boston

Contents

Preface

I am undertaking a historically oriented attempt to reconstruct the prehistory of modern positivism with the systematic intention of analyzing the connections between knowledge and human interests. In following the process of the dissolution of epistemology, which has left the philosophy of science in its place, one makes one's way over abandoned stages of reflection. Retreading this path from a perspective that looks back toward the point of departure may help to recover the forgotten experience of reflection. That we disavow reflection is positivism.

The analysis of the connection of knowledge and interest should support the assertion that a radical critique of knowledge is possible only as social theory. This idea is implicit in Marx's theory of society, even though it cannot be gathered from the self-understanding of Marx or of Marxism. Nevertheless I have not gone into the objective context in which the development of philosophy from Hegel to Nietzsche took place. Instead I have limited myself to following immanently the movement of thought. This has its logic, for only at the price of dilettantism could I anticipate a social theory at which I should first like to arrive through the self-reflection of science.[1] Now the first step in that direction has been taken. Thus this investigation cannot claim more than the role of a prolegomenon.

I first expounded the systematic perspectives guiding this investigation in my Frankfurt inaugural address of June, 1965, published as an appendix to the present volume.[2] The section on positivism, pragmatism, and historicism goes back to lectures in Heidelberg in the winter semester of 1963–64. Without my discussions with Karl-Otto Apel, which extend back to the time of my university studies, without his suggestions and disagreements, this theoretical framework would never have found its present form.[3]

In this framework psychoanalysis occupies an important place as an example. It seems to me necessary to state that my acquaintance with it is limited to the study of Freud's writings; I cannot draw upon the practical experiences of an analysis. Nevertheless I have learned much from the Wednesday discussions of the associates of the Sigmund-Freud-Institut that took place under the direction of Alexander Mitscherlich. I owe thanks to Alfred Lorenzer, who gave me access to the manuscript of his study of the methodological role of understanding in psychoanalysis. This manuscript has now been published in two parts by Suhrkamp Verlag as *Kritik des psychoanalytischen Symbolbegriffs* and *Sprachzerstörung und-Rekonstruktion.* I am indebted to him for more suggestions than I could indicate through specific references.

Jürgen Habermas
Frankfurt, 1971

Translator's Note

I should like to thank the following persons for their contribution, through discussion, reading, and encouragement, to the preparation of this translation: my colleagues Shierry Weber and Donna Huse of the Center for the Study of Technological Experience; Paul Breines; and Charlotte Riley. My original interest in the subject of this work arose under the teaching of Herbert Marcuse, Barrington Moore, Jr., Robert Paul Wolff, and Paul Tillich; to all of them I am much indebted.

Jeremy J. Shapiro

PART ONE

The Crisis of the Critique of Knowledge

If we imagine the philosophical discussion of the modern period reconstructed as a judicial hearing, it would be deciding a single question: how is reliable knowledge (*Erkenntnis*)[1] possible. The term "theory of knowledge," or "epistemology," was coined only in the 19th century; but the subject that it retrospectively denotes is the subject of modern philosophy in general, at least until the threshold of the 19th century. The characteristic endeavor of both rationalist and empiricist thought was directed likewise at the metaphysical demarcation of the realm of objects and the logical and psychological justification of the validity of a natural science characterized by formalized language and experiment. Yet no matter how much modern physics, which combined so effectively the rigor of mathematical form with the amplitude of controlled experience, was the model for clear and distinct knowledge, modern science did not coincide with knowledge as such. In this period what characterized philosophy's position with regard to science was precisely that science was accorded its legitimate place only by unequivocally philosophical knowledge. Theories of knowledge did not limit themselves to the explication of scientific method—they did not merge with the philosophy of science.

This was still the case when modern metaphysics, which was already organized around the problem of possible knowledge, was itself subjected to doubt. Even Kant, through whose transcendental-logical (*transzendentallogisch*)[2] perspective epistemology first became conscious of itself and thereby entered its own singular dimension, attributes to philosophy a sovereign role in relation to science. The critique of knowledge was still conceived in reference to a system of cognitive faculties that included practical reason and reflective judgment as naturally as critique itself, that is a theoretical reason that can dialectically ascertain not only its limits but also its own Idea. The comprehensive rationality of reason that becomes transparent to itself has not yet shrunk to a set of methodological principles.

It was with the elaboration of a metacritique that subjects the critique of knowledge to unyielding self-reflection, with Hegel's critique of Kant's transcendental-logical inquiry, that

3

philosophy was finally brought to the paradoxical point of not altering its position with regard to science but abandoning it completely. Hence I should like to put forth the thesis that since Kant science has no longer been seriously comprehended by philosophy. Science can only be comprehended epistemologically, which means as one category of possible knowledge, as long as knowledge is not equated either effusively with the absolute knowledge of a great philosophy or blindly with the scientistic self-understanding of the actual business of research (*Forschung*).[3] Both equations close off the dimension in which an epistemological concept of science can be formed—in which, therefore, science can be made comprehensible within the horizon of possible knowledge and legitimated. Compared with "absolute knowledge" scientific knowledge necessarily appears narrow-minded, and the only task remaining is then the critical dissolution of the boundaries of positive knowledge. On the other hand, where a concept of knowing that transcends the prevailing sciences is totally lacking, the critique of knowledge resigns itself to the function of a philosophy of science, which restricts itself to the pseudo-normative regulation of established research.

Philosophy's position with regard to science, which at one time could be designated with the name "theory of knowledge," has been undermined by the movement of philosophical thought itself. Philosophy was dislodged from this position by philosophy. From then on, the theory of knowledge had to be replaced by a methodology emptied of philosophical thought. For the philosophy of science that has emerged since the mid-nineteenth century as the heir of the theory of knowledge is methodology pursued with a scientistic self-understanding of the sciences. "Scientism" means science's belief in itself: that is, the conviction that we can no longer understand science as one form of possible knowledge, but rather must identify knowledge with science. The positivism that enters on the scene with Comte makes use of elements of both the empiricist and rationalist traditions in order to strengthen science's belief in its exclusive validity after the fact, instead of to reflect (*reflektieren*)[4] on it, and to account for the structure of the sciences on the basis of this belief. Modern positivism has solved this task with remarkable subtlety and indisputable success.

Every discussion of the conditions of possible knowledge today, therefore, must begin from the position worked out by analytic philosophy of science. We cannot return immediately to the dimension of epistemological investigation. Positivism has unreflectively leaped over this dimension, which is why it generally has regressed behind the level of reflection represented by Kant's philosophy. To me it seems necessary to analyze the context in which positivist doctrines originated before we can take up the current discussion. For a future systematic investigation of the basis in human interests of scientific knowledge cannot abstractly restore epistemology. Instead it can only return to a dimension that was first opened up by Hegel through the radical self-critique of epistemology and then once again obstructed.

In opposition to Kant, Hegel was able to demonstrate the phenomenological self-reflection of knowledge as the necessary radicalization of the critique of reason. But he did not develop it logically, owing, I believe, to his preoccupation with the postulates of the philosophy of identity (*Identitätsphiloso-phie*).[5] Marx, whose historical materialism really required the movement of Hegel's self-reflection, misunderstood his own conception and hence completed the disintegration of the theory of knowledge. Thus positivism could forget that the methodology of the sciences was intertwined with the objective self-formative process (*Bildungsprozess*)[6] of the human species and erect the absolutism of pure methodology on the basis of the forgotten and repressed.

CHAPTER ONE

Hegel's Critique of Kant: *Radicalization or Abolition of the Theory of Knowledge*

Hegel replaced the enterprise of epistemology with the phenomenological self-reflection of mind. He introduces the *Phenomenology of Mind* with an argument that returns in later contexts.[1] The critical philosophy (*Kritizismus*)[2] demands that the knowing subject ascertain the conditions of the knowledge of which it is in principle capable before trusting its directly acquired cognitions. Only on the basis of reliable criteria of the validity of our judgments can we determine whether we may also be certain with regard to our knowledge. But if this critique itself must claim to be knowledge, how can we critically investigate the cognitive faculty prior to knowing?

> What is demanded is thus the following: we should know the cognitive faculty before we know. It is like wanting to swim before going in the water. The investigation of the faculty of knowledge is itself knowledge, and cannot arrive at its goal because it is this goal already.[3]

Every consistent epistemology is caught in this circle from the beginning. This cannot be avoided by beginning the critique with presuppositions that remain provisionally unproblematic but that in principle can be taken as potential problems for subsequent investigation. This "problematic method," originally adopted by Reinhold, is still recommended today by positivists for methodological investigations. It is argued that one cannot at the same time take all principles as problematic. The set of presuppositions that defines the frame of reference of a given investigation should be assumed as unproblematic for the course of the investigation. The manifold repetition of this procedure is supposed to provide an adequate guarantee that in principle all presuppositions can be called into question. However, the choice of the first frame of reference and the sequence of the additional stages of investigation remain arbitrary. Radical doubt is excluded, because the procedure rests on a conventionalism that precludes the logical foundation of its premises. But the theory of knowledge, according to its philosophical claim, is an enterprise directed at the whole. It is concerned with the critical justification of the conditions of possible knowledge in general. It cannot renounce radical, that is unconditional doubt. The methodical (*methodisch*)[4] meaning of its approach would be inverted if it bound critique to conditions (that is if it allowed presuppositions) that are themselves the preconditions of the critique of knowledge without being subject to it. Because epistemology, in virtue of its claim to providing its own and the ultimate foundation, appears as the heir of First Philosophy (*Ursprungsphilosophie*),[5] it cannot dispense with the strategy of beginning without presuppositions.[6] This explains how Hegel can praise Reinhold, who clearly perceived the circular character of epistemology, while rejecting the problematic method that was to escape it. His "correct insight does not alter the character of such a method, but immediately expresses its inadequacy."[7]

Hegel's argument is conclusive. It is directed against the intention of First Philosophy. For the circle in which epistemology inevitably ensnares itself is a reminder that the critique of knowledge does not possess the spontaneity of an origin. As reflection it is instead dependent on something prior and given, which it takes as its object while simultaneously originating in it. Thus the critique of knowledge is condemned to being after the fact. It begins with data of consciousness that it first confronts empirically. But the choice of a starting point is not conventional. Sense-certainty is the name of the natural consciousness of a world of everyday life which we always find ourselves already inside, with inevitable contingency. Sense-certainty is objective in the sense that the recollecting power of reflection itself originates in this stratum of experience, whose dogmatic character it unmasks. In reflection consciousness cannot make anything transparent except the context of its own genesis. The circle that

Hegel charges to epistemology as a bad contradiction is justified in phenomenological experience as the form of reflection itself. It pertains to the structure of self-knowledge that one must have known in order to know explicitly. Only something already known can be remembered as a result and comprehended in its genesis. This movement is the experience of reflection. Its goal is that knowledge which the critical philosophy asserted as an immediate possession.

If this is so, then the critique of knowledge can no longer claim to fulfill the intention of First Philosophy. But it is not at all clear why abandoning this intention should entail abandoning the critique of knowledge itself. The latter has only to cast off its false consciousness by being turned against itself in metacritique. Hegel, however, believes that his argument affects not only this false consciousness but the epistemological approach as such:

> Meanwhile, if concern with falling into error
> creates mistrust in science, which goes to work
> without such misgivings and attains real knowledge,
> then it is not clear why conversely there should not
> be mistrust of this mistrust and why there should
> not be concern that this fear of erring is not
> error itself. In fact this fear presupposes many
> beliefs as true and bases its misgivings and conclusions
> on them. It is these presuppositions themselves that
> first need to be examined as to their truth.[8]

Hegel rightly criticizes the unacknowledged presuppositions of epistemology. However his demand that these, too, be subjected to critique accords with the strategy of unconditional doubt. Thus his argument cannot limit the mistrust expressed by the critical philosophy, which is the modern form of skepticism. Instead, it can only radicalize it. Phenomenology would have to reconstruct the standpoint of doubt (Zweifel) adopted by epistemology as the beaten path of despair (Verzweiflung). Hegel sees this; yet he asserts in the same breath that the fear of erring is error itself. Hence what starts out as immanent critique covertly turns into abstract negation. It is through the epistemological

circle that the theory of knowledge can cure its false consciousness and be brought to consciousness of itself as reflection. Hegel,
however, takes this circle as a sign of the untruth of the critical
philosophy as such. He sees through the absolutism of an epistemology based on unreflected presuppositions, demonstrates the
mediation of reflection by what precedes it, and thus destroys the
renewal of First Philosophy on the basis of transcendentalism.
Yet in so doing he imagines himself to be overcoming the critique
of knowledge as such. This opinion insinuates itself because from
the very beginning Hegel presumes as given a knowledge of the
Absolute while indeed the possibility of just this knowledge
would have to be demonstrated according to the criteria of a
radicalized critique of knowledge.

Accordingly there is something half-hearted about the
Phenomenology of Mind. The standpoint of absolute knowledge
is to proceed with immanent necessity from phenomenological
experience. But because it is absolute, it does not really need to
be justified by the phenomenological self-reflection of mind; and,
strictly speaking, it is not even capable of such justification. This
equivocation of the phenomenology of mind deprives Hegel's
critique of Kant of the force that it would have needed in order
to put forward a reflected theory of knowledge. The theory
of transcendental philosophy itself has not held its ground
against its positivist opponents.

Hegel directs himself against the organon[9] theory of
knowledge. Those who conceive of the enterprise of the critique
of knowledge as an examination of the means of knowledge start
with a model of knowledge that emphasizes either the activity of
the knowing subject or the receptivity of the cognitive process.
Knowledge appears mediated either by an *instrument* with whose
help we form objects or as a *medium* through which the light of
the world enters the subject.[10] Both versions accord in viewing
knowledge as transcendentally determined by the means of
possible knowledge. The model of knowing as a medium through
which the state of fact, which is true in itself, manifests itself in
refraction makes clear that even the contemplative self-understanding of theory, when examined from the viewpoint of the
critique of knowledge, must be re-interpreted along the lines of an

organon theory of knowledge. For Hegel the task of the critical philosophy appears as one of ascertaining the functions of the instrument or medium in order to be able to distinguish the inevitable contributions of the subject from the authentic objective content in the judgment that is the result of the cognitive process. The objection to this then lies at hand:

> If we remove from a formed thing what the
> instrument has done to it, then the thing—in this
> case the Absolute—is once again just what it was
> before this exertion, which thus was superfluous. . . .
> Or if the examination of knowing, which we represent to
> ourselves as a medium [instead of as the functioning of
> an instrument—Jürgen Habermas], makes us acquainted
> with the law of its refraction, it is just as useless to us to
> deduct it from the result. For knowing is not the
> refraction of the ray, but the ray itself through which
> truth reaches us.[11]

This objection is obviously valid only presupposing that there can be something like knowledge in itself or absolute knowledge independent of the subjective conditions of possible knowledge. Hegel imputes to epistemology a privative concept of subjectively tinged knowledge that can in fact only arise in confrontation with Hegel's own concept of absolute knowledge. However, for a critical philosophy that does not fear its own implications, there can be no concept of knowledge that can be explicated independently of the subjective conditions of the objectivity of possible knowledge: this is shown by Kant's principle of the synthetic unity of apperception as the highest principle of all employment of the understanding. Of course, we can feign the idea of a mode of knowledge that is not "ours," but we associate a meaning with this idea only to the extent that we derive it as a limiting concept from a variation of knowledge that is possible "for us." It remains derivative and cannot itself serve as a standard according to which we could relativize that from which it is derived. Transcendental philosophy's conception of knowledge mediated by an organon implies that the frame of reference within which the objects of knowledge are at all possible is first constituted by the functions of the instrument. The idea that Hegel imputes to transcendental philosophy, namely "that the Absolute is located on one side and knowing, located on the other, is still something real by itself and in separation from the Absolute,"—this idea belongs rather to Hegel's own frame of reference. For Hegel is referring to the absolute relation of subject and object. In this relation a mediating organon of knowledge can in fact be thought of only as the cause of subjective interference and not as the condition of the possible objectivity of knowledge. For critical philosophy it is otherwise. The organon produces the world within which reality can appear at all; thus under these conditions of its functioning it can always only disclose reality and not obscure it. Only presupposing that reality as such simply appears can this or that individual real element be obscured—unless we presume an absolute relation between reality and the cognitive process that is independent of that instrument. But from the presuppositions of transcendental philosophy we cannot even meaningfully talk of knowledge without identifying the conditions of possible knowledge. Accordingly Hegel's critique does not proceed immanently. For his objection to the organon theory of knowledge presupposes just what this theory calls into question: the possibility of absolute knowledge.

On the other hand, Hegel's critique also has its justifications. Unfolding the two cognitive models of the instrument and the medium brings to light a series of *implicit presuppositions* of a critique of knowledge that claims to be free of presuppositions. The latter must always already know more than it can know according to its own stated premises. The critique that knows knowledge to be mediated by an organon must include specific ideas both about the knowing subject and the category of correct knowledge. For Kant reconstructs the organization of the cognitive faculty, as the essential unity of the transcendental conditions under which knowledge is possible, by starting with a priori valid propositions and with an ego for which the validity of propositions exists. Already in our approach we secretly base the critique of knowledge on a specific concept of science and of the knowing subject. However, the only presupposition that modern skepticism will allow is the project of not accepting the thoughts of others on authority, but instead of examining everything oneself and autonomously following one's own conviction. The only thing standing at the beginning of critique is the radical project of unconditional doubt. From Descartes to Kant this doubt required no justification because it legitimated itself as an aspect of reason. And correspondingly consciousness that criticizes itself does not need to be trained in methodical doubt, because the latter is the medium in which consciousness constitutes itself as consciousness that is certain of itself. These are assertions claiming self-evidence that are no longer convincing today as basic assumptions of rationalism. Radical doubt that needs to be neither justified nor learned through practice is no longer conceded a transcendental role. At most it has a place in cognitive psychology. In recent philosophy of science, therefore, methodical doubt has been replaced by a critical attitude that is committed to the principles of rationalism but cannot itself be justified.[12] Rationalism is supposedly a method of belief, one opinion among others. Unaltered, however, is its function in the presuppositionless beginning of the critique of knowledge and thus for an absolutist self-understanding that transcendental philosophy shares with today's methodology. To the abstract resolve of unconditional doubt Hegel opposes a self-completing skepticism:

> The series of shapes that consciousness passes through on this course is . . . the complete history of the *self-formation* of consciousness into science. In the simple manner appropriate to it, that resolve presupposes this self-formation as immediately settled and completed. Against this untruth, however, this course of formation is the real accomplishment.[13]

Epistemology presumes to take nothing for granted except its pure project of radically doubting. In truth it bases itself on a critical consciousness that is the result of an entire process of self-formation. Thus it is the beneficiary of a stage of reflection that it does not admit and therefore also cannot legitimate.

The *first presupposition* with which epistemology begins

is a normative concept of science. It takes a given, specific category of knowledge as prototypical knowledge. Characteristically, in the preface to the *Critique of Pure Reason* Kant resorts to the examples of mathematics and contemporary physics. Both disciplines are distinguished by what appears to be relatively constant cognitive progress. They fulfill a criterion that Kant cloaks in the stereotyped phrase of the "sure march of science." In contrast, other disciplines, which have falsely claimed the name of science, are characterized by groping around with mere concepts. This includes metaphysics; measured against the pragmatic mark of cognitive progress, its method is without success. That is why Kant would like "us to undertake a complete revolution in it after the example of the geometers and natural scientists." From the very start the enterprise of a critique of pure speculative reason assumes the normative cogency of a *specific* category of knowledge. Presupposing that the statements of mathematics and contemporary physics are valid as reliable knowledge, the critique of knowledge can take principles that have proved themselves in these processes of inquiry and use them to draw conclusions about the organization of our cognitive faculty. It is true that Kant feels psychologically encouraged by the example of the natural scientists, who have understood that reason only comprehends what it itself produces according to its own plan, to transform metaphysics according to the same principle. But over and above this he depends systematically on this example, because the critique of knowledge only seems to be free from presuppositions. In fact it must begin with a prior, undemonstrated criterion of the validity of scientific statements, which nevertheless is accepted as cogent.

Modern methodology, too, gains pseudonormative force by first taking a particular category of traditional knowledge as the prototype of science. It then generalizes the procedures that make possible the reconstruction of this knowledge and converts them into a definition of science. Hegel opposes this by insisting that knowledge which first *presents itself* as science is primarily a manifestation of knowledge (*erscheinende Wissen*)[14]—one barren assurance is just as valid as another. Nor is science as it first manifests itself any more worthy of belief because we place our confidence in the claim that it is authentic or true science and decide against other forms of knowledge that appear with the same claim. The critique of knowledge must begin by abstaining from any prejudgment about what is to count as science. At first it confronts only competing claims of the manifestation of knowledge. That is why it has to abandon itself to the course taken by this knowledge in its manifestations:

> Skepticism directed at the entire compass of
> consciousness in its manifestations first makes . . .
> the mind skilled at examining what truth is. It does
> so by creating despair of so-called natural ideas,
> thoughts and opinions. It is a matter of indifference
> whether one calls these one's own or others'. The very
> consciousness that is to examine truth is still so
> filled with and caught in these ideas that it is in fact
> incapable of undertaking what it wants to.[15]

As the representation of knowledge in its manifestations the critique of knowledge takes up the thread of phenomenological experience in the everyday life-world in the formations that natural consciousness has given itself and in which we find ourselves:

> When knowledge in its manifestations becomes our
> object, its determinations are first taken up as they
> immediately present themselves; and they surely present
> themselves as they have just been formulated.[16]

Epistemological investigation does not thereby regress to the dogmatism of common sense. For now its critique is directed so unsparingly even against itself, that the standards that it uses for examination cannot simply be presupposed. By reconstructing the self-formative process of consciousness, the critique of knowledge observes how at every stage the standards of the preceding one disintegrate and new ones arise.

In this enterprise *the second presupposition* with which the critique of knowledge begins also becomes problematic: namely the assumption of a complete, fixed knowing subject or, in other words a normative concept of the ego. In order that judgment be passed on the errors through which reason had become at odds with itself in its trans-empirical employment, Kant wanted to institute a tribunal. He had no second thoughts about the genesis of the court. For nothing seemed more certain to him than the self-consciousness in which I am given to myself as the "I think" that accompanies all of my representations. Even if the transcendental unity of self-consciousness can only be comprehended in the actual course of the investigation as arising from the activities of original apperception, the identity of the ego must already be taken account of at its beginning on the basis of the undoubted transcendental experience of self-reflection. In contrast, Hegel perceives that Kant's critique of consciousness commences with a consciousness that is not transparent to itself. The observing consciousness of phenomenology knows that it itself is incorporated in the experience of reflection as one of its elements. Beginning with natural consciousness, its genesis must be reconstructed up to the point of view provisionally taken by the phenomenological observer. Then the position of the critique of knowledge can coincide with the constituted self-consciousness of a consciousness that has become aware of its own self-formative process; only in this way can it be purified of all that is contingent. For the consciousness that is about to begin the task of examination, the subject of epistemological investigation is not yet at hand. It is first given to itself only with the result of its self-ascertainment.

A critique of knowledge that has dissolved the normative conception of both science and the ego in radical doubt is relegated exclusively to what Hegel calls *phenomenological experience*. The latter moves in the medium of a consciousness that reflexively distinguishes between itself, for which an object is given, and the being-in-itself of the object. The transition from the naive intuition of the object-in-itself (*ansichseiend*)[17] to the reflexive knowledge that this being-in-itself exists for it (consciousness) enables consciousness to have a specific experience of itself via its object. This experience first exists only for us, the phenomenological observers:

> It is the *genesis* of the new object, which presents
> itself to consciousness without the latter knowing how

this occurs, that for us appears to take place, so to speak, behind its back. In this way a moment of *being-in-itself* or *being-for-us* enters into its movement; yet this moment does not present itself to the consciousness that is itself engaged in the experience. But the *content* of what originates for us exists *for it*, and we comprehend only its formal element or its pure genesis. This result of genesis exists *for it* only as object, whereas *for us* it is at the same time movement and becoming.[18]

The dimensions of *in itself, for it,* and *for us* designate the coordinate system in which the experience of reflection moves. But during the experiential process the values change in all dimensions, including the third. The phenomenologist's perspective, from which the path of knowledge in its manifestations presents itself "for us," can only be adopted in anticipation until this perspective itself is produced in phenomenological experience. "We," too, are drawn into the process of reflection, which at each of its levels is characterized anew by a "reversal of consciousness."

The *last* implicit *presupposition* with which an abstract critique of knowledge begins, however, thereby shows itself to be untenable: the distinction between theoretical and practical reason. The critique of pure reason assumes a different concept of the ego than does that of practical reason: the ego as the unity of self-consciousness versus the ego as free will. The separation of the critique of knowledge from a critique of rational action is considered self-evident. Yet this distinction becomes problematical if critical consciousness itself emerges only from the history of the development of consciousness. Then it is an element, even if the last one, in a self-formative process in which at every stage a new insight is confirmed in a new attitude. For reflection destroys, along with a false view of things, the dogmatic attitudes of a habitual form of life: this holds even for the first stage, the world of sense-certainty. In false consciousness, knowing and willing are still joined. The residues of the destructions of false consciousness serve as rungs on the ladder of the experience of re-flection. As shown by the prototypical area of experience in life history, the experiences from which one learns are negative. The reversal of consciousness means the dissolution of identifications, the breaking of fixations, and the destruction of projections. The failure of the state of consciousness that has been overcome turns at the same time into a new reflected attitude in which the situation comes to consciousness in an undistorted manner, just as it is. This is the path of determinate negation that guards against empty skepticism, "which always sees only *pure nothingness* in the result and abstracts from the circumstance that this nothing-ness is determined as the nothingness of *that from which it re-sults.*"[19] In clarifying what the reversal of consciousness means, Hegel repeats

> . . . that the result obtained from a non-veridical instance of knowledge cannot shrink to an empty nothingness but must be apprehended necessarily as the nothingness of *that of which it is the result:* a result that contains that which was true in the preceding instance of knowledge.[20]

This figure of determinate negation applies not to an im-manent logical connection but to the mechanism of the progress of a mode of reflection in which theoretical and practical reason are one. The affirmative moment that is contained in the very negation of an existing organization of consciousness becomes plausible when we consider that in this consciousness categories of apprehending the world and norms of action are connected. A *form of life* that has become an abstraction cannot be ne-gated without leaving a trace, or overthrown without practical consequences. The revolutionized situation contains the one that has been surpassed, because the insight of the new consists pre-cisely in the experience of revolutionary release from the old con-sciousness. Because the relation between successive states of a system is brought about by what is in this sense determinate‑ne-gation and not by either a logical or a causal relation, we speak of a self-formative process. A state defined by both cognitive perfor-mances and fixed attitudes can be overcome only if its genesis is analytically remembered. A past state, if cut off and merely repressed, would retain its power over the present. The relation described, however, secures continuity to a moral life context that is destroyed again at each new level of reflection. It makes possible a sustaining identity of the "mind" ("*Geist*") in the succession of abandoned identifications. This identity of the mind becomes conscious as a dialectical one. It contains *within* itself the distinction confidently presupposed by epistemology and cannot be defined in relation to this distinction between theoretical and practical reason.

Hegel radicalizes the approach of the critique of knowledge by subjecting its presuppositions to self-criticism. In so doing he destroys the secure foundation of transcendental consciousness, from which the a priori demarcation between transcendental and empirical determinations, between genesis and validity, seemed certain. Phenomenological experience moves in a dimension within which transcendental determinations themselves take form. It contains no absolutely fixed point. Only the experience of reflection as such can be elucidated under the name of self-formative process. Critical consciousness, after initially hastening forward, must work itself up to its present position through stages of reflection that can be reconstructed through a systematic repetition of the experiences that constituted the history of mankind. The *Phenomenology of Mind* attempts this reconstruction in three progressions: through the socialization process of the individual, through the universal history of mankind, and through this history as it reflects upon itself in the forms of absolute mind, that is religion, art, and scientific knowledge (*Wissenschaft*).[21]

The critical consciousness with which the theory of knowledge begins its examination is obtained as the result of phenomenological observation as soon as the latter becomes transparently aware of the genesis of its own standpoint by appropriating the self-formative process of the human species. Now Hegel asserts at the end of the *Phenomenology of Mind* that this critical consciousness is absolute knowledge. Hegel did not make good this assertion; indeed, he could not even carry out such a demonstration because he did not satisfy the formal conditions of a phenomenological passage through the history of nature. For in accordance with the approach of phenomenological investigation, absolute knowledge would be conceivable only as the result of a systematic repetition of the formative processes of the human species and nature at once.

Now it is not really probable that such a simple "mistake" could have crept into Hegel's thought. If, disregarding the preceding argument, he never entertained a doubt that the phenomenology of mind led, and had to lead, to the standpoint of absolute knowledge and thence to the concept of speculative scientific knowledge, it is rather an indication of a self-understanding of phenomenology that deviates from our interpretation. Through phenomenological investigation Hegel believes himself not to be radicalizing the epistemological approach but to be making it superfluous. He presumes that phenomenological experience always keeps and has kept within the medium of an absolute movement of the mind and therefore must terminate necessarily in absolute knowledge.[22] In contrast, we have followed his argument from the point of view of an immanent critique of Kant. If we are not guided by the presupposition of the philosophy of identity, the fateful union dissolves. True, Hegel's construction of consciousness in its manifestations, by radicalizing the epistemological approach, dispels transcendental philosophy's limitation of what merely seems to be unconditional doubt. But in no way does it guarantee us access to any sort of absolute knowledge. Unlike empirical experience, phenomenological experience does not keep within the bounds of transcendentally grounded schemata. Rather, the construction of consciousness in its manifestations incorporates the fundamental experiences in which transformations of such schemata of apprehending the world and of action themselves have been deposited. The experience of reflection preserves those outstanding moments in which the subject looks back over its own shoulder, so to speak, and perceives how the transcendental relation between subject and object alters itself behind its back. It recollects the emancipation thresholds of the history of mankind. However, this does not exclude contingent impacts upon the transcendental history of consciousness. Under contingent circumstances, the conditions under which any new transcendental framework for the appearance of possible objects is formed could be produced by the subject itself: for example, through progress in the forces of production, as Marx assumes. This would not bring about an absolute unity of subject and object. Only such a unity, however, would confer upon critical consciousness, in which phenomenological recollection culminates, the status of absolute knowledge.

Notwithstanding, Hegel advocated this view in 1807.

> By urging itself on to its true existence [in the course
> of phenomenological experience], it [consciousness]
> will attain a point at which it casts off its appearance
> of being affected with what is different from it,
> with what is only for it and as something other than
> itself, or where appearance becomes identical with
> essence, so that the description of consciousness
> coincides with this very point of the authentic scientific
> knowledge of mind; and finally, by apprehending this
> its own essence, it will express absolute knowledge
> itself.[23]

But already here a contradiction appears that is masked only rhetorically. If it is phenomenology that first produces the standpoint of absolute knowledge, and this standpoint coincides with the position of authentic scientific knowledge, then the construction of knowledge in its manifestations cannot itself claim the status of scientific knowledge. The apparent dilemma (Aporie) of knowing before knowledge, with which Hegel reproached epistemology, now returns in Hegel's thought as an actual dilemma: namely, that phenomenology must in fact be valid prior to every possible mode of scientific knowledge. Hegel first published the Phenomenology as the first part of a system of scientific knowledge. At that time he was convinced that the forms in which consciousness appeared followed one another with necessity, and "through this necessity this road to scientific knowledge is itself already scientific knowledge."[24] Yet Hegel could claim necessity for the progression of phenomenological experience only retrospectively from the standpoint of absolute knowledge. Seen from this perspective the relation of the phenomenology of mind to logic takes the following form:

> Consciousness is mind as concrete knowledge, which is, moreover, knowledge affected with externality. But, like the development of all natural and mental life, the forward movement of this object is based exclusively on the nature of the *pure essences* that make up the content of logic. As mind in its manifestations, which frees itself in this way from its immediacy and external concretion, consciousness becomes pure knowledge, which gives itself as an object these pure essences themselves, as they are in and for themselves.[25]

From this point of view, however, phenomenological investigation would lose its specific character and be reduced to the level of a metaphysical philosophy of mind and nature (*Realphilosophie des Geistes*).[26] If the progressive phenomenological movement of consciousness, like "all natural and mental life," were based on the logical structure of essences existing in and for themselves, then precisely the special relation that enables phenomenology to be an introduction to philosophy would be neglected: namely that the phenomenological observer, who cannot yet have attained the standpoint of logic, is himself incorporated in the self-formative process of consciousness. His dependent position is shown in that he must begin with sense certainty, which is something immediate.

Phenomenology does not depict the developmental process of mind, but rather the appropriation of this process by a consciousness that must first free itself from external concretion and attain pure knowledge through the experience of reflection. Thus it cannot itself already be scientific knowledge and yet must be able to claim scientific validity.

This ambiguity remains. We need to ground the concept of science phenomenologically only as long as we are not certain of the conditions of possible knowledge—or, possibly, of absolute knowledge. To this extent the method of phenomenological experience only radicalizes what was always the intention of the critique of knowledge. On the other hand, when phenomenology truly attains its declared goal, absolute knowledge, it makes itself superfluous. Indeed, it refutes the perspective of inquiry held by the critique of knowledge as such, although this perspective is its only legitimation. At best, then, we may regard phenomenology as a ladder which we must throw away after climbing it to the standpoint of the Logic. In a certain sense Hegel himself later also treated the *Phenomenology* in this way. He did not incorporate it into his system of the sciences. In its place in the *Encyclopedia* appears a so-called preliminary notion (*Vorbegriff*) of the science of logic.[27] Yet in the fall of 1831 Hegel began preparations for a second edition of the *Phenomenology* and made a note for himself reading, "Unusual early work, not to be revised." He obviously wanted to retain the phenomenology in its old form but for the same function as the new preliminary notion of the Logic and place it alongside the system as a whole. In this way scientific knowledge, which is expounded as a system, could explain its standpoint in relation to a consciousness that is still outside the system and that must still be motivated to decide to want to think purely.[28] As this sort of self-interpretation of science, which comprehends the necessity of a consciousness caught in appearance, phenomenology would have to evolve its thought process from the standpoint of speculative scientific knowledge. But it could do this only didactically and not scientifically. This later self-understanding of phenomenology rests on a re-interpretation of its original intention. Nevertheless Hegel could carry it out without violence, owing to the ambiguity that was always attached to phenomenology. It had to assume as uncertain the standpoint of absolute knowledge to which it was supposed to give rise and to which it could give rise only by radicalizing the critique of knowledge. Yet in fact it presupposed absolute knowledge with such certainty that it believed itself exempted from the labor of this critique from its first step.

Kant's critique of knowledge accepts an empirical concept of science in the form of contemporary physics and derives from it the criteria of possible science in general. Hegel shows that the critique of knowledge, if it unconditionally follows its own intention, must abandon such presuppositions; instead it must let the standard of critique emerge from the experience of reflection. Because he does not proceed logically but relativizes the critique of knowledge as such according to the presuppositions of the philosophy of identity, Hegel arrives at the concept of speculative scientific knowledge. In relation to this norm, sciences that proceed methodically, whether of nature or mind, can only prove themselves to be limitations of absolute knowledge and discredit themselves. Thus the paradoxical result of an *ambiguous radicalization of the critique of knowledge* is not an enlightened position of philosophy with regard to science. When philosophy asserts itself as authentic science, the relation of philosophy and science completely disappears from discussion. It is with Hegel that a fatal misunderstanding arises: the idea that the claim asserted by philosophical reason against the abstract thought of mere understanding is equivalent to the usurpation of the legitimacy of independent sciences by a philosophy claiming to retain its position as universal scientific knowledge. But the actual fact of scientific progress independent of philosophy had to unmask this claim, however misunderstood, as bare fiction. It was this that served as the foundation-stone of positivism. Only Marx could have contested its victory. For he pursued Hegel's critique of Kant without sharing the basic assumption of the philosophy of identity that hindered Hegel from unambiguously radicalizing the critique of knowledge.

CHAPTER TWO

Marx's Metacritique of Hegel: *Synthesis Through Social Labor*

In the last of the economic-philosophical manuscripts from his Paris period (1844) Marx comes to grips with the *Phenomenology of Mind*.* He focuses especially on the last chapter, on absolute knowledge. Marx follows the strategy of detaching the exposition of consciousness in its manifestations from the framework of the philosophy of identity. He does this in order to bring to light the elements of a critique that often "far surpasses Hegel's standpoint," elements that are already contained, although concealed, in the *Phenomenology*. In so doing he refers to paragraphs 381 and 384 of Hegel's *Encyclopedia*, in which the transition from the philosophy of nature to the philosophy of mind is delineated, making explicit the basic assumption that tacitly underlies the *Phenomenology*: "For us the mind has nature as its presupposition; it is the *truth* and thus the *absolute ground* (*Erstes*) of nature. In this truth nature has disappeared, and mind has emerged as the Idea existing for itself: both the *object* and the *subject* of the Idea is *the notion* (concept, *Begriff*)."[1] For Marx, on the contrary, it is nature that is the absolute ground of mind. Nature cannot be conceived of as the other of a mind that is at the same time in its own element (*bei sich*) in its other. For if nature were mind in the state of complete externalization, then as congealed mind it would have its essence and life not in itself but outside itself. There would be an advance guarantee that in truth nature could exist only as mind reflexively remembers it while returning to itself from nature. As Marx comments on the *Encyclopedia*,

---

* Karl Marx and Friedrich Engels, *Gesamtausgabe* (Berlin: Dietz, 1956–), I, 3:150 ff. This edition is cited in the Notes as MEGA.

Here externality is not to be understood as sensuousness
that externalizes itself and discloses itself to the light,
to sensuous man. This externality is meant here as an
alienation, a fault, a weakness that should not exist . . .
A being that is deficient not only for me or in my eyes
has something outside itself that it is lacking. That is, its
essence is different from itself. For the abstract thinker,
therefore, nature must eliminate itself, because it has
already been posited by him as a potentially eliminated
being.[2]

This seal placed on absolute knowledge by the philosophy of
identity is broken if the externality of nature, both objective en-
vironmental and subjective bodily nature, not only seems external to a consciousness that finds itself within nature but refers
instead to the immediacy of a substratum on which the mind contingently depends. Here the mind presupposes nature, but in the
sense of a natural process that, from within itself, gives rise likewise to the natural being man and the nature that surrounds him
—and not in the idealist sense of a mind that, as Idea existing for
itself, posits a natural world as its own self-created presupposition.[3]

Objective idealism attempts to render the being-in-itself
of nature comprehensible as a presupposition of absolute mind
that has not been discerned as such by subjective mind. What
Marx opposes to this is no coarse materialism. It is true that he
first appears to be renewing the naturalism of Feuerbach's anthropology.[4] In opposition to Feuerbach Marx certainly emphasizes,
beside the bodily attributes of an organism dependent on its environment (sensuous receptivity, need, emotionality, vulnerabil-
ity), the adaptive modes of behavior and active expressions of life
of an "active natural being." But as long as he attributes to "objective activity" the still unspecific meaning that man, like every
organism, "can only express his life through real, sensuous objects,"[5] Marx remains caught in the realm of naturalistic ideas.

The first thesis against Feuerbach, however, already goes
beyond this.[6] Here the meaning of speaking of man as an objective being is not anthropological[7] but epistemological: "the active

side" that idealism has developed in opposition to materialism is to be comprehended materialistically. When Marx sees as the main flaw of all previous materialism "that the object, reality, sensuousness is only apprehended in the form of the object or of intuition (*Anschauung*)[8] and not, however, as sensuous human activity, as practice (*Praxis*),[9] not subjectively," then "objective activity" has acquired the specific meaning of constituting the objectivity of possible objects of experience. As natural objects the latter share with nature the property of being-in-itself, but bear the character of produced objectivity owing to the activity of man. On the one hand Marx conceives of objective activity as a transcendental accomplishment; it has its counterpart in the construction of a world in which reality appears subject to conditions of the objectivity of possible objects of experience. On the other hand he sees this transcendental accomplishment as rooted in real labor (*Arbeit*)[10] processes. The subject of world constitution is not transcendental consciousness in general but the concrete human species, which reproduces its life under natural conditions. That this "process of material exchange" ("*Stoffwechselprozess*") takes the form of processes of social labor derives from the physical constitution of this natural being and some constants of its natural environment.

Marx calls labor a

> condition of human existence that is independent of
> all forms of society, a perpetual necessity of nature in
> order to mediate the material exchange between man
> and nature, in other words, human life.[11]

At the human level nature separates out into the *subjective nature* of man and the *objective nature* of his environment. At the same time nature mediates itself through the reproductive process of social labor:

> Labor is above all a process between man and nature,
> a process in which man through his own action
> mediates, regulates, and controls his material exchange
> with nature. He confronts the substance of nature

itself as a natural power. He sets in motion the natural
forces belonging to his corporeal being, that is his
arms and legs, head, and hand, in order to appropriate
nature in a form usable for his own life.[12]

The nature that surrounds us constitutes itself as *objective nature
for us* only in being mediated by the subjective nature of man
through processes of social labor. That is why labor, or work, is
not only a fundamental category of human existence but also an
epistemological category. The system of objective activities creates the factual conditions of the possible reproduction of social
life *and at the same time* the transcendental conditions of the
possible objectivity of the objects of experience. The category of
man as a tool-making animal signifies a schema both of action
and of apprehending the world. Although a natural process, labor is at the same time more than a mere natural process, for it
regulates material exchange with nature *and* constitutes a world:

> Man is not only a natural being, but a human natural
> being: that is a being that exists for itself[13] and is
> therefore a species-being and must confirm and activate
> itself as such both in its being and in its knowledge.
> Thus human objects are not natural objects as they are
> immediately given. Nor is the human mind (*Sinn*) in
> its immediate, objective form the same as human
> sensuousness. Nature is not immediately present
> adequately to the human being either objectively or
> subjectively.[14]

Thus in materialism labor has the function of synthesis.

As soon as we understand social labor as synthesis de-
nuded of its idealist meaning, however, we run into the danger
of a transcendental-logical misunderstanding. For the category of
labor then acquires unawares the meaning of world-constituting
life activity (*Lebenspraxis*) in general. This view arises especially
if we interpret Marx's writings on the nature of man in terms of the
analyses of the life-world found in Husserl's later works. A phenomenological strain of Marxism found expression in the Thirties

in several works of Herbert Marcuse, writing under the influence of Heidegger.[15] After the war this view found supporters among those influenced by Sartre[16] and governs the interpretation of Marx in several socialist countries.[17] Nevertheless, no matter how meaningful Marx finds "considering the labor process primarily independent of every specific social form,"[18] he never regarded it as the foundation for the construction of invariant meaning structures of possible social life-worlds. Social labor is fundamental only as the category of mediating objective and subjective nature. It designates the *mechanism* of the evolution of the species in history. Through the labor process what changes is not only the nature that has been worked on but, by means of the products of labor, the necessitous nature of the laboring subjects themselves. That is why after the sentence cited above, according to which "nature is not immediately present adequately to the human being either objectively or subjectively," Marx immediately adds,

> Just as everything natural must have its genesis, so man also has his own genetic act, namely history. For man, however, this act is as such a known genetic act and therefore one that surpasses itself through consciousness. History is the true natural history of man.[19]

Because the tool-making animal distinguishes itself from all other animal species through the reproductive form of social labor, the human species is not characterized by any invariant natural or transcendental structure, but only by a mechanism of humanization (*Menschwerdung*). The evolutionary concept of the "nature of man" unmasks philosophical anthropology as an illusion just as it does transcendental philosophy. In contrast to the fleeting aspects of individual performances, productions, and gratifications, labor processes give rise to something general that accumulates in the productive forces—Hegel had already observed this with regard to the tool. In their turn these enduring productions, or stored up forces of production, transform the world within which subjects relate to their objects. Therefore the species can have no fixed essence, either as a transcendental form of life or in the empirical form of a biologically conditioned basic pattern of culture:

> This sum of forces of production, capitals, and forms of social intercourse, which each individual and each generation confront as something given, is the real foundation of what philosophers have conceived as "substance" and the "essence of man"; of what they have apotheosized and combatted . . .[20]

When Marx sees in the history of industry, that is in the evolution of the system of social labor, "the open book of man's essential powers (Wesenskräfte), human psychology existing in sensuous form,"[21] what he has in mind is not an empirical structure but the context in which the history of the species is constituted. The stages of the manifestation of consciousness are determined by transcendental rules of apprehending the world and of action. In this framework a particular "objective nature" is given to each social system, regarded as a subject. But this framework itself changes historically in dependence on a "subjective nature" that is itself formed by the results of social labor. The famous sentence that the formation of the five senses is the work of all of previous history is meant literally by Marx. The materialist study of history is directed toward societal categories that determine both the real process of life and the transcendental conditions of the constitution of life-worlds.

In opposition to Hegel's position in the Phenomenology Marx holds the conviction that the self-reflection of consciousness discloses the fundamental structures of social labor, discovering therein the synthesis of the objectively active natural being man and the nature that is his objective environment. Marx did not arrive at an explicit concept of this synthesis. He had only a more or less vague conception of it. He would have found the very concept of synthesis suspect, although the first thesis on Feuerbach directly contains an injunction to learn from idealism insofar as it grasps the "active side" of the cognitive process. Nevertheless, from various indications we can extrapolate the way in which social labor is to be conceived as the synthesis of man and nature. We must clearly articulate this materialist concept of synthesis if we wish to understand how all the elements of a critique of knowledge radicalized by Hegel's critique of Kant are present in Marx and yet are not combined to construct a materialist epistemology.

Synthesis in the materialist sense differs from the concept developed in idealist philosophy by Kant, Fichte, and Hegel, primarily in that it does not generate a logical structure. It is not the accomplishment of a transcendental consciousness, the positing of an absolute ego, or the movement of an absolute mind. Instead it is the both empirical and transcendental accomplishment of a species-subject that produces itself in history. Kant, Fichte, and Hegel can recur to the material of spoken sentences, to the logical forms of judgment: the unity of subject and predicate is the paradigmatic result of the synthesis as which the activity of consciousness, ego, or mind is conceived. Thus logic provides the substance in which the achievements of synthesis have been sedimented. Kant takes formal logic in order to derive the categories of the understanding from the table of judgments. Fichte and Hegel take transcendental logic in order to reconstruct respectively the act of the absolute ego from pure apperception and the dialectical movement of the absolute notion (concept, *Begriff*) from the antinomies and paralogisms of pure reason. If, in contrast, synthesis takes place in the medium of labor rather than thought, as Marx assumes, then the substratum in which it leaves its residue is the system of social labor and not a connection of symbols. The point of departure for a reconstruction of synthetic accomplishments is not logic but the economy. Consequently what provides the material that reflection is to deal with in order to make conscious basic synthetic accomplishments is not the correct combination of symbols according to rules, but social life processes, the material production and appropriation of products. Synthesis no longer appears as an activity of thought but as one of material production. The model for the spontaneous reproduction process of society is the productions of nature rather than those of mind. That is why for Marx the *critique of political economy* takes the place held by the *critique of formal logic* in idealism. Marx declares decisively that the much renowned "unity of man with nature" has always existed in industry and has existed differently in every epoch according to the lesser or greater development of industry. The same holds for man's "struggle" with nature until the development of his productive forces to an adequate basis.[22]

This synthesis through social labor is not an absolute one. Anything like absolute synthesis can be conceived only on the presuppositions of the philosophy of identity. Hegel's model of mind that recognizes itself in nature as in its other combines two relations of reflection: the self-reflective relation of the isolated subject to itself and the intersubjective relation of a subject that knows and recognizes a subject in the other just as the latter does with regard to the former. In the absolute identity of mind and nature the moment of difference in unity is retained from the first relation just as the moment of unity in difference is retained from the second. Absolute mind is the identity of mind and nature in the mode in which the subject knows itself to be identical with itself in self-consciousness. But this unity implies just as well the non-identity of mind and nature in the mode in which one subject knows itself to be absolutely different from another. It follows from this that absolute difference is still conceived as a relation between subjects. Therefore what unites the identity of mind and nature with their non-identity can itself be conceived according to that type of synthesis through which the identity of an ego comes into being. One of the two moments that is mediated defines the category of mediation itself: as absolute, synthesis is still conceived after the pattern of self-reflection.

Marx, on the contrary, does not view nature under the category of another subject, but conversely the subject under the category of another nature. Hence, although their unity can only be brought about by a subject, he does not comprehend it as an absolute unity. The subject is originally a natural being instead of nature being originally an aspect of the subject, as in idealism. Therefore unity, which can only come about through the activity of a subject, remains in some measure imposed on nature by the subject. The resurrection of nature cannot be logically conceived within materialism, no matter how much the early Marx and the speculative minds in the Marxist tradition (Walter Benjamin, Ernst Bloch, Herbert Marcuse, Theodor W. Adorno) find themselves attracted by this heritage of mysticism. Nature does not conform to the categories under which the subject apprehends it in the unresisting way in which a subject can conform to the understanding of another subject on the basis of reciprocal recognition under categories that are binding on both of them. The unity of the social subject and nature that comes into being "in industry" cannot eradicate the autonomy of nature and the remainder of complete otherness that is lodged in its facticity. As the correlate of social labor, objectified[23] nature retains both *independence* and *externality* in relation to the subject that controls it. Its independence manifests itself in our ability to learn to master natural processes only to the extent that we subject ourselves to them. This elementary experience is expressed in the language of natural "laws" that we must "obey." The externality of nature manifests itself in the contingency of its ultimate constants. No matter how far our power of technical control over nature is extended, nature retains a substantial core that does not reveal itself to us.

The process of production regulated in systems of social labor is a form of synthesis of man and nature that binds the objectivity of the possible objects of experience to the objective activity of subjects on the one hand, but does not eliminate the independence of its existence on the other:

> This activity, this continuous sensuous working and creating, this production is so much the foundation of the entire sensuous world as it now exists that if it were interrupted for even a year, Feuerbach would encounter a tremendous transformation not only in the natural world but would quite soon also be without the entire human world and his own perceptual faculty, and indeed his own existence. Nevertheless the priority of external nature remains, and of course all of this does not apply to the original . . . men; but this distinction has meaning only to the extent that one regards man as distinguished

> from nature. Moreover, that prehistoric nature is in any case not the nature in which Feuerbach lives, not the nature that today exists nowhere except perhaps on a few Australian coral islands. . . .[24]

Marx is assuming something like a nature in itself. It is prior to the world of mankind. It is at the root of laboring subjects as natural beings and also enters into their labor processes. But as the subjective nature of man and the objective nature of their environment, it is already part of a system of social labor that is divided up into two aspects of the same "process of material exchange." While epistemologically we must presuppose nature as existing in itself, we ourselves have access to nature only within the historical dimension disclosed by labor processes. Here nature in human form mediates itself with objective nature, the ground and environment of the human world. "Nature in itself" is therefore an abstraction, which is a requisite of our thought: but we always encounter nature within the horizon of the world-historical self-formative process of mankind. Kant's "thing-in-itself" reappears under the name of a nature preceding human history.

This conception has the important epistemological function of pointing to the contingency of nature as a whole; in opposition to the idealist attempt to reduce nature to a mere externalization of mind, it preserves nature's immovable facticity despite nature's historical embeddedness in the universal structure of mediation constituted by laboring subjects.

This discussion can be summarized as follows. Synthesis through social labor neither generates a logical structure nor creates an absolute unity of man and nature. Like Kant's original apperception, the materialist concept of synthesis preserves the difference between form and matter. Of course the forms are categories not primarily of the understanding but of objective activity; and the unity of the objectivity of possible objects of experience is formed not in transcendental consciousness but in the behavioral system of instrumental action. Nevertheless, the matter that is given is first shaped in the labor process as in the cognitive process: "In his production man can only proceed like nature herself, that is only by changing the forms of substances."[25] For the labor process is one of "forming objects, of subjecting them to a subjective end; their transformation into results and containers of subjective activity."[26] Yet if we compare the elements of the labor process with those of the cognitive process—that is if we compare the material of labor, the instruments of labor, and the labor force with the material of sensation, the categories of the understanding, and the imagination—then the characteristic *difference between Kant and Marx* becomes clear. The synthesis of the material of intuition by the imagination receives its necessary unity through categories of the understanding. As pure concepts of the understanding these transcendental rules of synthesis make up the internal and inalterable inventory of consciousness as such. The synthesis of the material of labor by labor power receives its actual unity through categories of man's manipulations. As instruments in the broadest sense, these technical rules of synthesis take on sensuous existence and belong to the historically alterable inventory of societies.[27]

The materialist concept of synthesis thus retains from Kant the fixed framework within which the subject forms a substance that it encounters. This framework is established once and for all through the equipment of transcendental consciousness or of the human species as a species of tool-making animals. On the other hand, in distinction from Kant, Marx assumes empirically mediated rules of synthesis that are objectified as productive forces and historically transform the subjects' relation to their natural environment.[28] What is Kantian about Marx's conception of knowledge is the invariant relation of the species to its natural environment, which is established by the behavioral system of instrumental action—for labor processes are the "perpetual natural necessity of human life." The conditions of instrumental action arose contingently in the natural evolution of the human species. At the same time, however, with transcendental necessity, they bind our knowledge of nature to the interest of possible technical control over natural processes. The objectivity of the possible objects of experience is constituted within a conceptual-perceptual scheme rooted in deep-seated structures of human action; this scheme is equally binding on all subjects that keep alive through labor. The objectivity of the possible objects of experience is thus grounded in the identity of a natural substratum, namely that of the bodily organization of man, which is oriented toward action, and not in an original unity of apperception, which, according to Kant, guarantees with transcendental necessity the identity of an ahistorical consciousness in general. The identity of societal subjects, in contrast, alters with the scope of their power of technical control. This point of view is fundamentally un-Kantian. The knowledge generated within the framework of instrumental action takes on external existence as a productive force. Consequently both nature, which has been reshaped and civilized in labor processes, and the laboring subjects themselves alter in relation to the development of the productive forces. The actual stage of development of the productive forces defines the level at which each generation must bring about anew the unity of subject and object.

The Kantian component of the concept of synthesis through social labor can be elaborated in an instrumentalist theory of knowledge.[29] The latter would have to make conscious the transcendental structure of labor processes within which, and only within which, the organization of experience and the objectivity of knowledge become possible from the standpoint of the technical controllability of nature. In Marx there are only a few methodological pointers toward such a theory. They were first elaborated in pragmatism, especially by Peirce[30] and Dewey.[31] But they suffice to render comprehensible the affirmative relation of materialism to the natural sciences. For the technically exploitable knowledge that is produced and tested in research processes of the natural sciences belongs to the same category as the pragmatic knowledge of everyday life acquired through trial and error in the realm of feedback-controlled action (*erfolgskontrolliertes Handeln*).[32] Marx once wrote to Kugelmann, "Natural laws can absolutely not be abolished. What can change in different historical states is only the form in which these laws take effect."[33] Only because the conditions of the objectivity of possible natural-scientific knowledge are rooted in a deep-seated structure of human action can statements of laws at all claim universal validity. In contrast, the historically changeable form is grounded in the level of development of the forces of production. At the same time this level designates that of a cumulative learning process and thus determines the conditions under which new technical knowledge arises. This knowledge is itself potentially a productive force that reacts back upon the subject via the nature to which it is applied.

This is where the second, non-Kantian component of the concept of synthesis through social labor comes into play. This component is developed in the interpretation that Fichte gives to Kant's concept of the original synthetic unity of apperception —naturally on idealist presuppositions.

Kant was faced with the problem of how synthetic unity in the manifold of representations comes into being for a finite understanding which is not given the manifold of intuition through its own self-activity. On the premise that subject and object are not identical, knowledge by the understanding is possible only when an original synthesis brings the manifold of given representations under the unity of an apperception. The synthesis of representations is brought about by my representing to myself the identity of consciousness in these representations. This occurs in self-consciousness. Thus in order to show the possibility of a cognitive faculty divided into sensibility and understanding, Kant must assume a faculty that combines all my representations, considered as collectively belonging to me, in a self-consciousness. We ascertain this spontaneous faculty of imagination in the experience of the ego being identical with itself. Fichte takes this deduction of pure apperception and turns it upside down. That is, he starts with the act of self-consciousness as the original transcendental experience, and thus with the absolutely certain, and inquires how this self-reflection is to be conceived. Fichte covers Kant's path in reverse in order to prove the identity of ego and non-ego and thus precisely to contest the presupposition on which Kant saw himself compelled to ascend to the transcendental unity of self-consciousness. According to Kant, pure apperception produces the representation "I think," which must be able to accompany identically all other representations, without this representation itself being able to be accompanied by and reflected by a further one.[34] What Fichte demands is just this reflection that goes one step further than self-consciousness.

What then emerges, however, is that whoever wants radically to think himself must depart from the dimension of mere thinking and representing and spontaneously carry out the act of self-consciousness, producing it with his own existence. Self-consciousness is not an ultimate *representation* that must be able to accompany all other representations: it is an *action* that goes back inside itself and thus in its own accomplishment simultaneously makes itself transparent—an act that becomes transparent to itself in the course of its own achievement.

Fichte's train of thought is as follows. Self-consciousness constitutes itself by my retaining myself as an identical ego in all my representations while at the same time abstracting from the entire content of what is thought. If the ego, however, in returning to itself, becomes conscious of itself, then there must already be an ego there at its basis and preceding it, to which it returns. Then, though, self-consciousness would not be original; instead it would first have to be derived from something like the ego. Yet it is only through self-consciousness that we can attain certainty about the ego: the ego is only the being-for-itself of the ego (Ich ist nur Fürsichsein des Ich). Then, however, we must penetrate behind the situation in which we obtain the representation of self-consciousness through abstraction from all that does not belong to the ego. We must construct the ego in the very act of self-consciousness itself: Ego exists only insofar as it posits itself. The ego as self-consciousness cannot coincide with the ego which experiences being or non-ego come into existence outside itself. Rather, the ego that I merely encounter knows itself as ego only insofar as it is posited by itself:

> In thinking of your present self-positing, which has
> been elevated to clear consciousness, you must
> conceive of another such positing having preceded
> it without clear consciousness; the present one
> refers to the latter and is conditioned by it.[35]

The original ego posits the ego by positing a non-ego in opposition to itself. As original ego it is nothing outside of this action of returning into itself. Since consciousness is always consciousness of something, it is precisely self-consciousness that remains beneath the threshold of clear consciousness; yet in being accomplished it is purely and simply certain.[36]

This interpretation given by Fichte with stubborn logic to Kant's pure apperception sheds light on the identity of socially laboring subjects as it is conceived by materialism. As an identical ego they find themselves confronting an environment that obtains its identity in labor processes; this environment is not ego. Although the transcendental framework within which nature appears objectively to these subjects does not change, the identity of their consciousness is formed in each case in dependence on the historical stage of development of the forces of production and an environment formed at this stage by their production. Each generation gains its identity only via a nature that has already been formed in history, and this nature is in turn the object of its labor. The system of social labor is always the result of the labor of past generations. It continually establishes a new "proportion between labor and natural substance." The present subject has in some sense been "posited" by the totality of preceding subjects, that is placed in a position to come to grips with nature at its historically determined level. Yet it cannot regard this totality as an alien subject. For the labor processes through which it has been constituted itself belong to the very same production in which it is itself engaged and which it is merely carrying forward.[37] In its labor the present subject comprehends itself by knowing itself to have been produced as by itself through the production of past subjects.

At any stage the social subject confronted by its environment relates to past processes of production and reproduction as a whole just as the ego confronted with its non-ego relates to the deed of action returning to itself, which as the absolute ego produces itself as ego by positing a non-ego in opposition to itself. Only in its process of production does the species first *posit* itself *as* a social subject. Production, that activity which Marx apostrophizes as continuous sensuous labor and creation, gives rise simultaneously to the specific formations of nature with which the social subject finds itself confronted and the forces of production that put the subject in a position to transform historically given nature in its turn, thereby forming its own identity. The identity of consciousness, which Kant understood as the unity of transcendental consciousness, is identity *achieved through labor*. It is not an immediate faculty of synthesis, or pure apperception, but an act of self-consciousness in Fichte's sense. That is why a social subject attains consciousness of itself in the strict sense only if it becomes aware of itself in its production or labor as the self-generative act of the species in general and knows itself to have been produced by the "labor of the entire previous course of world history."

In distinction to Fichte, of course, Marx refers the unconscious production of non-ego and ego only to the historical world of mankind. Actual nature is always presupposed as a substratum of the activity of positing in both its objective and subjective aspects:

> The original conditions of production appear as natural presuppositions, *natural conditions of the producer's existence*. . . . These *natural conditions of existence*, to which he relates as to an inorganic body belonging to himself, are themselves of a double nature: 1. subjective and 2. objective. He exists as member of a family, clan, tribe, etc.—which then take on varying historical forms through mixture with and conflict with others; and as such a member he relates to a particular nature (say earth, ground, and soil) as his own inorganic existence, as the condition of his production and reproduction.[38]

Marx restricts Fichte's absolute ego to the contingent human species. Its act of self-generation, the activity in which it constitutes itself, is thus absolute only in relation to historical formations of the ego and the non-ego, to societal subjects and their material environment. Production is conditioned on both sides by "natural presuppositions." The material to be worked on enters labor processes "from without," while the organism of the human laborer enters it "from beneath." From the materialist standpoint synthesis is an accomplishment relativized with regard to the sphere of world history. Marx relegates Fichte to an area bounded by Kant's transcendental philosophy on the one side and Darwin's theory of evolution on the other.

Already before Darwin, Marx is familiar with an interpretation, in terms of an anthropological theory of cognition, of transcendental philosophy in its instrumentalist construction. Synthesis through social labor presupposes the evolution of nature to the human stage—that is a finite natural production that can no longer be comprehended idealistically as synthesis. For the transcendental framework that is posited with the behavioral system of instrumental action and makes synthesis possible is grounded in the species-specific bodily organization of man as such. Without the particular physical equipment of the hominids, the "process of material exchange" could never have assumed the form of labor at the human level. Men "begin to distinguish themselves from animals as soon as they begin *to produce* their means of subsistence, a step that is conditioned by their bodily organization." "The first state of affairs of which to take note is therefore the bodily organization of these individuals and the relation it sets up between them and the rest of nature."[39] The absolute ego of social production is founded in a history of nature that brings about the tool-making animal as its result. Therefore Marx can view the history of the human species as a "real portion of natural history, of nature's becoming man."[40] However, Marx does not say *how* we can comprehend history as a continuation of natural history. We can speak of "nature's becoming man" both as the natural evolution of the human species to the threshold of culture and as the world-historical process of humanization (*Menschwerdung*). But in the first case "nature" is in the subjective genitive whereas in the second it is in the objective genitive. The materialist concept of synthesis allows us to make the historical evolution of systems of social labor plausible *at the same time* as a history of transcendental consciousness. But it is still an open question how to conceive natural history's production, which is the basis for the self-generative act of the human species, in relation to social production—in other words, how it can be comprehended as the prehistory of the history of transcendental consciousness.

The materialist concept of synthesis through social labor marks the systematic position occupied by Marx's conception of the history of mankind in the intellectual current that begins with Kant. In a turn of thought peculiarly determined by Fichte, Marx adopts the intention of Hegel's objection to the Kantian approach to the critique of knowledge. In so doing he is impervious to the philosophy of identity, which precludes epistemology as such. Notwithstanding, the philosophical foundation of this materialism proves itself insufficient to establish an unconditional phenomenological self-reflection of knowledge and thus prevent the positivist atrophy of epistemology. Considered immanently, I see the reason for this in the *reduction of the self-generative act of the human species* to labor. Alongside the forces of production in which instrumental action is sedimented, Marx's social theory also incorporates into its approach the institutional framework, the relations of production. It does not eliminate from practice the structure of symbolic interaction and the role of cultural tradition, which are the only basis on which power (*Herrschaft*) and ideology can be comprehended. But this aspect of practice is not made part of the philosophical frame of reference. It is in this very dimension, however, which does not coincide with that of instrumental action, that phenomenological experience moves. In this dimension appear the configurations of consciousness in its manifestations that Marx calls ideology, and in it reifications are dissolved by the silent force of a mode of reflection to which Marx gives back the Kantian name of critique.

Thus in Marx's works a peculiar disproportion arises between the practice of inquiry and the limited philosophical self-understanding of this inquiry. In his empirical analyses Marx comprehends the history of the species under categories of material activity *and* the critical abolition of ideologies, of instrumental action *and* revolutionary practice, of labor *and* reflection at once. But Marx interprets what he does in the more restricted conception of the species' self-reflection through work alone. The materialist concept of synthesis is not conceived broadly enough in order to explicate the way in which Marx contributes to realizing the intention of a really radicalized critique of knowledge. In fact, it even prevented Marx from understanding his own mode of procedure from this point of view.

CHAPTER THREE

The Idea of the Theory of Knowledge as Social Theory

The interpretive scheme set forth by Marx for the *Phenomenology of Mind* contains the program for an instrumentalist translation of Hegel's philosophy of absolute reflection:

> The greatness of Hegel's phenomenology and its end result—the dialectic of negativity as motive and productive principle—is thus . . . that Hegel grasps the self-generation of man as a process, objectification as de-objectification, as alienation (*Entäußerung*) and the overcoming of this alienation; in other words, that he grasps the essence of labor and comprehends objective man, who is true man because of his reality, as the result of his own labor.[1]

The idea of the self-constitution of the species through labor is to serve as the guide to appropriating the *Phenomenology* while demythologizing it. As we have shown, the assumptions of the philosophy of identity kept Hegel from reaping the real harvest of his critique of Kant, and they dissolve on this materialist basis. Ironically, however, the very viewpoint from which Marx correctly criticizes Hegel keeps him from adequately comprehending the import of his own studies. By turning the construction of the manifestation of consciousness into an encoded representation of the self-production of the species, Marx discloses the mechanism of progress in the experience of reflection, a mechanism that was concealed in Hegel's philosophy. It is the development of the forces of production that provides the impetus to abolishing and surpassing a form of life that has been rigidified in positivity and become an abstraction. But at the same time, Marx deludes himself about the nature of reflection when he reduces it to labor. He identifies "transformative abolition (*Aufheben*), as objective

43

movement which reabsorbs externalization," with the appropriation of essential powers that have been externalized in working
on material.

Marx reduces the process of reflection to the level of
instrumental action. By reducing the self-positing of the absolute
ego to the more tangible productive activity of the species, he
eliminates reflection as such as a motive force of history, even
though he retains the framework of the philosophy of reflection.
His re-interpretation of Hegel's *Phenomenology* betrays the paradoxical consequences of taking Fichte's philosophy of the ego
and undermining it with materialism. Here the appropriating
subject confronts in the non-ego not just a product of the ego but
rather some portion of the contingency of nature. In this case the
act of appropriation is no longer identical with the reflective re-
integration of some previously externalized part of the subject
itself. Marx preserves the relation of the subject's prior positing
activity (which was not transparent to itself), that is of hypostatization, to the process of becoming conscious of what has been
objectified, that is of reflection. But, on the premises of a philosophy of labor, this relation turns into the relation of production
and appropriation, of externalization and the appropriation of externalized essential powers. *Marx conceives of reflection according to the model of production.* Because he tacitly starts with this
premise, it is not inconsistent that he does not distinguish between the logical status of the natural sciences and of critique.

In fact, Marx does not completely obliterate the distinction between the natural sciences and the sciences of man. The
outlines of an instrumentalist epistemology enable him to have
a transcendental-pragmatistic conception of the natural sciences.
They represent a methodically guaranteed form of the kind of
knowledge which, on a pre-scientific level, is accumulated in the
system of social labor. In experiments, assumptions about the
lawlike connection of events are tested in a manner fundamentally identical with that of "industry," that is of pre-scientific situations of feedback-controlled action. In both cases, the transcendental viewpoint of possible technical control, subject to which
experience is organized and reality objectified, is the same. With
regard to the epistemological justification of the natural sciences

Marx stands with Kant against Hegel, although he does not identify them with knowledge as such. For Marx as for Kant the criterion of what makes science scientific is methodically guaranteed cognitive progress. Yet Marx did not simply assume this progress as evident. Instead, he measured it in relation to the degree to which natural-scientific information, regarded as in essence technically exploitable knowledge, enters the process of production:

> The natural sciences have developed an enormous
> activity and appropriated an ever growing body of
> material. Philosophy has remained just as foreign to
> them as they remained foreign to philosophy. Their
> momentary union [criticizing Schelling and Hegel] was
> only a fantastic illusion . . . In a much more practical
> fashion, natural science has intervened in human life and
> transformed it by means of industry . . . Industry is the
> real historical relation of nature, and thus of natural
> science, to man.[2]

On the other hand, Marx never explicitly discussed the specific meaning of a science of man elaborated as a critique of ideology and distinct from the instrumentalist meaning of natural science. Although he himself established the science of man in the form of critique and not as a natural science, he continually tended to classify it with the natural sciences. He considered unnecessary an epistemological justification of social theory. This shows that the idea of the self-constitution of mankind through labor sufficed to criticize Hegel but was inadequate to render comprehensible the real significance of the materialist appropriation of Hegel.

Invoking the model of physics, Marx claims to represent "the economic law of motion of modern society" as a "natural law." In the epilogue[3] to the second edition of *Capital* (Volume I) he quotes with approval the methodological evaluation of a Russian reviewer. While the latter goes along with Comte in emphasizing the difference between economics and biology on the one hand and physics and chemistry on the other, and calls attention in particular to the restriction of the validity of economic laws to specific historical periods,[4] he nevertheless equates this social theory with the natural sciences. Marx has only one concern,

> to demonstrate through precise scientific investigation
> the necessity of definite orders of social relations and to
> register as irreproachably as possible the facts that serve
> him as points of departure and confirmation . . . Marx
> considers the movement of society as a process of natural
> history, governed by laws that are not only independent
> of the will, consciousness, and intention of men but
> instead, and conversely, determine their will,
> consciousness, and intentions.[5]

In order to prove the scientific character of his analysis, Marx repeatedly made use of its analogy to the natural sciences. He never gives evidence of having revised his early intention, according to which the science of man was to form a unity with the natural sciences:

> Natural science will eventually subsume the science of
> man just as the science of man will subsume natural
> science: there will be a *single* science.[6]

This demand for a natural science of man, with its positivist overtones, is astonishing. For the natural sciences are subject to the transcendental conditions of the system of social labor, whose structural change is supposed to be what the critique of political economy, as the science of man, reflects on. Science in the rigorous sense lacks precisely this element of reflection that characterizes a critique investigating the natural-historical process of the self-generation of the social subject and also making the subject conscious of this process. To the extent that the science of man is an analysis of a constitutive process, it necessarily includes the self-reflection of science as epistemological critique. This is obliterated by the self-understanding of economics as a "human natural science." As mentioned, this abbreviated methodological self-understanding is nevertheless a logical consequence of a frame of reference restricted to instrumental action.

If we take as our basis the materialist concept of synthesis through social labor, then both the technically exploitable knowledge of the natural sciences, the knowledge of natural laws, as well as the theory of society, the knowledge of laws of human natural history, belong to the same objective context of the self-constitution of the species. From the level of pragmatic, everyday knowledge to modern natural science, the knowledge of nature derives from man's primary coming to grips with nature; at the same time it reacts back upon the system of social labor and stimulates its development. The knowledge of society can be viewed analogously. Extending from the level of the pragmatic self-understanding of social groups to actual social theory, it defines the self-consciousness of societal subjects. Their identity is reformed at each stage of development of the productive forces and is in turn a condition for steering the process of production:

> The development of fixed capital indicates the extent to which general social knowledge has become an *immediate force of production*, and therefore [!] the conditions of the social life process itself have come under the control of the general intellect.[7]

So far as production establishes the only framework in which the genesis and function of knowledge can be interpreted, the science of man also appears under categories of knowledge for control (*Verfügungswissen*). At the level of the self-consciousness of social subjects, knowledge that makes possible the control of natural processes turns into knowledge that makes possible the control of the social life process. In the dimension of labor as a process of production and appropriation, reflective knowledge (*Reflexionswissen*) changes into productive knowledge (*Produktionswissen*). Natural knowledge congealed in technologies impels the social subject to an ever more thorough knowledge of its "process of material exchange" with nature. In the end this knowledge is transformed into the steering of social processes in a manner not unlike that in which natural science becomes the power of technical control.

In the preliminary studies for the *Critique of Political*

Economy there is a model according to which the history of the species is linked to an automatic transposition of natural science and technology into a self-consciousness of the social subject (general intellect)—a consciousness that controls the material life process. According to this construction the history of transcendental consciousness would be no more than the residue of the history of technology. The latter is left exclusively to the cumulative evolution of feedback-controlled action and follows the tendency to augment the productivity of labor and to replace human labor power—"the realization of this tendency is the transformation of the means of labor into machinery."[8] The epochal turning-points in the evolution of technology show how all capacities of the human organism combined in the behavorial system of instrumental action are gradually transferred to the means of labor: First the capacities of the executing organs, then those of the sense organs, the energy production of the human organism, and finally the capacities of the controlling organ, the brain. The stages of technical progress can in principle be foreseen. In the end the entire labor process will have separated itself from man and reside only in the means of labor.[9]

The self-generative act of the human species is complete as soon as the social subject has emancipated itself from necessary labor and, so to speak, takes its place *alongside* scientized production. At that point labor time and the quantity of labor expended also become obsolete as a measure of the value of goods produced. The spell of materialism cast upon the process of humanization by the shortage of available means and the compulsion to labor will be broken. The social subject (as ego) will have permeated and appropriated the nature objectified through labor (the non-ego), as much as is conceivable under the conditions of production (the activity of the "absolute ego"). Along with the materialist interpretation of his theory of knowledge, Fichte's thought has been translated into a Saint-Simonian perspective. An unusual passage from the *Grundrisse der Kritik der Politischen Ökonomie*, which does not recur in the parallel investigations in *Capital*, fits into this framework:

> To the degree . . . that large-scale industry develops, the creation of social wealth depends less on labor time

and the quantity of labor expended than on the power of the instruments that are set in motion during labor time and which themselves in turn—their powerful effectiveness—themselves in turn are in no proportion to the immediate labor time that their production costs. Rather they depend on the general level of science and technological progress, or the application of science to production. (The development of this science, especially natural science, and all others along with it, is itself in turn proportional to the development of material production.) For example, agriculture becomes the mere application of the science of material exchange as it is to be regulated most advantageously for the entire social body. Real wealth manifests itself rather—and large industry reveals this—in the tremendous disproportion between the labor time expended and its product just as in the qualitative disproportion between labor that had been reduced to a pure abstraction and the power of the productive process that it oversees. As man relates to the process of production as overseer and regulator, labor no longer seems so much to be enclosed within the process of production. (What holds for machinery holds just as well for the combination of human activities and the development of human intercourse.) The laborer no longer inserts a modified natural object (Naturgegenstand) between the object (Objekt) and himself. Instead he inserts the natural process that he has transformed into an industrial one as a medium between himself and inorganic nature, of which he takes command. He takes his place alongside the process of production instead of being its chief agent. In this transformation what appears as the keystone of production and wealth is neither the immediate labor performed by man himself nor the time he labors but the appropriation of his own general productive force, his understanding of nature and its mastery through his societal existence—in a word, the development of the social individual. . . .

Therewith production based on exchange value

collapses, and the immediate material process of production sheds the form of scantiness and antagonism. The free development of individualities and therefore not the reduction of necessary labor time in order to create surplus labor, but rather the reduction of society's necessary labor to a minimum, which then has its counterpart in the artistic, scientific, and other education of individuals through the time that has become free for all of them and through the means that have been created.[10]

Here it is from the methodological perspective that we are interested in this conception of the transformation of the labor process into a scientific process that would bring man's "material exchange" with nature under the control of a human species totally emancipated from necessary labor. A science of man developed from this point of view would have to construct the history of the species as a synthesis through social labor—and only through labor. It would make true the fiction of the early Marx that natural science subsumes the science of man just as much as the latter subsumes the former. For, on the one hand, the scientization of production is seen as the movement that brings about the identity of a subject that knows the social life process and then also steers it. In this sense the science of man would be subsumed under natural science. On the other hand, the natural sciences are comprehended in virtue of their function in the self-generative process of the species as the exoteric disclosure of man's essential powers. In this sense, natural science would be subsumed under the science of man. The latter contains principles from which a methodology of the natural sciences resembling a transcendental-logically determined pragmatism could be derived. But this science does not question its own epistemological foundations. It understands itself in analogy to the natural sciences as productive knowledge. It thus conceals the dimension of self-reflection in which it must move regardless.

Now the argument which we have taken up was not pursued beyond the stage of the "rough sketch" ("Rohentwurf") of Capital. It is typical only of the philosophical foundation of

Marx's critique of Hegel, that is production as the "activity" of a self-constituting species. It is not typical of the actual social theory in which Marx materialistically appropriates Hegel on a broad scale. Even in the Grundrisse we find already the official view that the transformation of science into machinery does not by any means lead of itself to the liberation of a self-conscious general subject that masters the process of production. According to this other version the self-constitution of the species takes place not only in the context of men's instrumental action upon nature but simultaneously in the dimension of power relations that regulate men's interaction among themselves. Marx very precisely distinguishes the *self-conscious control* of the·social life process by the combined producers from an *automatic regulation* of the process of production that has become independent of these individuals. In the former case the workers relate to each other as combining with each other of their own accord. In the latter they are merely combined,

> so that the aggregate labor as a totality is *not* the work
> of the individual worker, and is the work of the various
> workers together only insofar as they are combined
> and not insofar as they relate to each other as combining
> of their own accord.[11]

Taken by itself, scientific-technical progress does not yet lead to a reflexive comprehension of the traditional, "natural" operation of the social life process in such a way that self-conscious control could result:

> In its combination this labor [of scientized production]
> appears just as much in the service of an alien will and an
> alien intelligence, which directs it. It has its *psychic*
> (*seelenhaft*) *unity* outside itself and its material unity
> subordinated to the *unity of machinery*, of fixed capital,
> which is *grounded in the object*. Fixed capital, as an
> *animated monster*, objectifies scientific thought and is in
> fact the encompassing aspect. It does not relate to the
> individual worker as an instrument. Instead he exists as

an animated individual detail, a living isolated accessory to the machinery.[12]

The institutional framework that resists a new stage of reflection (which, it is true, is prompted by the progress of science established as productive force) is not immediately the result of a labor process. It is to be comprehended much rather as a form of life that has been rigidified to the point of abstraction: in Hegel's phenomenological language, a form of the manifestation of consciousness. What this represents is not immediately a stage of technological development but rather a relation of social force, namely the power of one social class over another. The relation of force usually appears in *political form*. In contrast, the distinctive feature of capitalism is that the class relation is *economically* defined through the free labor contract as a form of civil law. As long as this mode of production exists, the most progressive scientization of production could not lead to the emancipation of a self-conscious subject that knows and regulates the social life process. Of necessity it would only sharpen the "litigant contradiction" ("*prozessierende Widerspruch*") of that mode of production:

> On the one hand it [capital] thus calls to life all the powers of science and of nature as of social combination and social intercourse, to make the creation of wealth (relatively) independent of the labor time expended on it. On the other, it wants to take the gigantic social forces generated in this way and measure them against labor time and confine them within the bounds required in order to preserve as value the value already created.[13]

The *two versions* that we have examined make visible an indecision that has its foundation in Marx's theoretical approach itself. For the analysis of the development of economic formations of society he adopts a concept of the system of social labor that contains more elements than are admitted to in the idea of a species that produces itself through social labor. Self-constitution through social labor is conceived *at the categorial level* as a process of production, and instrumental action, labor in the sense of material activity, or work designates the dimension in which natural history moves. *At the level of his material investigations*, on the other hand, Marx always takes account of social practice that encompasses both work and interaction. The processes of natural history are mediated by the productive activity of individuals and the organization of their interrelations. These relations are subject to norms that decide, with the force of institutions, how responsibilities and rewards, obligations and charges to the social budget are distributed among members. The medium in which these relations of subjects and of groups are normatively regulated is cultural tradition. It forms the linguistic communication structure on the basis of which subjects interpret both nature and themselves in their environment.

While *instrumental action* corresponds to the constraint of external nature and the level of the forces of production determines the extent of technical control over natural forces, *communicative action* stands in correspondence to the suppression of man's own nature. The institutional framework determines the extent of repression by the unreflected, "natural" force of social dependence and political power, which is rooted in prior history and tradition. A society owes emancipation from the external forces of nature to labor processes, that is to the production of technically exploitable knowledge (including "the transformation of the natural sciences into machinery"). Emancipation from the compulsion of internal nature succeeds to the degree that institutions based on force are replaced by an organization of social relations that is bound only to communication free from domination. This does not occur directly through productive activity, but rather through the revolutionary activity of struggling classes (including the critical activity of reflective sciences). Taken together, both categories of social practice make possible what Marx, interpreting Hegel, calls the self-generative act of the species. He sees their connection effected in the system of social labor. That is why "production" seems to him the movement in which instrumental action and the institutional framework, or "productive activity" and "relations of production," appear merely as different aspects of the same process.[14]

However, if the institutional framework does not subject all members of society to the same repressions, then the tacit expansion of the frame of reference to include in social practice both work *and* interaction must necessarily acquire decisive importance for the construction of the history of the species and the question of its epistemological foundation. If production attains the level of producing goods over and above elementary needs, the problem arises of distributing the surplus product created by labor. This problem is solved by the *formation of social classes*, which participate to varying degrees in the burdens of production and in social rewards. With the cleavage of the social system into classes that are made permanent by the institutional framework, the social subject loses its unity: "To regard society as *one* single subject is, moreover, to regard it falsely—speculatively."[15]

As long as we regard the self-constitution of the species through labor only with respect to the power of control over natural processes that accumulates in the forces of production, it is meaningful to speak of the social system in general and to speak of the social subject in the singular. For the level of development of the forces of production determines the system of social labor as a whole. In principle the members of a society all live at the same level of mastery of nature, which in each case is given with the available technical knowledge. So far as the identity of a society takes form via this level of scientific-technical progress, it is the self-consciousness of "the" social subject. But as we now see, the self-formative process of the species does not coincide with the genesis of this subject of scientific-technical progress. Rather, this "self-generative act," which Marx comprehended as a materialistic activity, is accompanied by a self-formative process mediated by the interaction of class subjects either under compulsory integration or in open rivalry.

While the constitution of the species in the dimension of labor appears linearly as a process of production and the growth of complexity, in the dimension of the struggle of social classes it takes place as a process of oppression and self-emancipation. In both dimensions each new stage of development is characterized by a supersession of constraint: through eman-

cipation from external natural constraint in one and from repressions of internal nature in the other. The course of
scientific-technical progress is marked by the epochal innovations
through which functional elements of the behavioral system of
instrumental action are reproduced step by step at the level of
machines. The limiting value of this development is thus defined:
the organization of society itself as an automaton. The course of
the social self-formative process, on the other hand, is marked not
by new technologies but by stages of reflection through which
the dogmatic character of surpassed forms of domination and
ideologies are dispelled, the pressure of the institutional framework is sublimated, and communicative action is set free as
communicative action. The goal of this development is thereby
anticipated: the organization of society linked to decision-making
processes on the basis of discussion free from domination. Rais-
ing the productivity of technically exploitable knowledge, which
in the sphere of socially necessary labor leads to the complete
substitution of machinery for men, has its counterpart here in the
self-reflection of consciousness in its manifestations to the point
where the self-consciousness of the species has attained the level
of critique and freed itself from all ideological delusion. The two
developments do not converge. Yet they are interdependent;
Marx tried in vain to capture this in the dialectic of forces of
production and relations of production. In vain—for the meaning
of this "dialectic" must remain unclarified as long as the materialist concept of the synthesis of man and nature is restricted to the
categorial framework of production.

If the idea of the self-constitution of the human species
in natural history is to combine both *self-generation through productive activity* and *self-formation through critical-revolutionary
activity*, then the concept of synthesis must also incorporate a second dimension. The ingenious combination of Kant and Fichte
then no longer suffices.

Synthesis through labor mediates the social subject with
external nature as its object. But this process of mediation is in-
terlocked with synthesis through struggle, which, in each case,
mediates two partial subjects of society that make each other into
objects—in other words, two social classes. Knowledge, the syn-

thesis of the material of experience and forms of the mind, is only one aspect of both processes of mediation. Reality is interpreted from a technical viewpoint in the former and from a practical viewpoint in the latter. Synthesis through labor brings about a theoretical-technical relation between subject and object; synthesis through struggle brings about a theoretical-practical relation between them. Productive knowledge arises in the first, reflective knowledge in the second. The only model that presents itself for synthesis of the second sort comes from Hegel. It treats of the dialectic of the moral life, developed by Hegel in his early theological writings, in political writings of the Frankfurt period, and in the Jena philosophy of mind, but which he did not incorporate into his system.[16]

In his fragment on the spirit of Christianity, Hegel unfolds the dialectic of the moral life through the example of the punishment that befalls one who destroys a moral totality. The "criminal" annuls the complementarity of unconstrained communication and the reciprocal gratification of needs by putting himself as an individual in place of the totality. In so doing he sets off a process of fate that turns upon him. The struggle ignited between the conflicting parties and the hostility against the other who has been injured and oppressed render perceptible the lost complementarity and past friendship. The criminal is confronted with the negating power of his past life. He experiences his guilt. The guilty one must suffer under the violence of the repressed and sundered life, which he has himself provoked, until he experiences in the repression of the other's life the deficiency of his own, and, in his turning away from the other subject, his alienation from himself. This *causality of fate* is ruled by the power of the suppressed life. The latter can only be reconciled if the experience of the negativity of the sundered life gives rise to yearning for what has been lost and compels the guilty one to identify with the existence of the other, against which he is struggling, as that which he is denying in his own. Then both parties recognize their rigidified position in relation to each other as the result of detachment and abstraction from their common life context. And in the latter, the dialogic relation of recognizing oneself in the other, they experience the common ground of their existence.

Marx could have employed this model and constructed the disproportional appropriation of the surplus product, which has class antagonism as its consequence, as a "crime." The punitive causality of fate is executed upon the rulers as class struggle coming to a head in revolutions. Revolutionary violence reconciles the disunited parties by abolishing the alienation of class antagonism that set in with the repression of initial morality. In his work on municipal government and in the fragment of the introduction to his work on the German constitution Hegel developed the dialectic of the moral life with regard to political conditions in Würtemberg and the old German Empire. The positivity of rigidified political life mirrors the disruption of a moral totality; and the revolution that must occur is the reaction of suppressed life, which will visit the causality of fate upon the rulers.

Marx, however, conceives the moral totality as a society in which men produce in order to reproduce their own life through the appropriation of an external nature. Morality is an institutional framework constructed out of cultural tradition; but it is a framework for processes of production. Marx takes the dialectic of the moral life, which operates on the basis of social labor, as the law of motion of a defined conflict between definite parties. The conflict is always about the organization of the appropriation of socially created products, while the conflicting parties are determined by their position in the process of production, that is as classes. As the movement of class antagonism, the dialectic of the moral life is linked to the development of the system of social labor. The overcoming of abstraction, that is the critical-revolutionary reconciliation of the estranged parties, succeeds only relative to the level of development of the forces of production. The institutional framework also incorporates the constraint of external nature, which expresses itself in the degree of mastery of nature, the extent of socially necessary labor, and in the relation of available rewards to socially developed demands. Through the repression of needs and wishes, it translates this constraint into a compulsion of internal nature, in other words into the constraint of social norms. That is why the relative destruction of the moral relation can be measured only by the difference between the *actual* degree of institutionally *demanded* repression and the degree of repression that is necessary at a given level of the forces of production. This difference is a measure of objectively super-fluous domination. It is those who establish such domination and defend positions of power of this sort who set in motion the cau-sality of fate, divide society into social classes, suppress justified interests, call forth the reactions of suppressed life, and finally experience their just fate in revolution. They are compelled by the revolutionary class to recognize themselves in it and thereby to overcome the alienation of the existence of *both* classes. As long as the constraint of external nature persists in the form of economic scarcity, every revolutionary class is induced, after its victory, to a new "injustice," namely the establishment of a new class rule. Therefore the dialectic of the moral life must repeat itself until the materialist spell that is cast upon the reproduction of social life, the Biblical curse of necessary labor, is broken tech-nologically.

Even then the dialectic of the moral life does not auto-matically come to rest. But the inducement by which it is hence-forth kept in motion assumes a new quality. It now stems not from scarcity, but rather only from the masochistic gratification of a form of domination that impedes taming the struggle for existence, which is objectively possible, and puts off uncoercive in-teraction on the basis of communication free from domination. This domination is then reproduced only for its own sake. It hin-ders alteration of the aggregate state of natural history—the tran-sition to a history freed from the dialectic of the moral life, which could unfold in the medium of dialogue on the basis of produc-tion relieved of human labor.

Unlike synthesis through social labor, the dialectic of class antagonism is a movement of reflection. For the dialogic relation of the complementary unification of opposed subjects, the re-establishment of morality, is a relation of *logic* and of *life conduct* (*Lebenspraxis*) at once. This can be seen in the dialectic of the moral relation developed by Hegel under the name of the *struggle for recognition.* Here the suppression and renewal of the dialogue situation are reconstructed as a moral relation. The gram-matical relations of communication, once distorted by force, exert force themselves. Only the result of dialectical movement eradicates this force and brings about the freedom from constraint contained in dialogic self-recognition-in-the-other: in the language of the young Hegel, love as reconciliation. Thus it is not unconstrained intersubjectivity itself that we call dialectic, but the history of its repression and re-establishment. The distortion of the dialogic relation is subject to the causality of split-off symbols and reified grammatical relations: that is, relations that are removed from public communication, prevail only behind the backs of subjects, and are thus also empirically coercive.

Marx, confronted with contemporary capitalism, analyzes a social form that no longer institutionalizes class antagonism in the form of immediate political domination and social force; instead, it stabilizes it in the legal institution of the free labor contract, which congeals productive activity into the commodity form. This commodity form is objective illusion, because it makes the object of conflict unrecognizable for both parties, capitalists as well as wage laborers, and restricts their communication. The commodity form of labor is ideology, because it simultaneously conceals and expresses the suppression of an unconstrained dialogic relation:

> The mystery of the commodity form, therefore, is simply that it takes the social characteristics of men's own labor and reflects them back to men as the objective characteristics of the products of labor themselves, as the social natural properties of these things. It thus also reflects the social relation of the producers to the totality of labor as a social relation of objects, one that exists independently of the producers. Through this quid pro quo the products of labor become commodities and natural supernatural (*sinnlich übersinnliche*) or social things. Thus the light impression something makes on the optic nerve does not appear as a subjective stimulus of the optic nerve itself but as the objective form of a thing outside the eye. But in vision light really is projected from one thing, the external object, onto another thing, the eye. It is a physical relation between physical things. On the contrary, the commodity form,

> and the value relation of the products of labor in which
> it is expressed, have absolutely nothing to do with their
> physical nature and the concrete (*dingliche*) relations
> arising from it. Here it is only the specific social relation
> of men themselves that assumes for them the
> phantasmagoric form of a relation of things. Hence in
> order to find an analogy we must take flight to the
> obscure region of the religious world. Here the products
> of the human mind appear endowed with their own life,
> as independent forms that enter into relations with one
> another and with men. In the commodity world, the
> same holds for the products of the human hand. This I
> call the fetishism that clings to the products of labor as
> soon as they are produced as commodities, and which
> therefore is inseparable from commodity production.[17]

The institutionally secured suppression of the communication
through which a society is divided into social classes amounts to
fetishizing the true social relations. Thus, according to Marx, the
distinguishing feature of capitalism is that it has brought ideologies from the heights of mythological or religious legitimations of
tangible domination and power down into the system of social
labor. In liberal bourgeois society the legitimation of power is
derived from the legitimation of the market, that is from the
"justice" of the exchange of equivalents inherent in exchange relations. It is unmasked by the critique of commodity fetishism.

    I have chosen this example because it is central to Marx's
theory of society. It shows that the transformation of the institutional framework, viewed as the movement of class antagonism,
is a dialectic of the consciousness of classes in its manifestations.
Particularly a social theory that conceives the self-constitution of
the species from the *double* perspective of synthesis through the
struggle of classes and their social labor, therefore, will be able to
analyze the natural history of production only in the framework
of a reconstruction of the manifestations of the consciousness of
these classes. The system of social labor develops only in an objective connection with the antagonism of classes; the development of the forces of production is intertwined with the history

of revolutions. The results of this class struggle are always sedimented in the institutional framework of a society, in social form. Now, as the repeated dialectic of the moral life, this struggle is a process of reflection writ large. In it the forms of class consciousness arise: not idealistically in the self-movement of an absolute mind but materialistically on the basis of objectifications of the appropriation of an external nature. This reflection, in which an existing form of life is convicted of its abstraction and thereby revolutionized, is prompted by the growing potential of control over the natural processes objectified in work. The development of the forces of production at any time augments the disproportion between institutionally demanded and objectively necessary repression, thereby making conscious the existing untruth, the felt disruption of a moral totality.

This has two consequences for the methodological status of social theory. On the one hand the science of man is continuous with the self-reflection of class consciousness in its manifestations. Like the *Phenomenology of Mind* it is guided by the experience of reflection in reconstructing the course of the manifestation of consciousness, although the latter is now seen as prompted by developments of the system of social labor. But, on the other hand, this science of man also resembles Hegel's *Phenomenology* in knowing itself to be involved in the self-formative process that it recollects. The knowing subject must also direct the critique of ideology at itself. The natural sciences merely extend in methodical form the technically exploitable knowledge that has accumulated prescientifically within the transcendental framework of instrumental action. The science of man, however, extends in methodical form the reflective knowledge that is already transmitted prescientifically within the same objective structure of the dialectic of the moral life in which this science finds itself situated. In this structure, the knowing subject can only cast off the traditional form in which it appears to the degree that it comprehends the self-formative process of the species as a movement of class antagonism mediated at every stage by processes of production, recognizes itself as the result of the history of class consciousness in its manifestations, and thereby, as self-consciousness, frees itself from objective illusion.

For Marx, the phenomenological exposition of consciousness in its manifestations, which served Hegel only as an *introduction* to scientific knowledge, becomes the frame of reference in which the analysis of the history of the species *stays* confined. Marx did not adopt an epistemological perspective in developing his conception of the history of the species as something that has to be comprehended materialistically. Nevertheless, if social practice does not only accumulate the successes of instrumental action but also, through class antagonism, produces and reflects on objective illusion, then, as part of this process, the analysis of history is possible only in a phenomenologically mediated (*gebrochen*) mode of thought. The science of man itself is critique and must remain so. For after arriving at the concept of synthesis through a reconstruction of the course of consciousness in its manifestations, there is only one condition under which critical consciousness could adopt a perspective that allowed disengaging social theory from the epistemological mediation of phenomenological self-reflection: that is if critical consciousness could apprehend and understand itself as absolute synthesis. As it is, however, social theory remains embedded in the framework of *phenomenology*, while the latter, under materialist presuppositions, assumes the form of the *critique of ideology*.

If Marx had reflected on the methodological presuppositions of social theory as he sketched it out and not overlaid it with a philosophical self-understanding restricted to the categorial framework of production, the difference between rigorous empirical science and critique would not have been concealed. If Marx had not thrown together interaction and work under the label of social practice (*Praxis*), and had he instead related the materialist concept of synthesis likewise to the accomplishments of instrumental action and the nexuses of communicative action, then the idea of a science of man would not have been obscured by identification with natural science. Rather, this idea would have taken up Hegel's critique of the subjectivism of Kant's epistemology and surpassed it materialistically. It would have made clear that ultimately a radical critique of knowledge can be carried out only in the form of a reconstruction of the history of the species, and that conversely social theory, from the viewpoint of the self-constitution of the species in the medium of social labor and class struggle, is possible only as the self-reflection of the knowing subject.

On this foundation philosophy's position with regard to science could have been explicitly clarified. Philosophy is preserved in science as critique. A social theory that puts forth the claim to be a self-reflection of the history of the species cannot simply negate philosophy. Rather, the heritage of philosophy issues in the critique of ideology, a mode of thought that determines the method of scientific analysis itself. Outside of critique, however, philosophy retains no rights. To the degree that the science of man is a material critique of knowledge, philosophy, which as pure epistemology robbed itself of all content, indirectly regains its access to material problems. As philosophy, however, the universal scientific knowledge that philosophy wanted to be succumbs to the annihilating judgment of critique.[18]

Marx did not develop this idea of the science of man. By equating critique with natural science, he disavowed it. Materialist scientism only reconfirms what absolute idealism had already accomplished: the elimination of epistemology in favor of unchained universal "scientific knowledge"—but this time of scientific materialism instead of absolute knowledge.

With his positivist demand for a natural science of the social, Comte merely needed to take Marx, or at least the intention that Marx believed himself to be pursuing, at his word. Positivism turned its back to the theory of knowledge, whose philosophical self-liquidation had been carried on by Hegel and Marx, who were of one mind in this regard. In so doing, positivism regressed behind the level of reflection once attained by Kant. In continuity with pre-critical traditions, however, it successfully set about the task, which epistemology had abandoned and from which Hegel and Marx believed themselves exempted, of elaborating a methodology of the sciences.

PART TWO

Positivism, Pragmatism, Historicism

Positivism marks the end of the theory of knowledge. In its place emerges the philosophy of science. Transcendental-logical inquiry into the conditions of possible knowledge aimed as well at explicating the meaning of knowledge as such. Positivism cuts off this inquiry, which it conceives as having become meaningless in virtue of the fact of the modern sciences. Knowledge is implicitly defined by the achievement of the sciences. Hence transcendental inquiry into the conditions of possible knowledge can be meaningfully pursued only in the form of methodological inquiry into the rules for the construction and corroboration of scientific theories. True, Kant had also tacitly adopted from contemporary physics a normative concept of science. Leaving aside the point that this assumption already contradicts the intention of an unprejudiced critique of knowledge, Kant took the form of modern science as the starting point of an investigation into the constitution of possible objects of causal-analytic knowledge. Positivism loses sight of this dimension, because it conceives of the fact of modern science not so much as eliminating the question of the meaning of knowledge in general but as prejudging its answer. Positivism certainly still expresses a philosophical position with regard to science, for the scientistic self-understanding of the sciences that it articulates does not coincide with science itself. But by making a dogma of the sciences' belief in themselves, positivism assumes the prohibitive function of protecting scientific inquiry from epistemological self-reflection. Positivism is philosophical only insofar as is necessary for the immunization of the sciences against philosophy. For methodology by itself does not suffice; it must also prove itself as epistemology or, better, as its legitimate and reliable executor. Positivism stands and falls with the principle of scientism, that is that the meaning of knowledge is defined by what the sciences do and can thus be adequately explicated through the methodological analysis of scientific procedures. Any epistemology that transcends the framework of methodology as such now succumbs to the same sentence of extravagance and meaninglessness that it once passed on metaphysics.

The replacement of epistemology by the philosophy of

science is visible in that the knowing subject is no longer the system of reference. From Kant through Marx the subject of cognition was comprehended as consciousness, ego, mind, and species. Therefore problems of the validity of statements could be decided only with reference to a synthesis, no matter how much the concept of synthesis changed with that of the subject. Explicating the meaning of the validity of judgments or propositions was possible through recourse to the genesis of conditions that are not located in the same dimension as that of the contents of the judgments or propositions. Questions about the conditions of possible knowledge were answered with a universal genetic history. Each history reports on the deeds and destinies of a subject, even where it is through them that the subject is first formed. But the philosophy of science renounces inquiry into the knowing subject. It orients itself directly toward the sciences, which are given as systems of propositions and procedures, that is, as a complex of rules according to which theories are constructed and corroborated. For an epistemology restricted to methodology, the subjects who proceed according to these rules lose their significance. Their deeds and destinies belong at best to the psychology of the empirical persons to whom the subjects of knowledge have been reduced. The latter have no import for the immanent elucidation of the cognitive process. The obverse of this restriction is the development through which logic and mathematics become independent, self-sufficient formal sciences, so that henceforth the problems of their foundations are no longer discussed in connection with the problem of knowledge.[1] As the methodology of research, the philosophy of science presupposes the validity of formal logic and mathematics. As autochthonous sciences these in turn are severed from the dimension in which the genesis of their fundamental operations can be made the subject of inquiry.

Once epistemology has been flattened out to methodology, it loses sight of the constitution of the objects of possible experience; in the same way, a formal science dissociated from transcendental reflection becomes blind to the genesis of rules for the combination of symbols. In Kantian terms, both ignore the synthetic achievements of the knowing subject.[2] The positivistic attitude conceals the problems of world constitution. *The meaning of knowledge itself becomes irrational*—in the name of rigorous knowledge. In this way the naive idea that knowledge describes reality becomes prevalent. This is accompanied by the copy theory of truth, according to which the reversibly univocal correlation of statements and matters of fact must be understood as isomorphism. Until the present day this objectivism has remained the trademark of a philosophy of science that appeared on the scene with Comte's positivism. Transcendental-logical inquiry into the meaning of knowledge is replaced by positivistic inquiry into the meaning of "facts" whose connection is described by theoretical propositions. Ernst Mach radicalized this manner of posing the question and developed the philosophy of science on the basis of a doctrine of elements that is supposed to elucidate the facticity of facts as such.

Positivism so lastingly repressed older philosophical traditions and so effectively monopolized the self-understanding of the sciences that, given the self-abolition of the critique of knowledge by Hegel and Marx, the illusion of objectivism can no longer be dispelled by a return to Kant but only immanently—by forcing methodology to carry out a process of self-reflection in terms of its own problems. Objectivism deludes the sciences with the image of a self-subsistent world of facts structured in a lawlike manner; it thus conceals the a priori constitution of these facts. It can no longer be effectively overcome from without, from the position of a repurified epistemology, but only by a methodology that transcends its own boundaries. The beginnings of this sort of *self-reflection of the sciences* can be found in the works of Charles Sanders Peirce and Wilhelm Dilthey. The pragmatist and historicist critiques of meaning emerged from the contexts of the methodology of the natural and cultural sciences respectively. Nevertheless, Peirce (1839–1914) and Dilthey (1833–1911), contemporaries of Mach (1834–1916), were each in his way still so much under the spell of positivism, that in the end they do not quite escape from objectivism and cannot comprehend as such the foundation of the knowledge-constitutive interests toward which their thought moves.

CHAPTER FOUR

Comte and Mach: *The Intention of Early Positivism*

Positivism first appears in the form of a new philosophy of history. This is paradoxical. For the scientistic content of positivist doctrine, according to which legitimate knowledge is possible only in the system of the empirical sciences, is obviously at odds with the form in which positivism originated; namely the philosophy of history. Comte's law of three stages provides a rule according to which the intellectual development of both individuals and the species as a whole is supposed to take place. This developmental law obviously has a logical form that does not correspond to the status of lawlike hypotheses in the empirical sciences. The knowledge that Comte invokes in order to interpret the meaning of positive knowledge does not itself meet the standards of the positive spirit.[1] This paradox disappears as soon as we discern the intention of early positivism: the pseudo-scientific propagation of the cognitive monopoly of science.

Epistemology could not be replaced by the philosophy of science without some mediation. Because the philosophical concept of knowledge had been liquidated, the meaning of science would have become irrational, had positivism not supplied science with a meaning in terms of the philosophy of history. Henceforth the phenomenon of scientific-technical progress obtains supreme significance. The knowing subject's reflection upon itself is replaced by the investigation, from the perspective of the philosophy of history, of an empirical state of affairs, that is the analysis of both the history of modern inquiry and the social consequences of institutionalized scientific progress. As soon as knowledge is regarded as sufficiently defined by the example of the modern sciences, science can no longer be comprehended within the horizon of possible and a priori reflected knowledge. Thus the only remaining basis for elucidating the meaning of science is the process of the birth of modern scientific inquiry

71

and the social functions of a mode of inquiry that revolutionizes the entire context of life. Because the concept of knowledge becomes irrational, the methodology of the sciences and the scientific rationalization of life conduct must interpret each other reciprocally. This is the real job of early positivism. It justifies the sciences' scientistic belief in themselves by constructing the history of the species as the history of the realization of the positive spirit:

> What is at issue is man's actual influence on the external world, the gradual development of which constitutes without doubt one of the main aspects of social evolution. Indeed, it can even be said that without its development this entire evolution would have been impossible. . . . The political as well as moral and intellectual development of humanity is absolutely inseparable from its material progress. . . . Hence it is clear that the impact of man on nature depends mainly on the knowledge it has acquired regarding the real laws of inorganic phenomena, although biological philosophy certainly plays a role. . . . Physics . . . and chemistry even more so . . . (constitute) the real basis of human power . . . , whereas astronomy, despite the important part it plays, contributes only through its indispensable foresight and cannot bring about any direct modification of the surrounding milieu. . . .[2]

Marx, also, analyzes the role of scientific-technical progress in the self-constitution of the human species. But he adopts the idealist concept of knowledge and reduces it to synthesis through social labor, grounding technical control over nature and sociocultural evolution precisely from an epistemological perspective. In contrast, Comte must attach to the contingent circumstance of scientific progress a philosophy of history that can illuminate a concept of science detached from epistemology and blinded through positivism.

Comte borrowed from Condorcet and Saint-Simon the main features of the construction according to which the mind of individuals as well as the species goes through a theological and a metaphysical stage before entering the era of the positive spirit. The simultaneously historical and systematic hierarchy of the six basic sciences, that is mathematics and astronomy, physics and chemistry, and finally biology and sociology, with which Comte renews the encyclopedic concept of the sciences, is equally un-original. Even less can Comte claim to have made discoveries in the realm of methodology; the methodological ideas of his philosophy of science are more or less commonplaces of the empiricist and rationalist traditions. The boring character of early positivism can be accounted for as a result of its eclectic combination of familiar elements. Nevertheless, it revolutionized philosophy's position with regard to the sciences. Its specific achievement is to take assertions of precritical epistemology and pry them out of the system of reference of the perceiving and judging subject, and to reduce them to stipulations of a methodology of the sciences by putting scientific-technical progress, as the subject of a scientistic philosophy of history, in the place of the epistemological subject. Comte's provisional systematization of science, which he introduces as an encyclopedic law, makes it possible to take these methodological principles, which have been isolated from their epistemological contexts, and refer them directly to the process of the development of the modern sciences and a progressive rationalization of social relations.

The philosophy of science could only make any headway at all in the wake of a scientistic philosophy of history. This is because the epistemological background of the concept of science could not be liquidated without at least compensating the philosophical concept of knowledge, which was metaphysically devalued, with an explication of the meaning of science. Of course, analytic philosophy of science has long gotten rid of this apparently remaining metaphysical residue. Nevertheless, as soon as methodology reflects on itself it must have recourse to a theory of scientific progress; this can be seen in the logically consistent thought of Karl Popper.[3] The dimension still unhesitatingly annexed by early positivism is in no way an accident associated with the origins of the philosophy of science. On the contrary, it marks a path that is necessary for the reduction of epistemology to the philosophy of science. Insofar as the latter can be induced to self-reflection, it must traverse this path backwards.

Comte's philosophy of science can be reduced to methodological rules, all of which are supposed to be covered by the term "positive": the "positive spirit" is linked to procedures that guarantee scientific objectivity (*Wissenschaftlichkeit*). In his discourse on the spirit of positivism, Comte provides a semantic analysis of the word. He uses "positive" to refer to the actual in contrast to the merely imaginary (*réel-chimérique*), what can claim certainty in contrast to the undecided (*certitude-l'indécision*), the exact in contrast to the indefinite (*le précis—le vague*), the useful in contrast to the vain (*l'utile—l'oiseux*), and, finally, what claims relative validity in contrast to the absolute (*le relative—l'absolu*).[4]

The contrast between the factual and the merely imaginary provides the criterion for a strict separation between science and metaphysics. Our intelligence should direct itself at "really attainable objects of research while . . . excluding unfathomable mysteries."[5] Positivism wants to eliminate orientations of inquiry that are meaningless because they are undecidable; this is to be done by restricting to "facts" the object domain (*Objektbereich*)[6] of possible scientific analyses. But Comte does not attempt to distinguish between facts and fancies directly by means of an ontological definition of the factual. Everything that can become the object of rigorous science counts as a fact. Therefore the delimitation of the object domain of science leads back to the question of how science itself is to be defined. At the only level positivism allows, science can be defined only by the methodological rules according to which it proceeds.

First, positivism adopts the basic rule of the empiricist schools that all knowledge has to prove itself through the *sense certainty* of systematic observation that secures intersubjectivity. Only perception can claim evidence with regard to reality. Observation is thus the "only possible foundation of cognitions that are really obtainable and wisely suited to our actual needs."[7] Sense experience defines access to the domain of facts. Science that makes statements about reality is always empirical science.

Nevertheless, positivism does not regard the certainty of knowledge as guaranteed exclusively by its empirical basis. Me-

thodical certainty is just as important as sense certainty. While the reliability of metaphysical knowledge was based on the unity and interconnectedness of being as a whole, the reliability of scientific knowledge is guaranteed by unity of method. Science is directed at the manifold of facts, which are in principle infinite and which can never be comprehended in their totality. Therefore, the unity of knowledge can no longer be lodged objectively in a world that fits together into a system by itself. Instead it must be grounded subjectively in a systematic procedure of the investigator: "In this sense we need seek no other unity than that of . . . the positive method."[8] Science asserts the priority of method over substance, because we can reliably inform ourselves about substance only with the aid of scientific modes of procedure. The certainty of knowledge demanded by positivism thus means simultaneously the empirical certainty of sensory evidence and the methodical certainty of obligatorily unitary procedure.

The demand for *precision in knowledge* goes beyond this. The exactitude of our knowledge is guaranteed only by the formally cogent construction of theories that allow the deduction of lawlike hypotheses. In distinction from erudition that accumulates facts, scientific theories

> consist essentially of laws and not of facts, although the latter are indispensable for their justification and confirmation. Thus no isolated fact, no matter of what sort, can really be incorporated into science before it is at least correctly connected with some other conception through the aid of a rational hypothesis.[9]

Existential statements about facts obtain scientific value only if they are "correctly connected" with theoretical statements. For only the analytic interconnection of universal propositions and the logical connection of observation statements with such theories secure the precision of our knowledge. Comte comprehends the relevance of deductive connections as opposed to mere description. He sees

> that the positive mind, without mistaking the necessary predominance of reality observed in all form, always

strives as much as possible to expand the area of rational
inference at the cost of experimentation. . . . Scientific
progress consists mainly in decreasing gradually the
number of separate and independent laws through an
unceasing extension of their connections.[10]

Only in this way can an "increasing harmony between our conceptions and observations" be attained.[11] Comte knows himself
to be the heir of the rationalist tradition. He himself compares
the chapter in which he summarizes his thoughts on the positive
method with Descartes' *Discourse on Method*.[12] On the other
hand, the reason that he can freely combine rationalist and empiricist principles is that they are functioning not as components
of a theory of knowledge, but as normative rules of scientific
procedure, through which science itself receives its definition.

Positivism's additional demand for the *utility of knowledge* derives from this combination of the two epistemologically
opposed traditions. From empiricism Comte borrows the viewpoint that scientific cognitions must be technically utilizable. He
is convinced that "all of our sound theories [are necessarily re-
lated] to the continuous improvement of our individual and collective conditions of life—in opposition to the vain gratification
of a sterile curiosity."[13] Hence the talk of harmony between science and technology. Science makes possible technical control
over processes of both nature and society:

It is important above all . . . that previously the
fundamental relation of science and technology
necessarily could not be grasped adequately by even the
best minds, owing to the insufficient extension of natural
science, which remained foreign to the most important
and most difficult areas of inquiry immediately relevant
to human society. Indeed, in this way the rational
comprehension of the effect of man upon nature was
essentially restricted to the inorganic world. . . . Once
this huge gap is adequately filled—a process that is
beginning today—the fundamental significance of this
great practical goal [of the sciences] for the continual

stimulation and often even the better direction of the
highest theories . . . will be recognized. For technology
will then be no longer exclusively geometrical,
mechanical, or chemical, etc., but also and primarily
political and moral.[14]

Comte adopts the old principle formulated by Bacon for future
natural sciences and extends its validity to future social sciences:
"To see in order to foresee: that is the permanent distinguishing
feature of true science."[15] But he observes that the power of control over nature and society can be multiplied only by following
rationalist principles—not through the blind expansion of empirical research, but through the development and the unification
of theories. Only acquaintance with laws allows us to both explain and foresee facts:

> It is really in the laws of phenomena that science
> consists, for which the actual facts, no matter how exact
> and numerous, always provide only the indispensable
> raw material. . . . Thus one can say without any
> exaggeration that genuine science—far from consisting of
> simple facts—always aims as much as possible at freeing
> us from immediate [empirical] research by replacing
> the latter with that rational foresight which represents in
> every respect the hall-mark of the positive spirit. . . .
> This significant property of all our sound theories is just
> as important for their practical utility as for their
> intrinsic value. For the immediate investigation of fixed
> phenomena would not suffice to permit us to change
> their course if it did not lead us to foresee the latter
> adequately.[16]

If certainty, precision, and utility are the criteria of the scientific
character of our statements, then it follows that our knowledge
is in principle *unfinished and relative*, in accordance with the
"relative nature of the positive spirit." The knowledge of laws,
checked by experience, methodically arrived at, and convertible
into technically exploitable predictions, is relative knowledge in-

sofar as it can no longer pretend to know what there is in its essence, that is absolutely. Scientific knowledge is not, like metaphysics, the knowledge of ultimate origins (*Ursprungswissen*).

> The fundamental revolution that characterizes the generation of our spirit consists essentially in everywhere replacing the unattainable determination of authentic causes [that is final causes or substantial forms] with the simple investigation of *laws*, that is of the constant relations existing between observable phenomena. . . . Not only must our positive investigations universally and essentially be restricted to the systematic judgment of what is, by renouncing the discovery of its ultimate origin and final designation, but it is also important to realize that this study of phenomena, instead of somehow being capable of becoming absolute . . . , must always remain *relative* to our organization and our situation.[17]

Comte, however, does not conceive the relativity of knowledge in the epistemological sense as a question of the constitution of a world of possible objectifications of reality. Rather he asserts only the abstract antithesis of science and metaphysics. Early positivism retains in singularly uncritical fashion the metaphysical separation of the world into a realm of authentic, unchanging, and necessary being on the one hand and a realm of changing and accidental appearances on the other. Only, in opposition to a theory that professed to be concerned with the essence of things, positivism declares its disinterest in a realm of essences that has been unmasked as illusion—in other words, in fancies. Conversely, the field of phenomena that had been neglected by pure theory is now the object domain of science. Under the name of the positive, exclusive reality is now claimed for phenomena which had previously been considered trivial. Compared with the brute facts and the relations between them, the essences of metaphysics are now declared unreal. Thus the elements of the metaphysical tradition are preserved; in positivist polemics they have only exchanged their roles. The positivist argument is based, it is true, on the correct observation that with the origins of the modern empirical sciences, the classical metaphysical concepts of substance have been replaced by concepts of relation, and theories that were intended to replicate being as a whole have been supplanted by theories that causally explain empirical regularities. But the positivist interpretation of this is itself still immersed in metaphysics. Whereas the latter had taken for granted a correspondence between the universe and the human mind and assumed a relation of conformity between the cosmos of being and the logos of man, positivism boasts of "universally putting the *relative* in place of the absolute."[18] In opposition to the affinity of essences and contemplation it asserts a necessary disproportion between being and consciousness:

> When one . . . recognizes the necessary imperfection of our diverse theoretical means, one sees that, far from being able to completely investigate any real existence, we have no guarantee of the possibility of being able to establish all real existences even in a very superficial manner. . . .[19]

Paradoxically, early positivism is repeatedly compelled to move within the metaphysical antitheses of essence and appearance— of the totality of the world and absolute knowledge on the one hand and contingent manifoldness and relative knowledge on the other—while simultaneously declaring the positions advanced by metaphysics to be meaningless. The critique of metaphysics does not lead to a substantive discussion of theories of the major philosophical tradition. Comte refuses from the very beginning to go into the problems posed by metaphysics. They are not reflected upon, but merely supplanted. By restricting the realm of decidable questions to the explanation of facts, positivism removes metaphysical problems from discussion. Comte adopts the expression "undiscussable." Already for Comte the critique of ideology assumes the form of the *presumption of meaninglessness*. Rationally undecidable opinions cannot really be refuted. They do not hold up to the indifference stubbornly asserted by positivism in matters of belief, and are obliterated:

> Undoubtedly, no one has ever logically proven the nonexistence of Apollo, Minerva, etc., nor that of the

oriental fairies or of the various creations of poetry. But this has in no way kept the human mind from irrevocably abandoning old dogmas when they finally ceased to correspond to its overall situation.[20]

Positivism does not come to grips with metaphysics but simply knocks the bottom out of it. It declares metaphysical assertions meaningless and, letting them stand as such, abandons them to a self-generating "disuse." Yet it is only through metaphysical concepts that positivism can render itself comprehensible. By being unreflectively put aside, they retain their substantial power even over their adversary.

This apparent paradox can be rendered comprehensible in the context of the overall positivist argument. The scientistic self-understanding of the sciences, which has gained predominance as the philosophy of science, replaces the philosophical concept of knowledge. Knowledge becomes identical with scientific knowledge (*wissenschaftliche Erkenntnis*). Science is delimited from other cognitive activities primarily through its object domain. In turn, the object domain can be defined only by methodological rules of inquiry. Since these rules, however, are derived by projecting individual rules of pre-critical epistemology onto the level of methodology, they can be suited for a definition of science only if they have already been selected according to an implicit preunderstanding of science. This preunderstanding has emerged critically from science's self-delimitation from metaphysics. Nevertheless, once epistemology has been displaced, the only system of reference available for the explicit demarcation between science and metaphysics is the very metaphysical system that has been withdrawn from circulation. We have seen that the law of three stages introduces a normative concept of science via the philosophy of history. It is the background ideology that has made possible the replacement of epistemology by the philosophy of science. Once the latter is established in the form of a methodology of the sciences, however, it must be possible to provide on this basis a systematic definition of science in the form of a demarcation between science and metaphysics. Since the path of reflection on the meaning of knowledge is blocked off and the meaning of science is prejudged according to the model of replicating reality, the only remaining possibility is that of elucidating the possibility of the objectivism that has been adopted as a foundation. If science differs from metaphysics in describing facts and relations between facts, the problem of demarcation leads to the problem of what the significance of the positivity of facts actually is. Epistemology, having been disavowed, revenges itself with an unsolved problem that now has to be dealt with by an ironically restored ontology of the factual.

Ernst Mach's doctrine of elements is an excellent example of positivism's attempt to justify the object domain of the sciences as the exclusive sphere to which reality can be attributed. But the positivist concept of fact first attains ontological dignity by being burdened with the critical burden of proof against a shadowy world of metaphysical illusion. On the one hand, the realm in which substantial forms and pure structures, that is the essence of things in contrast to the things themselves, had been identified, is cleared away and reduced to the sphere of phenomena. At the same time, however, this sphere of the changeable and accidental can be distinguished as authentic and exclusive reality only with the aid of the nullified categories of metaphysics. This dilemma is expressed in the concept of facticity, where the two are forcibly integrated: the prosaic significance of the immediately given and the emphatic significance of true being, in relation to which the earlier meaning of essence dissolves into empty illusion. What began in the late works of Schelling and is affirmed by Kierkegaard as the "existence" of historical man finds in positivism an unnoticed variant: According to Moritz Schlick, Mach's follower, there is only one reality, "and it is always essence." In the positivist concept of fact the existence of the immediately given is asserted as the essential. Mach's doctrine of elements is an attempt to explicate the world as the sum total of facts and, at the same time, the facts as the essence of reality.

Facts are given evidently in sense experience. Simultaneously they have the immovability and indisputability of something given intersubjectively. The facticity of the facts is evidence both of the certainty of subjective perception and of the external existence of a matter of fact, mandatory for all subjects. Facts contain both moments: the immediate power of conviction of sensations in an ego and the impingement of bodies or things independent of the ego. Therefore Mach looks for a foundation of the facts that permits developing a concept of the real that falls short of phenomenalism and physicalism. Sensations and bodies are evidence of facts, which are composed of elements that are indifferent in relation to our distinction between the psychic and the physical. The things that belong to the physical world are constructed of the same elements as sensations situated in a human body that we identify as ego. Mach largely uses "element" and "sensation" synonymously, but the decisive aspect of his monistic approach is that, in connection with an ego, elements are *sensations*, whereas in relation to one another they are characteristics of *bodies*:

> I can resolve all of my physical attributes into elements that cannot be further analyzed: colors, notes, pressures, temperatures, odors, spaces, times, etc. These elements reveal themselves dependent on circumstances both outside and inside my [bodily] environment. If and only if the latter is the case, we also call these elements sensations.[21]

Mach takes the following example. "A color is a physical object as soon as we take account of (for example) its dependence on the light that is the source of illumination (i.e., of other colors, temperatures, spaces, etc.). But if we regard its dependence on the retina (the elements of the perceiving ego), it is a psychological object, a sensation." From this he concludes that "the great gap between physical and psychological inquiry thus exists only for the conventional, stereotypical point of view. . . . It is not the material that is different in the two areas, but the orientation of investigation."[22] In drawing this conclusion, Mach divests color of its subjective quality in both cases. Both investigations proceed within a physicalist system of reference, regardless of whether we *talk* of bodies or sensations. Yet this implication of the doctrine of elements for the strategy of inquiry is its less interesting meaning. Its real intention comes to light only when we view it in relation to the positivist strategy of avoiding epistemological questions.

If the elements out of which reality is constructed were sensations, as the empiricist school assumes, then it would be difficult to deny the function of consciousness, in whose horizon sensations are always given. It would be difficult to avoid the standpoint of immanence in consciousness (*Bewusstseinsimmanenz*), which has idealistic implications, as is shown by the example of Berkeley, one relevant to Mach's development.[23] In that case, however, the basis of the immediately given as the authentic reality sought by positivism would slip away. The elements of reality would be not sensations but the consciousness in which they are connected. The facts would once again have to be grounded in a construction *behind* the facts; in other words, they would have to be interpreted metaphysically. Via sensualism Mach would slip back unintentionally into theory of knowledge. To positivism, though, the reflexive priority of the knowing subject over objects appears as regression. If reality is the totality of facts, then we must conceive the ego as a relatively constant, although accidental complex of sensations, which originates in elements just as much as do all things existing independently of us. We must not succumb to the epistemological constraint of conceiving the unanalyzable ego-complex as the unity and foundation of elementary sensations:

> What is primary is not the ego but the elements
> (sensations) . . . The elements form the ego. . . . If we
> are not content with knowing the connection of elements
> (sensations) and ask, "Who has this connection of
> sensations, who is having sensation?", then we are subject
> to the old custom of incorporating every element
> (every sensation) in an *unanalyzed* complex. Thus we
> sink back unnoticed into an older, deeper, and more
> limited standpoint. It is often observed that a psychic
> event that is not the experience of a specific subject is
> inconceivable, as though the essential role of the unity of
> consciousness were thereby proved. . . . It could be said

equally that a physical event that does not occur . . . in
the world is inconceivable. It must be allowable to
abstract . . . from this environment in one case as in the
other . . . We need think only of the sensations of the
lower animals, to which we would scarcely ascribe a
clearly defined subject. The subject is built up out of
sensations; then, of course, it can in turn react to
sensations.[24]

Mach reifies the knowing ego as a fact among facts in order not
to have to conceive the facts as derivative by being related back
to an ego. Mach would like to carry out the reduction of consciousness to elements in which something like an ego first
originates; but then these elements cannot themselves be conceived as correlates of consciousness, that is as sensations. Nevertheless, since the facticity of elements is proved by sense certainty, the positivist concept of fact must acquire the form of
sensory evidence at the same time that perceiving subjects are
eliminated:

The entire internal and external world [is composed]
of a *small number of homogeneous elements* in either
more transitory or more permanent combination. These
elements are *customarily called sensations.* But
since this appellation already contains a *one-sided
theory,* we prefer to talk simply of elements.[25]

Reality exists *in itself* as the totality of all elements and
all combinations of elements. *For us* it exists as a mass of bodies
in correspondence with our ego. Under the symbols "body" and
"ego" we subsume relatively constant combinations of elements
for specific practical purposes. This classification is a makeshift
for provisional orientation. It belongs to the natural worldview.
Science, which transcends practical aims, dissolves these schematizations, which have utility in life, and discerns their merely
subjective validity. "Body" and "ego" can never be definitively
delimited from the mass of elements and combinations of elements. The scientific worldview knows only facts and relations

between facts, under which cognitive consciousness must also be subsumed:

> Through their great *practical* significance not only for the individual but for the whole species, the combinations "ego" and "body" assert themselves instinctively and appear with elementary force. In particular cases, however, in which practical goals are not at issue and *knowledge* is a goal in itself, this delimitation can prove insufficient, cumbersome, and untenable.[26]

It is not on account of its materialism that Mach's doctrine of elements can fulfill the task positivism sets itself (of grounding science, objectivistically understood, in an ontology of the factual). The reason is rather that its shallow materialism blocks off epistemological inquiry into the subjective conditions of the objectivity of possible knowledge. The only reflection admissible serves the self-abolition of reflecting on the knowing subject. The doctrine of elements justifies the strategy of "*thinking nothing of one's ego*, and resolving it into a transitory combination of changing elements."[27] It unmasks the fictions of the natural life-world and denounces as humbug the process of reflection that arises therein.

The leveling out of subjectivity has its counterpart in the effacement of the distinction between essence and appearance. Facts are all there is. Facts in the emphatic sense are sensations hypostatized as building blocks of the physical world and of consciousness; these sensations fill the universe uninterruptedly. In the final instance, they are both the immediately and certainly given and the immovably and indisputably objective. Mach objectifies sensations into what exists in itself; the reality of facts is the world of completely reified consciousness. Consequently, every conceivable form of transcendence is retracted. In its unconcealedness, facticity knows no opposition of essence and appearance, of being and illusion, because the facts themselves have been elevated to the status of essence:

> If we consider the elements red, green, warm, cold, etc.,

which are physical elements in their dependence on
circumstances outside of my environment and psychic
elements in dependence on internal ones, but
immediately given and identical in both senses, then in
this simple objective situation the problem of illusion
and reality has lost its meaning. We have here before us
at the same time the elements of the real world and the
elements of the ego[28]. . . .

The popular conception of an antithesis between illusion
and reality has had a very stimulating effect on scientific
and philosophical thought. . . . But because this
conception was not thought through to the end, it has
had an improper influence on our worldview. Although
we are part of the world, it got away from us completely
and was expelled from our field of vision.[29]

The doctrine of elements comprehends reality as the
totality of facts. The unity of things and of consciousness is
unmasked as a fiction, albeit a useful one, and is reduced to complexes of facts. Then, however, we cannot go behind science
itself, which describes lawlike relations between facts. It is absolutely primary and, as such, cannot be surpassed by reflection on
the conditions of the objectivity of science. The general categorial framework for scientistic concept formation, as proposed
by Mach, implies the prohibition of considering science itself
problematic. The objectivity of knowledge cannot be conceptualized from the perspective of the knowing subject; rather, it can
be derived only from the object domain. The doctrine of elements establishes the primacy of science over reflection; the
latter is meaningful only when it negates itself.

Pursuing the analysis of our experiences to the level of
elements has the advantage principally of reducing the
two problems of the "unfathomable thing" and the
"inscrutable ego" to their simplest, most transparent
form and making them recognizable as pseudo-problems.
By disposing of things whose investigation has

absolutely no meaning, we make whatever really can be investigated by the specialized sciences stand out that much more clearly: the manifold, universal dependence of elements on one another.[30]

Stipulating the object domain suffices as a criterion of the demarcation between science and metaphysics: all statements intending to describe facts and relations between facts are to be considered scientific. The positivist criterion of demarcation is *copying reality*.

Although the concept of fact is elucidated by means of the doctrine of elements, the function of knowledge itself remains in obscurity. Because Mach only undertakes reflection in order to direct it against itself, dissolve the subjective conditions of metaphysics, and destroy prescientific schematizations, he can define truth only by the objectivist principle that our "*intellectual* need is satisfied as soon as our thoughts are capable of completely reproducing the sensory facts."[31] In the framework of an ontology of the factual, knowledge can be defined only negatively: The replication of what is the case must not be obscured by admixtures of subjectivity. The cognitive act itself is designated with the trivial commonplaces of traditional realism and its copy theory of knowledge: "All science aims . . . at representing *facts* in *thoughts*."[32] In other places Mach speaks also of the adaptation of thought to the facts. Inquiry he terms the intentional adaptation of thoughts.[33] Here Mach is thinking of the mimetic adaptation of thought to the facts and not of the adaptation of an organism to its environment.

The doctrine of elements offers a far-reaching interpretation of reality, while contenting itself with a minimal definition of knowledge. Its own status is contradictory. By explicating the totality of facts as the object domain of the sciences and delimiting science from metaphysics through its replication of the facts, it cannot justify any reflection that goes beyond science, including itself. The doctrine of elements is the reflected form of science, but one that prohibits any reflection going beyond science. Mach offers the meagre information that "this is not a new philosophy or metaphysics, but rather an attempt to accord with a momentary striving of the positive sciences for mutual interconnection."[34] Nevertheless, he does not restrict himself to methodology as an auxiliary science; in truth he explicates reality as the sum total of what is the case. He stipulates the meaning of the facticity of facts in order to be able to eliminate on principle all statements that may assert no claim to scientific status. In this regard, the doctrine of elements can understand itself as reflection that destroys the obscurities of reflection and restricts knowledge to science. Reflection can abolish itself, however, only by granting science a legitimate object domain. Therefore it cannot already claim, as it must nonetheless, to be science itself.

This problem remains. On scientistic presuppositions, positivism suspends the theory of knowledge in favor of a philosophy of the sciences, because it measures knowledge only in terms of the actual achievements of the sciences. How, then, *prior* to all science, can the doctrine of elements make statements about the object domain of science as such, if we only obtain information about this domain *through* science? Yet we can reliably distinguish this information from mere speculation only if we are always in a position, by virtue of prior knowledge of the object domain, to distinguish science, which copies the facts, from metaphysics. Only via an ontology of the factual does the doctrine of elements lead to a scientistic foundation of science that excludes every form of metaphysics as meaningless. This circle is concealed by objectivism, which expresses itself in unreflectively prohibiting the self-reflection of knowledge. In this way a tacit epistemology of common sense, according to which knowledge replicates reality or copies facts in thoughts, is immunized against possible doubt. Through this theory we can see how the doctrine of elements comes into being and what status it assumes.

Mach chooses physics and a natural-science oriented psychology as models because their scientific status is adequately authenticated by consensus. Mach projects both of them onto one level, in order to derive a system of reference in which they are compatible. This integration of the most general characteristics of possible objects of physics and contemporary experimental psychology results in the basic assumptions of the doctrine of elements. The latter defines the totality of facts that can be made in any way the object of analysis in the empirical sciences; it thus serves in turn for the demarcation between science and metaphysics. Mach does not investigate the dependence of the object domain of these model sciences on both a categorial framework and measurement operations or, consequently, inquire into the constitution of facts by method and by research technique. Instead, Mach takes integrated and generalized systems of reference and hypostatizes them as the organization of reality itself. Methodical rules for the apprehension of reality are projected onto it and then interpreted as an ontology of the factual.

This procedure can be justified only if we presume from the beginning that the model sciences, about whose scientific character consensus prevails, adequately describe reality as what it is. This is the basic assumption of objectivism. It is based on the conviction that the factual cognitive progress of model sciences such as physics proves them to be the only reliable category of knowledge (Wissen). The scientific creed encourages the objectivist assumption that scientific information apprehends reality descriptively. On this assumption, however, it does not appear meaningful to regard the objects of empirical-analytic inquiry as constituted or to consider the transcendental conditions of objectification as an independent variable in relation to the object domain. To the contrary, generalized systems of reference of existing model sciences, ontologically interpreted, provide the basis to which the knowing subject and all its cognitive activities can be empirically reduced. Modern positivism rejects this solution proposed by Mach as psychologistic. But with regard to the central perspective, the arguments are repeated, despite a thorough critique of psychologism, by those who do not incline to conventionalism.

Objectivism, which makes a dogma of the prescientific interpretation of knowledge as a copy of reality, limits access to reality to the dimension established by the scientific system of reference through the methodical objectification of reality. It prohibits discerning the a priori element of this system of reference and calling into question in any way its monopoly of knowledge. As soon as this occurs, however, the objectivist barrier of the philosophy of science falls. As soon as we renounce misleading ontologizing, we can understand a given scientific system of reference as the result of interaction between the knowing subject and reality.

The first to tread the dimension of a self-reflecting philosophy of science was Charles Sanders Peirce. Like Dilthey, he explicitly takes up the set of questions and linguistic usage introduced by Kant. Peirce is aware that he is pursuing methodology in the epistemological mode. He even borrows the expression "theory of cognition" literally from German.[35]

CHAPTER FIVE

Peirce's Logic of Inquiry: *The Dilemma of a Scholastic Realism Restored by the Logic of Language*

Peirce does not succumb to the objectivist attitude of early positivism. This may have been due in part to his familiarity with the philosophical tradition, especially with late Medieval Scholasticism and with Berkeley and Kant. But the crucial factor was his reflection on the basic experience of positivism, which motivated his thought from the very beginning. The methodically secured progress of natural-scientific knowledge had given Kant occasion to investigate the transcendental conditions of knowledge as such; it had led Comte and the positivists to identify all of knowledge with science. Peirce was the first to gain clarity about the systematic meaning of this experience. Scientific progress does not only motivate us psychologically to take science seriously as the exemplary form of knowledge, it is itself the exemplary feature of science. The intersubjectively acknowledged cognitive progress of the theoretical natural sciences is also the *systematic* feature that distinguishes modern science from other categories of knowledge.

What separates Peirce from both early and modern positivism is his understanding that the task of methodology is not to clarify the logical structure of scientific theories but the logic of the procedure with whose aid we *obtain* scientific theories. We term information scientific if and only if an uncompelled and permanent consensus can be obtained with regard to its validity. This consensus does not have to be definitive, but has to have definitive agreement as its goal. The genuine achievement of modern science does not consist primarily in producing true, that is correct and cogent statements about what we call reality. Rather, it distinguishes itself from traditional categories of knowledge by a method of arriving at an uncompelled and permanent consensus of this sort about our views:

91

Investigation differs entirely from these methods in that the nature of the final conclusion to which it leads is in every case destined from the beginning, without reference to the initial state of belief. Let any two minds investigate any question independently and if they carry the process far enough they will come to an agreement which no further investigation will disturb.[1]

Although we cannot state at any time which individual result of previous investigation can claim definitive validity, nevertheless the scientific method gives us the certainty that every adequately formulated question must find a definitive answer if the process of inquiry is carried far enough. Therefore the status of scientific statements has two implications: the structure of scientific method guarantees both the revisability of all individual statements and the possibility in principle of an ultimate answer to every emerging scientific question.

Peirce takes as his starting point only the fact of the cognitive progress of modern science, which has not previously been seriously contested by anyone. He changes this fact into a principle by concluding that the institutionalization of the process of inquiry has once and for all defined the course we must take in order to arrive at our beliefs, which we call cognitions only because they find uncompelled and intersubjective recognition. As long as the process of inquiry as a whole has not come to an end, we cannot definitively distinguish true from false propositions in the totality of all prevailing results. Nevertheless, because we are convinced of the fact of cognitive progress, it must be that the scope of the areas of reality about which we have obtained true information has increased in proportion to the progress of inquiry. Accordingly, it follows that all future processes of inquiry will converge upon a state that, although temporally indeterminate, can be anticipated in principle, in which all prevailing views will be true propositions about reality.

Nevertheless, Peirce can assert this only if he already claims definite validity in the present for one belief, namely the assumption of actual progress in scientific knowledge. Now the fact that an uncompelled consensus has existed about this opinion until the present does not exclude its future revision per se. On the other hand, Peirce is armed with the argument that we must consider a well-founded and intersubjectively recognized view true as long as its validity has not been rendered problematical by an unforeseen experience. The methodical intention of doubt for its own sake he considers abstract. Previously the process of inquiry has been carried on in the certainty that there is cognitive progress, and no fact has shaken this interpretation. Strictly speaking, however, the common-sense argument that excludes programmatic doubt already presupposes the pragmatist assumption that is at issue: that we may rely on the effective functioning of a self-regulating, cumulative learning process. In his review of an edition of Berkeley's works, Peirce explains this basic belief as follows:

> All human thought and opinion contains an arbitrary, accidental element, dependent on the limitations in circumstances, power, and bent of the individual; an element of error, in short. But human opinion universally tends in the long run to a definite form, which is the truth. Let any human being have enough information and exert enough thought upon any question, and the result will be that he will arrive at a certain definite conclusion, which is the same that any other mind will reach under sufficiently favorable circumstances. . . . There is, then, to every question a true answer, a final conclusion, to which the opinion of every man is constantly gravitating. He may for a time recede from it, but give him more experience and time for consideration, and he will finally approach it. The individual may not live to reach the truth; there is a residuum of error in every individual's opinions. No matter; it remains that there is a definite opinion to which the mind of man is, on the whole and in the long run, tending. On many questions the final agreement is already reached, on all it will be reached if time enough is given.[2]

Peirce extrapolates from the experience of cognitive progress to a collective, directional learning process of the human species, which has assumed methodical form at the level of organized inquiry. In so doing he assumes the fact that scientific method guarantees lawlike progress in inquiry. True, this assumption is not seriously disputed in fact. Nevertheless, when Peirce wants to demonstrate its indisputability, he must demonstrate methodologically the conditions of the possibility of institutionalized cognitive progress. In this sense his philosophy of science can be understood as the attempt to elucidate the *logic of scientific progress*.

Peirce carries out the methodology of the sciences in the form of logical investigations. In so doing he employs the concept of logic in an unusual way. He does not restrict himself to the analysis of formal relations between symbols, in other words to the logical form of propositions and systems of propositions. Neither does he return to the dimension of epistemology opened up by Kant. The logic of inquiry is situated as it were between formal and transcendental logic. It goes beyond the realm of the formal conditions of the validity of propositions, but falls short of the cognitively constitutive determinations of a transcendental consciousness as such. The logic of inquiry develops a methodological concept of truth. It explicates the rules according to which true statements about reality are obtained: "Logic is the doctrine of truth, its nature and the manner in which it is to be discovered."[3] Like transcendental logic, the logic of inquiry extends to the structure of the constitution of knowledge. But, as a process of inquiry, this logical structure materializes under empirical conditions: "Science is to mean for us a mode of life. . . ."[4] In the process of inquiry, the logical connections of symbols and the empirical connections of actions are integrated into a "mode of life."

> . . . If I am asked to what the wonderful success of modern science is due, I shall suggest that to gain the secret of that, it is necessary to consider science as living, and therefore not as knowledge already acquired but as the concrete life of the men who are working to find out the truth.[5]

Peirce conceives science within the horizon of methodical inquiry, and he comprehends inquiry as a life process. The logical analysis of inquiry, therefore, is concerned not with the activities of a transcendental consciousness as such but with those of a subject that sustains the process of inquiry as a whole, that is with the community of investigators, who endeavor to perform their common task communicatively,

> . . . we have, broadly speaking, nothing to do with the nature of the human mind. Only as there are some faculties which must belong to any mind which can investigate at all, these must come under our consideration.[6]

On the other hand, because it comprehends the process of inquiry as a world-constituting life activity (*Lebenspraxis*), the logic of inquiry is committed to the attitude of a transcendental logic. It can no longer regress to the objectivist attitude in which knowledge appears as a description of reality that can be detached from the knowing subject. Peirce discerns that it is only under the conditions of the process of inquiry as a whole that reality is first constituted as the object domain of the sciences. He is immune to the ontologizing of facts. If the only propositions that count as *true* are those about which an uncompelled and permanent consensus can be generated by means of scientific method, then *reality* means nothing but the sum of those states of fact about which we can obtain final opinions. Reality is a transcendental concept. The constitution of the objects of possible experience is prescribed, however, not by the categorial organization of a transcendental consciousness but by the mechanism of the process of inquiry as a self-regulating, cumulative learning process.[7]

Peirce hurries to emphasize that this *concept of reality* of the logic of inquiry, corresponding to the methodological *concept of truth*, does not include any idealist elements. Although it is meaningless to speak of an unknowable reality, nevertheless reality exists independently of our actual knowing:

> . . . [I]t may be said that this view is directly opposed to the abstract definition which we have given of

reality, inasmuch as it makes the characters of the real depend on what is ultimately thought about them. But the answer to this is that, on the one hand, reality is independent, not necessarily of thought in general, but only of what you or I or any finite number of men may think about it; and that, on the other hand, though the object of the final opinion depends on what that opinion is, yet what that opinion is does not depend on what you or I or any man thinks. Our perversity and that of others may indefinitely postpone the settlement of opinion; it might even conceivably cause an arbitrary proposition to be universally accepted as long as the human race should last. Yet even that would not change the nature of the belief, which alone could be the result of investigation carried sufficiently far; and if, after the extinction of our race, another should arise with faculties and disposition for investigation, that true opinion must be the one which they would ultimately come to . . . the opinion which would finally result from investigation does not depend on how anybody may actually think. But the reality of that which is real does depend on the real fact that investigation is destined to lead, at last, if continued long enough, to a belief in it.[8]

The concept of reality corresponding to the logic of inquiry is as far removed from Kant's transcendental concept of nature as from Comte's positivist concept of a world of facts. The system of reference is rather a process of inquiry that commences when prevailing views become problematic and that supplies a reliable strategy for arriving at unproblematic views, in other words, for eliminating emergent doubts in favor of new certainties. Of course, methodical doubt that calls the totality of our beliefs into question is abstract: only within a horizon of unproblematic convictions and in a specific case can we subject a particular part of our assumptions to the process of inquiry. But there is not a single belief that we can identify a priori as one of which we can in principle be certain that it has definitive validity and will never

be doubted in the future. Universal doubt is replaced by potentially general doubt, from which no fact and no principle is
exempt. Therefore thought, to which the being of reality corresponds as knowability, cannot rely on an absolute beginning or
an unshakable foundation:

> It is false to say that reasoning must rest either on first
> principles or on ultimate facts. For we cannot go behind
> what we are unable to doubt, but it would be
> unphilosophical to suppose that any particular fact will
> never be brought into doubt.[9]

Peirce directs himself likewise against both empiricist and
rationalist attempts at ultimate foundations (*Ursprungsdenken*):
The ultimate given provided by the evidence of sense perception
is as deceptive as the ultimate foundation provided by the evidence of highest truths. If we had intuitive access to something
immediate, then we would necessarily be able to distinguish with
immediate certainty intuitions from discursive cognitions.

But the controversies about the true sources of intuitive
knowledge have never led to a satisfactory consensus. This shows
that we do not dispose of an intuitive faculty for convincingly
identifying anything immediate. Peirce comes to the conclusion
that there can be no knowledge that is not mediated by prior
knowledge.[10] The cognitive process is discursive at every stage.
Peirce speaks of a chain of reasoning—"but the beginning and
the end of this chain are not distinctly perceived."[11] There are
neither fundamental propositions that qualify as principles once
and for all, without being justified by other propositions, nor ultimate elements of perception that are immediately certain and
unaffected by our interpretations. Even the simplest perception
is the product of a judgment, which means an implicit inference.[12]

We cannot meaningfully conceive of anything like
uninterpreted facts. Yet the facts cannot be exhaustively reduced
to our interpretations. On the one hand, every empirical basis on
which we can conceivably rely is mediated by implicit inferential

interpretations. These inferences, no matter how rudimentary, are tied to representational signs. Consequently, even perceptions already occur in the dimension of semiotic representation.[13]

On the other hand, the empirical basis cannot be totally mediated by thought. Besides the logical laws it obeys, the process of reasoning linked to signs depends on information inputs. It does not proceed immanently, but incorporates impulses deriving from experience. Otherwise Peirce would have to abandon in idealist fashion the difference between thought and a contingently experienced reality. Because all knowledge is discursive, it is true that in thought we cannot jump out of the dimension of mediation. No matter how far we retrace our inferences to their premises, we remain caught in the compass of our interpretations. Even the apparently ultimate data resolve themselves in turn into interpretations. Nevertheless, the process through which old beliefs that have become problematic are transformed into new, recognized interpretations is prompted only by independent original stimuli, which attest to reality's resistance to false interpretations and turn into stimuli of thought processes.

This conception leads to a difficulty that recapitulates the problems of the "thing in itself" on a new level. The concept of truth held by the logic of inquiry, which links the validity of statements to the method of attaining consensus, leads as shown to a concept of reality derived from the logic of language. It restricts reality to the realm of facts that in principle can be represented by convincing inferences. If in this sense "being" is identified with "cognizability," then the category of a thing in itself is meaningless: "We have no conception of the absolutely incognizable."[14] Notwithstanding, what is incorporated in the interpretations of our inferential thought is something immediate, although it cannot be represented by it as unmediated and ultimately given. Against a total mediation of the empirical basis, which would absorb the facticity of reality and particular qualities into the immanence of a self-contained thought process, Peirce must assert the independence of singular original stimuli that are unmediated by symbols. "Reality" cannot be ascribed to them, although all of our statements about "the real" are in some measure grounded in them. The concept of reality that Peirce derives from his methodological concept of truth prohibits any thought of something evidently ultimate and unmediated, of which he nevertheless writes that "the Unanalyzable, the Inexplicable, the Unintellectual runs in a continuous stream through our lives."[15] Facticity, reality, and qualitative manifoldness must be grounded in immediately present states of consciousness, and yet, because they do not represent anything, they have no correspondence in reality. What corresponds only to private determinations of a continuous stream of consciousness is not "real." Peirce does not pass over this difficulty.

> At any moment we are in possession of certain information, that is, of cognitions which have been logically derived by induction and hypothesis from previous cognitions which are less general, less distinct, and of which we have a less lively consciousness. These in their turn have been derived from others still less general, less distinct, and less vivid; and so on back to the ideal first, which is quite singular, and quite out of consciousness. This ideal first is the particular thing-in-itself. It does not exist *as such*. That is, there is no thing which is in-itself in the sense of not being relative to the mind, though things which are relative to the mind doubtless are, apart from that relation. The cognitions which thus reach us by this infinite series of inductions and hypotheses (which though infinite *a parte ante logice*, is yet as one continuous process not without a beginning *in time*) are of two kinds, the true and the untrue, or cognitions whose objects are *real* and those whose objects are *unreal*. And what do we mean by the real? It is a conception which we must first have had when we discovered that there was an unreal, an illusion; that is, when we first corrected ourselves. Now the distinction for which alone this fact logically called, was between an *ens* relative to private inward determinations, to the negations belonging to idiosyncrasy, and an *ens* such as would stand in the long run. The real, then, is that which, sooner or later, information and reasoning

would finally result in, and which is therefore
independent of the vagaries of me and you.[16]

Peirce denies a thing in itself in the sense of transcendental
philosophy, a reality that *affects* our senses while yet merely
appearing under the transcendental conditions of possible objectivity and thus unknowable as such. The predicate "real" has no
explicable meaning apart from states of fact about which we can
make true statements. That is why the "ideal first," which must
be assumed as the source of information inputs, cannot be considered real. For, in contrast to the general determinations about
which general consensus can be obtained, the stream of subjective
experiences is the contingent. Truth is public. No determination
that holds only privately for an individual subject can refer to
what is real. Only beliefs that hold independently of personal
idiosyncrasies and affirm their intersubjective validity in the face
of indefinitely repeated doubt represent real matters of fact.
Therefore we cannot accord existence in itself to singular expressions of emotion or absolutely private sensations and elevate them
to the basis of reality. Only to the extent that they enter into
symbolically mediated inferences and become part of interpretations can they obtain cognitive content and thus be true or false.

This argument is compelling, but it does not solve the
problem as it has been posed. For the ideal first, even if it cannot
be conceived as a thing in itself, is not just nothing. Rather, it
possesses facticity and the particular qualities of reality. Moreover, it is not meaningful to place the affection of the senses on
the same level with idiosyncrasies. These psychic events are not
private opinions. To the contrary, they completely lack the status
of opinions; they fall short of the threshold of intentionality. Yet
are they not the ground of all intentionality? Are not actual
experiences the source of the information that enters the implicit
inferences of perception and of judgment and that is elaborated
by thought processes into definitive beliefs? True, only that
"which will be thought to exist in the final opinion is real, and
nothing else. What is the power of external things, to affect the
senses?"[17]

In order to escape the metaphysical trap of traditional

epistemology, the danger of hypostatization, Peirce must reformulate this question in terms of his frame of reference, that is the logic of inquiry. As the sum total of all possible predicates appearing in true statements about reality, reality is no longer determined by the constitutive activities of a transcendental consciousness per se but by what is in principle a finite process of inferences and interpretations, namely the collective efforts of all those who ever participate in the process of inquiry. With regard to methodical progression to a universe of valid, that is general and permanently recognized beliefs, the power of affecting the senses present in actual experiences obviously functions to render prevailing opinions problematic and stimulate efforts to obtain unproblematic beliefs. The affection of the senses, in which the *facticity* and *immediate quality* of reality assert themselves, is thus a permanent occasion for transforming old interpretations into new ones. Then, however, the affecting power of things (to which we may not ascribe existence in themselves) is nothing other than the constraint of reality, which motivates us to revise false statements and generate new ones. Thus,

> to assert that there are external things which can be
> known only as exerting a power on our sense, is nothing
> different from asserting that there is a general *drift* in
> the history of human thought which will lead it to one
> general agreement, one catholic consent.[18]

The constraint of reality, embodied in the qualitative immediacy of singular sensations and feelings, is the occasion for constituting reality in the form of true statements. Yet it does not itself belong to reality. But how, then, can we say anything at all about it? By explicating the meaning of something that is not part of reality and thus cannot be the object of a true belief, we are insinuating once again the concept of a thing in itself. Peirce could counter that the constraint of reality dissolves to the extent that we obey its motivating force, advance the process of inquiry, and form true beliefs about reality. The constraint of reality would then be a complementary concept to the idea of the process of inquiry. In contrast to reality as the totality of all knowable matters of fact, this concept denotes the disproportion factually existing at a given time between our beliefs and reality. But Peirce did not argue in this fashion. Instead, he attempts a justification in terms of the logic of language.

Had Peirce argued in the manner suggested, he would have realized the necessity of using the *logic of inquiry* to compensate for his denial, on grounds of the *logic of language*, of a "thing in itself." Non-intentional contents of experience are converted into symbolic representations owing to a synthesis that a consistent pragmatism can develop only in the framework of a logic of the process of inquiry. Peirce, on the contrary, approached the problem immediately on the level of his linguistic concept of reality. For if reality is defined by the totality of possible true statements, and if these statements are symbolic representations, then why should the structure of reality not be elucidated in relation to the structure of language?

Now we can distinguish two functions of language, the connotative (representative) and the denotative. Peirce calls real the connotations of all predicates appearing in true propositions. The individual objects to which a true predicate is ascribed in a particular case, are denotations. They do not belong as such to the connotative content. In this way an aspect of reality that cannot enter into the predicative content of statements about reality can be designated by means of the logic of language. Peirce distinguishes the "forces" that constitute the denotative employment of a sign from the universal relations that form its connotative content. The *facticity* of reality does not correspond to any linguistic content: consequently we cannot make any direct statements about it. Nonetheless, it can be grasped indirectly, because it can be correlated with the *index function* of language.

Nevertheless, the correlate of the denotative function of language is not completely the same as what is called, in epistemological contexts, the affection of our senses by things outside us. It is true that the denotative employment of a sign attests to the facticity of facts, in other words the mere way in which an existence that the subject immediately encounters forces itself upon him. But it does not take account of the substantive qualities that are also present in singular states of consciousness.

The constraint of reality expresses itself not only in the resistance of things in general, but in specific resistance to specific interpretations. Thus, alongside the facticity of things, it includes a substantive moment without which the influx of information would indeed be unthinkable. Peirce consequently does not hesitate to introduce yet a third category alongside the representative and denotative function of symbolically mediated knowledge: pure quality.

> Thus, we have in thought three elements: first, the
> representative function which makes it a
> *representation*; second, the pure denotative application,
> or real connection, which brings one thought into
> *relation* with another; and third, the material quality,
> or how it feels, which gives thought its *quality*.[19]

In another passage there is a formulation suggesting that all three categories, representation, denotation, and quality, were derived likewise from linguistic functions. A sign can appear as a symbol, which represents, as an index, which refers, and as an icon, which is an image of its object:

> Now a sign has, as such, three references: first, it is a
> sign *to* some thought which interprets it; second, it
> is a sign *for* some object to which in that thought it
> is equivalent; third, it is a sign, *in* some respect or
> quality, which brings it into connection with its object.[20]

It is not easy to discern in what respect the third function of language distinguishes itself from the first. If we take a statue or portrait as an example of an iconic employment of signs, then it is true that they both differ from usual word-symbols in that the material (*dinglich*) substratum of the sign shares certain features with the objects designated, so that we can detect a relation of resemblance. But the copy function fulfilled by such iconic signs is, notwithstanding, only a special case of the representative function. Genetically we can imagine representation as an abstraction from copying, but both are representation. Quality is a third, independent feature of linguistic structure, distinct from representation and denotation only if it refers as such to the material substratum of the sign. Thus we read a few pages later:

> Since a sign is not identical with the thing signified
> . . . it must plainly have some characters which belong
> to it in itself, and have nothing to do with its
> representative function. These I call the *material*
> qualities of the sign. As examples of such qualities, take
> in the word "man," its consisting of three letters—in
> a picture, its being flat and without relief.[21]

Taken in this sense, quality does, to be sure, define a property of linguistic signs. Stripped of the context of iconic employment, however, this category no longer describes a function of language. It does not contribute to clarifying the concept of reality in terms of the logic of language. For in this respect "quality" has meaning as a category of language only as long as it stands for the immediate, that is for the non-intentional content of experience, which is mediated and given symbolic representation. The intangibility of the immediate for the logic of language is shown precisely by the circumstance that it is given in singular sensations, which for their part are completely irrational:

> Whatever is wholly incomparable with anything else
> is wholly inexplicable, because explanation consists
> in bringing things under general laws or under natural
> classes. Hence every thought, in so far as it is a feeling
> of a peculiar sort, is simply an ultimate, inexplicable
> fact.[22]

As singular events, states of consciousness have no cognitive content. They are psychic events through which an organism reacts to its environment. They represent nothing. Peirce believes that this construction does not contradict his postulate that uninterpreted facts are not admissible,

for on the one hand, we never can think, "This is

present to me," since, before we have time to make
the reflection, the sensation is past, and, on the other
hand, when once past, we can never bring back the
quality of the feeling as it was *in and for itself*, or
know what it was like *in itself*, or even discover the
existence of this quality except by a corollary from our
general theory of ourselves, and then not in its
idiosyncrasy, but only as something present. But, as
something present, feelings are all alike and require no
explanation, since they contain only what is
universal. So that nothing which we can truly predicate
of feelings is left inexplicable, but only something
which we cannot reflectively know. So that we do not
fall into the contradiction of making the Mediate
immediate. Finally, no present actual thought (which
is a mere feeling) has any meaning, any intellectual
value; for this lies not in what is actually thought,
but in what this thought may be connected with in
representation by subsequent thoughts; so that
the meaning of a thought is altogether something
virtual.[23]

Thus Peirce distinguishes between feelings, which are
generalized expressions, and emotions, which are immediate
psychic movements, possessing no intentional content and incapable of representation. Correspondingly, Peirce views sensations in two ways. As unique psychic events they belong to
organic life processes, and as cognitive contents they enter the
process of reasoning mediated by signs:

Thus, the sensation, so far as it represents something,
is determined, according to a logical law, by previous
cognitions; that is to say, these cognitions determine
that there shall be a sensation. But so far as the
sensation is a mere feeling of a particular sort, it is
determined only by an inexplicable, occult power; and
so far, it is not a representation, but only the material
quality of a representation.[24]

Now what is at issue, however, is precisely how psychic events, linked to isolated, singular states, are related to the symbolically generalized sensations that are already components of interpretations. Peirce's answer, in the same passage, is in terms of the logic of language: The singular sensation

> is not a representation, but only the material quality
> of a representation. For just as in reasoning from
> definition to definitum, it is indifferent to the logician
> how the defined word shall sound, or how many letters
> it shall contain, so in the case of this constitutional
> word, it is not determined by an inward law how it
> shall feel in itself. A feeling, therefore, as a feeling, is
> merely the *material quality* of a mental sign.[25]

Peirce would like to conceive the relation of non-intentional experiential content to symbolic representation on the model of language: they relate to each other as the material substratum of a sign to its symbolic content.[26] But this model contributes to solving our problem, that is how the pre-symbolic influx of information content enters into the symbolically mediated process of reasoning, only if we view the quality of a sign not only as its *substratum* but also as a *copy* determined by the relation of resemblance—in other words, as icon. Since the copy function is, as indicated, only a special case of the representative function, psychic events would in this way have merely acquired by subreption just what they lack—symbolic content. The concept of quality is supposed to accomplish two incompatible purposes: To account for the moment of immediacy in singular sensations on the one hand and yet include an elementary representative function on the other. The attempt to derive this "quality" from the logic of language must fail. Either quality corresponds to the substratum of the sign and is not iconic, or it retains its image character, in which case it must be classified as a representative symbol and is no longer immediate. Thus quality cannot, like facticity, be derived from the structure of language. While the latter can be associated with the denotative function of language, the former has no equivalent that could identify, in terms of the logic of language, statements about the presence of the properties of things in singular sensations and emotions. The concept of reality (*Realität*) defined in terms of the logic of language, with its two dimensions of reality (*Wirklichkeit*) (as the totality of all true connotations) and facticity (as the common element in all correct denotations) does not suffice to explain how thought processes transform the presymbolic influx of information content. The inferences that in the long run bring about a convergence of opinions are fed with singular sensations and emotions: they do not signalize only *whether* a fact is present, but *which* fact is present. This layer of immediate qualities goes beyond the concept of reality derived from the logic of language. Therefore Peirce must either expand this concept ontologically or return from the dimension of language as such to the system of reference of the logic of inquiry, in order to analyze the logical rules of reasoning in the objective context of the process of inquiry as rules for the constitution of a world.

Peirce attempts both, but he does not clearly realize the incompatibility of these two perspectives. The ontological interpretation assumes the form of a doctrine of categories, in which the fundamental determinations of reality are no longer derived from the structure of language but introduced phenomenologically.[27] In the present context we can neglect the ontology of Peirce's later period. What interests us is only the reason that led Peirce first to hypostatize the concept of reality based on the logic of language in opposition to the concept of truth based on the logic of inquiry, and then to elaborate this approach ontologically by constructing his doctrine of categories. The impetus originates in a set of problems connected with the dissolution of the thing-in-itself—in the restoration of Scholastic realism.

Peirce understands reality as what corresponds to the totality of true propositions. True means for him interpretations that have stood up to indefinitely repeated tests and are intersubjectively recognized in the long run. From his definition of reality Peirce can conclude that everything real is knowable and that, insofar as we know reality, we know it as it is. Accordingly, universal matters of fact (*Sachverhalte*) must exist. The basic assumption of nominalism is inconsistent with Peirce's concept of reality.

Nevertheless, universal matters of fact have no existence independent of the categories in which we speak of them:

> To make a distinction between the true conception
> of a thing and the thing itself is . . . only to regard one
> and the same thing from two different points of view;
> for the immediate object of thought in a true judgment
> is the reality.[28]

Peirce arrives at the conviction that what reality *is* coincides with what we can truly *state* about it. A Kantian "phenomenalism," omitting the thing-in-itself, seemed to him to accord with the principles of realism:

> It is plain that this view of reality is inevitably
> realistic; because general conceptions enter into all
> judgments, and therefore into true opinions.
> Consequently a thing in the general is as real as in the
> concrete. It is perfectly true that all white things
> have whiteness in them, for that is only saying, in
> another form of words, that all white things are white;
> but since it is true that real things possess whiteness,
> whiteness is real. It is a real which only exists by virtue of
> an act of thought knowing it, but that thought is not
> an arbitrary or accidental one dependent on any
> idiosyncrasies, but one which will hold in the final
> opinion. This theory involves a phenomenalism. But it
> is the phenomenalism of Kant, and not that of Hume.[29]

Peirce would like to adhere to Kant because the universal relations that constitute reality can only be meaningfully conceived in relation to the possible true interpretations of a "community of all intelligible beings." On the other hand, eliminating the thing-in-itself makes it possible to change perspective. Reality can be considered not only from the transcendental point of view of the genesis of true statements; conversely the genesis of true statements can also be rendered comprehensible from the ontological point of view of a reality of universals existing in themselves:

This theory of reality is instantly fatal to the idea
of a thing in itself,—a thing existing independent of all
relation to the mind's conception of it. Yet it would by
no means forbid, but rather encourage us, to regard the
appearances of sense as only signs of the realities. Only,
the realities which they represent would not be the
unknowable cause of sensation, but *noumena*, or
intelligible conceptions which are the last products
of the mental action which is set in motion by sensation.
The matter of sensation is altogether accidental;
precisely the same information, practically, being
capable of communication through different senses.
And the catholic consent which constitutes the truth
is by no means to be limited to men in this earthly
life or to the human race, but extends to the whole
communion of minds to which we belong, including
some probably whose senses are very different from ours,
so that in that consent no predication of a sensible
quality can enter, except as an admission that so
certain sorts of senses are affected.[30]

The realistic hypostatization of what is represented in true
statements leads to a view that construes reality itself according to
the model of language. It is "symbolic" in the sense that any multiplicity of stimuli specific to a particular sense (the singular) refers to a universal relation existing independent of actual states
of consciousness. The universal is represented by its contingent
particularizations in the same way that the meaning of a word is
represented by the manifold material substrata that can function
as word-signs. The concrete is a referential context that, while
subjective, unmediated, contingent, inconstant, and accidental,
always points to the same universals, which are objective as well
as necessary and immutable for the community of all intelligible
beings. Through concrete sensory phenomena we are "brought"
to the existing universal.

    Ontological propositions about the structure of reality
unintentionally elucidate the process of mediation through which
we come to know reality. Yet in fact this concept of reality was

first introduced only as the correlate of a process of inquiry that guarantees the cumulative acquisition of definitively valid statements. As soon as we remember this point of departure, Scholastic realism of Peirce's stamp can be seen through as the ontologizing of an originally *methodological* problem. Indeed for Peirce the problem of the relation of the universal and the particular presented itself outside of the tradition. That is, it appeared not as a logical-ontological problem, but rather in connection with the methodological concept of truth as a problem of the logic of inquiry. Under the impression of actual cognitive progress in the natural sciences, Peirce had defined truth in the following manner: First, so that universal propositions, above all, could be true; second, so that no certainty is possible about the definitive validity of every individual opinion *before* the completion of the process of inquiry; and third, so that to the degree that the sciences advance, there is, nonetheless, an objective accumulation of opinions whose validity does not have to be revised again before the completion of the process of inquiry as a whole—"although we can never be absolutely certain of doing so in any special case."[31] From this state of affairs Peirce infers the existence of the universal or general: ". . . it follows that since no cognition of ours is absolutely determinate, generals must have a real existence."[32]

The fact of scientific progress induces Peirce to define universal propositions exclusively in relation to the anticipated end of the process of inquiry as a whole and yet to assume at the same time that, in increasing measure, we objectively arrive at true statements even *before* the consummation of this process—despite subjective uncertainty about the truth value of every single one of these statements. If this is so, however, then we must be able per se to infer a universal matter of fact from a given, finite number of singular cases, although *for us* the validity of this procedure cannot be compelling, but at best probable. Regarded from the perspective of the logic of inquiry, synthetic inferences must be possible. This is the methodological context in which Peirce came upon the problem of the relation of universal and particular.

At first glance, realism can render the possibility of synthetic inference comprehensible ontologically through its view that the universal exists not only as a concept of the knowing subject but in itself, and in such a manner that the concrete cases "in" which it exists "point" to it. In contrast, the perspective of the logic of inquiry compels Peirce to adopt a concept of reality *derived* from the methodological concept of truth. He has to link the existence of universals to the universal propositions in which they are formulated. Thus Peirce sees himself forced to reconcile realism with the principles of a transcendental philosophy that has been turned into a logic of inquiry. What he actually does, however, once having taken the logic of inquiry as his point of departure, is detach from it a concept of reality limited by the logic of language and remain satisfied with the observation that reality is constituted under conditions of the grammatical form of universal propositions. On this presupposition, the metaphysical version of realism seems to be convertible into a metalinguistic one. But the limit of linguistic transcendentalism reveals itself, as indicated, in the element of immediate qualitative manifoldness, which, like that of facticity, first guarantees being's independence from our interpretations. In the end, therefore, the logic of language must be replaced by a doctrine of categories that tacitly abandons the transcendental approach and restores ontology in an only barely concealed manner. On this basis, however, the identity of concept and object (*Sache*), which Peirce had first derived from a methodological conception of truth and thus understood as an *interpretation of the fact of scientific progress*, can only be justified in terms of an idealism that is not unlike Hegel's. Peirce did not explicitly draw this conclusion in his later philosophy. But, if I am not mistaken, the conception of a progressive embodiment of ideas, which dominates Peirce's later philosophy, cannot evade the difficult concept of nature as an absolute subject. Thus we shall return to the starting point of Peirce's argumentation, the logic of inquiry.

The conditions of the possibility of synthetic reasoning can be investigated in the dimension of the process of inquiry itself. The problem of the relation of the universal and the particular does not need to be displaced prematurely from the methodological to the ontological level. Then, however, it poses itself in a different form: What are the properties of the transcendental conditions of a process of inquiry in whose framework reality is objectified such that we apprehend the general in the singular—that is, that we can infer the validity of universal propositions from a finite number of singular cases? From this transcendental perspective it is not meaningful to talk in the language of Scholastic realism about the existence of the universal. Rather, within the framework posited with the process of inquiry we constitute the objects of possible experience such that reality is disclosed in a definite constellation of the universal and the particular. This constellation can be demonstrated in the modes of inference on which the progress of inquiry logically depends.

CHAPTER SIX

The Self-Reflection of the Natural Sciences: *The Pragmatist Critique of Meaning*

Peirce speaks of reasoning not in the narrow sense of the logical derivation of statements from other statements. Rather, it extends to the process of argument with whose aid we obtain true statements about reality. The logical forms of inference are not rules for the deductive acquisition of analytically correct propositions but rather for methodically arriving at synthetically valid statements. The forms of inference necessary for the logic of inquiry are rules according to which, under the condition of incoming information, statements can be transformed into other statements. Every individual bit of information, however, must be capable of being traced back in turn to other inferences of this sort, at least to implicit ones. For we do not have the support of either first principles or ultimate facts. Yet the input of information is to provide the two elements that characterize statements about a reality that exists in itself, namely qualitatively new content and the factual validity of propositions. If this is so, then the transformation of beliefs that have been rendered problematic into valid interpretations must take place according to rules that make possible the as it were osmotic translation of non-intentional experiential contents into symbolic representation—in other words, according to rules of synthesis.

Peirce distinguishes three forms of inference: deduction, induction, and abduction. Deduction proves that something must behave in a certain manner; induction that something does in fact behave in a certain manner; and abduction that something probably will behave in a certain manner. Abduction is the form of argument that extends our knowledge. It is the rule according to which we introduce new hypotheses. Thus only abductive thinking impels the process of inquiry onward. Through deduction we develop consequences of hypotheses by recourse to ini-

113

tial conditions. We apply the hypotheses to individual cases and deduce predictions of events that must occur if the hypothesis is correct. Through induction we examine whether and with what probability the predictions can be confirmed. Induction is the logical form of the actual process of inquiry, insofar as it tests the factual validity of hypotheses. The analytically cogent form of inference, deduction, is the least important from the perspective of a logic of scientific progress. For we do not acquire any *new* information deductively.[1]

It is abduction and induction that are important for the logic of inquiry. It is through them that the information input from experience enters our interpretations. The content of our theories about reality is extended abductively through the discovery of new hypotheses, whereas we inductively check the agreement of our hypotheses with the facts:

> Abduction is the process of forming an explanatory hypothesis. It is the only logical operation which introduces any new idea; for induction does nothing but determine a value, and deduction merely evolves the necessary consequences of a pure hypothesis. . . . Its [abduction's] only justification is that from its suggestion deduction can draw a prediction which can be tested by induction, and that, if we are ever to learn anything or to understand phenomena at all, it must be by abduction that this is to be brought about.[2]

Abductive inference takes into consideration that aspect of reality which cannot be grasped through the logic of language and which Peirce's doctrine of categories conceives of as Firstness or quality. Inductive inference takes account of the other aspect, the facticity of reality, which corresponds to the denotative function of language and later appears as the category of Secondness:

> The Deductions which we base upon the hypothesis which has resulted from Abduction produce conditional predictions concerning our future experience. That is to say, we infer by Deduction that if the

hypothesis be true, any future phenomena of certain descriptions must present such and such characters. We now institute a course of quasi-experimentation in order to bring these predictions to the test, and thus to form our final estimate of the value of the hypothesis, and this whole proceeding I term Induction.[3]

Peirce distinguishes the analytic form of syllogism, *deduction*, from abduction and induction, the so-called synthetic forms of inference. Logically these two forms can be regarded as variations of the necessary syllogism. If we take the syllogism *Barbara* as a typical example of deduction, we can view the universal proposition of the major premise as a lawlike hypothesis, the singular case of the minor premise as an expression for the initial conditions of a lawlike hypothesis, and the conclusion as a prediction. I deduce the prediction from the law as the result (effect) of a case (cause). Peirce speaks of *abduction* not when I derive the result deductively from a law and a case but rather when I derive the case from a result and a law. By result we mean in this connection an unforeseen fact that could not have been predicted on the basis of prevailing interpretations. It is inexplicable because we lack the hypothesis with whose aid we could infer the cause from the result. The special achievement of abduction, therefore, is the discovery and invention of a suitable hypothesis that allows this inference of the case from result and law.[4] Finally, *induction* refers not to our deductively inferring the result from law and case, or abductively inferring the case from result and law, but rather to our inferring a law from case and result. The case comprises the experimentally produced or quasi-experimentally chosen conditions of a prediction, and the result is the consequence of an experiment that confirms a conditional prediction. These two make it possible to infer the validity of the hypothesis according to which we can derive the result from the case, or the prediction from the conditions.

In the logic of inquiry, the interconnection of the three modes of inference represents the rules according to which we must proceed if the process of inquiry is to fulfill the purpose by which it is defined: namely of leading in the long run to true statements about reality. More difficult than apprehending these rules descriptively is explaining why they guarantee fulfilling it *in fact*. The form of inference that leads to correct propositions in an immanent and cogent manner, that is deduction, owes this merit to its analyticity. But this means that it provides no new information and is sterile for cognitive progress. On the other hand, the synthetic modes of inference, on which this progress is based, are not cogent. We cannot comprehend a priori why they should be valid. ". . . Only we know that, by faithfully adhering to that mode of inference, we shall, on the whole, approximate to the truth."[5]

Occasionally Peirce considers an empirical explanation for the validity of abduction and induction in the logic of inquiry. Like regularities of organic behavior, these rules that are productive in the acquisition of information could be the result of natural selection.

> How is the existence of this faculty accounted for?
> In one sense, no doubt, by natural selection. Since it
> is absolutely essential to the preservation of so delicate
> an organism as man's, no race which had it not has
> been able to sustain itself. This accounts for the
> prevalence of this faculty . . . But how can it be possible?[6]

Yet in the end Peirce sees that the question of the validity of logical rules cannot be answered immediately on empirical grounds, but first requires a transcendental-logical answer:

> . . . What makes the facts usually to be, as inductive
> and hypothetic conclusions from true premises
> represent them to be? Facts of a certain kind are
> usually true when facts having certain [logical] relations
> to them are true; what is the cause of this? That is
> the question.[6]

This question is a transcendental-logical question about the conditions of possible knowledge. This is shown in that the validity of abduction and induction can neither be demonstrated through formal logic nor explained empirically (or ontologically with reference to the structure of reality):

> On the one hand, no determination of things, no *fact*,
> can result in the validity of probable argument; nor,
> on the other hand, is such argument reducible to that
> form which holds good, however the facts may be.[7]

It is not within Kant's system of reference, however, that Peirce repeats Kant's question. It is not into the possibility of synthetic judgments a priori that he inquires but rather into the possibility of synthetic thinking in general. Kant supposed that the synthetic judgments in terms of which he inquired how knowledge is transcendentally possible were as cogently valid as analytic judgments. Peirce says only that synthetic inferences must be valid in fact if something like a process of inquiry that is contingent as a whole is possible. Since we are compelled to view reality as the correlate of a process of inquiry that is successful in the long run, we can be assured of the factual validity of synthetic thought through the mere existence of anything real at all. Inquiring into the conditions of its possibility is "equivalent to asking why there is anything real. . . ."[8] Peirce believes himself capable of answering this question with his theory of reality:

> [I]f nothing real exists, then, since every question
> supposes that something exists—for it maintains its
> own urgency—it supposes only illusions to exist. But
> the existence even of an illusion is a reality; for an
> illusion affects all men, or it does not. In the former
> case, it is a reality according to our theory of reality; in
> the latter case, it is independent of the state of mind
> of any individuals except those whom it happens to
> affect. So that the answer to the question, Why is
> anything real? is this: That question means, "supposing
> anything to exist, why is something real?" The answer
> is, that that very existence is reality by definition. . . .
> Thus, I claim to have shown, in the first place, that

it is possible to hold a consistent theory of the validity
of the laws of ordinary logic.[9]

It is easy to see, however, that Peirce's argument is circular. With a concept of reality derived from the logic of inquiry,
Peirce already presupposes that the existence of anything independent of synthetic inferences is inconceivable. It then naturally
follows from any matter of fact at all, insofar as it is taken as
existing, that the modes of inference at issue are valid. Yet
Nietzsche developed a perspectivistic concept of truth and an ir-
rationalistic concept of reality that shows that it is certainly possible to *conceive* a reality that can be resolved into a plurality of
fictions relative to multiple standpoints. It is constituted as a
manifold of what in principle can be any number of perspectives.
Against the background of this concept, which is antithetical to
what Peirce means by reality, his tautology becomes clear. If we
assume that reality is not constituted independently of the rules
to which the process of inquiry is subject, then we cannot refer
to this reality to justify the validity of the rules of the process of
inquiry, that is the modes of inference.[10]

What speaks for their validity is primarily no more—although no less—than the basic belief that until now there has
been a cumulative learning process and that this process would
necessarily lead to complete knowledge of reality if it were continued long enough in methodical fashion as a process of inquiry.
This belief underlies the postulate of hope for the realization of
the empirical conditions under which the process of inquiry can
in fact be completed. But this does not answer the question,
"What makes the facts usually to be, as inductive and hypothetical conclusions from true premises represent them to be?"

If we comprehend the process of inquiry as the system of
reference for the possible objectification of reality, then the validity of its logical rules can be none other than the validity of
transcendental rules. At the same time, the modes of inference
cannot be viewed simply as transcendentally necessary because
they are not valid universally, at all places and times. They only
justify the validity of a method that leads to true statements *in
the long run*. The synthetic forms of inference allow justifiable

conclusions that are not necessarily true or probable. They owe their validity exclusively to the circumstance that they are the results of a method "which if steadily persisted in must bring the reasoner to the truth of the matter or must cause his conclusion in its changes to converge to the truth as its limit."[11] The logical rules of the process of inquiry do not by any means ground the conditions of possible knowledge with transcendental necessity. Otherwise the judgments implied in them would be synthetic judgments a priori. But they do establish a procedure that increases intersubjectively recognized beliefs if it is carried out continuously under empirical conditions. If this method is the sole guarantee of obtaining true statements, then these rules, as specifications of a method, have the function of transcendental conditions of possible objects of experience. But, unlike transcendental conditions, they cannot be derived from the constitution of consciousness per se. They remain contingent as a whole.

Among all methods that lead to validated beliefs, the method of inquiry has proved itself to be the most successful in fact. Besides scientific method, Peirce discusses three other methods. He calls them the method of tenacity, the method of authority, and the a priori method. All of them have advantages, but they are surpassed by the scientific method if the only criterion of evaluation is in what way can we best arrive at definitively valid beliefs—in other words, beliefs that all future events will not render problematic but rather confirm? It is on this criterion that the meaning of the "validity" of the conclusions produced by the process of inquiry depends. Whereas for Kant the determinations of transcendental consciousness, forms of intuition, and categories of the understanding define the conditions of the objectivity of knowledge and thus the meaning of the truth of statements, for Peirce this concept of truth is not derivable merely from the logical rules of the process of inquiry, but rather only from the *objective life context* in which the process of inquiry fulfills specifiable functions: the settlement of opinions, the elimination of uncertainties, and the acquisition of unproblematic beliefs—in short, the fixation of belief. The objective context in which the three modes of inference fulfill this task is the behavioral system of purposive-rational action. For the definition of a belief is that we orient our behavior according to it. ". . . Belief consists mainly in being deliberately prepared to adopt the formula believed in as the guide to action."[12] The "essence of belief is the establishment of a habit; and different beliefs are distinguished by the different modes of action to which they give rise."[13]

A belief is a behavioral rule, but not the habitually determined behavior itself. Behavioral certainty is the criterion of its validity. A belief remains unproblematic as long as the modes of behavior that it guides do not fail in reality. As soon as a behavioral habit is rendered uncertain by the resistance of reality, doubt arises with regard to the orientation that guides behavior. The undermining of habits awakens doubt in the validity of the corresponding beliefs. And this doubt motivates efforts to find new beliefs that will restabilize the disturbed behavior.[14] The results of synthetic reasoning have a function only in the behavioral system of this purposive-rational, feedback-controlled, and habitual behavior. True beliefs define the realm of future behavior that the actor has under control.[15]

Valid beliefs are universal propositions about reality that, under given initial conditions and on the basis of conditional predictions, can be transformed into technical recommendations. This and only this is the content of pragmatism:

> Pragmatism is the principle that every
> theoretical judgment expressible in a sentence in the
> indicative mood is a confused form of thought whose
> only meaning, if it has any, lies in its tendency to enforce
> a corresponding practical maxim expressible as a
> conditional sentence having its apodosis in the
> imperative mood.[16]

A pragmatistic criterion of meaning can be derived from this basic assumption, one that makes it possible to eliminate meaningless statements[17] and render more precise the meaning of vague concepts. But the intention of what Peirce called pragmatism and then, in order to set it off from psychologistic misinterpretations, pragmaticism, has a more far-reaching aim. The issue is not the derivation of a criterion of meaning but rather the central question of a logic of inquiry that is guided by reflection on the basic experience of positivism: *how is scientific progress possible?* Pragmatism answers this question by legitimating the validity of synthetic modes of inference on the basis of the transcendental structure of instrumental action.

Beliefs are crystallized in concepts. These concepts can be explicated in universal judgments having the form of lawlike hypotheses. These in turn are to be understood in terms of the conclusions that can be derived from them as conditional predictions. The correction and amplification of concepts occurs in processes of syllogistic reasoning, in which abduction, deduction, and induction supplement each other and mutually presuppose each other. Concepts and judgments can be explicated in syllogisms just as syllogisms can be condensed into judgments and concepts. But this "movement of the concept"[18] is neither absolute nor self-sufficient. It acquires its meaning only from the system of reference of possible *feedback-controlled action*. Its goal is the elimination of behavioral uncertainty. All logical forms (concept, judgment, and syllogism) therefore refer with transcendental necessity to the pragmatistic meaning of universal relations represented by signs. The primary form of relation is expressed in the conditional prediction of what events will occur under specifiable conditions, which means in principle conditions that can be manipulated. Thus the meaning of the validity of statements is determined with reference to possible technical control of the connection of empirical variables. Statements refer to "the 'would-acts,' 'would-dos' of habitual behavior; and no agglomeration of actual happenings can ever completely fill up the meaning of a 'would-be.' "[19] Correspondingly, the purpose of hypotheses is also the maintenance and extension of feedback-controlled action: "Its [a hypothesis's] end is, through subjection to the test of experiment, to lead to the avoidance of all surprise and to the establishment of positive expectation that shall not be disappointed."[20] Thus the modes of inference are not just embedded secondarily in the behavioral system of instrumental action; rather the latter implies the conditions of their validity. At one point Peirce criticizes De Morgan's propositional logic with the argument that "formal logic must not be too purely formal; it must represent a fact of psychology, or else it is in danger of degenerating into a mathematical recreation."[21] This is not meant psychologistically, for Peirce repeatedly protests energetically against the confusion of intentional contents with psychic events. But at the same time he insists that logical forms pertain categorically to the fundamental life processes in whose context they assume functions. In this sense Peirce comprehends the three modes of inference as functions of a life process.

From this point of view deduction has the function of a "decision." The conclusion to which it leads "is" a specific behavioral reaction resulting from the application of a general rule of behavior to a singular case: "The cognition of a result [meaning the conclusion of a syllogism in the modus Barbara] is of the nature of a decision to act in a particular way on a given occasion."[22] To emphasize that the cycle of operations of feedback-controlled action is a life process, Peirce sets forth an analogy between reactions of animal behavior occurring in accordance with the reflex-arc model and the purposive-rational action of man, mediated by processes of inference:

> In point of fact, a syllogism in Barbara virtually takes place when we irritate the foot of a decapitated frog. The connection between the afferent and efferent nerve, whatever it may be, constitutes a nervous habit, a rule of action, which is the physiological analogue of the major premise. The disturbance of the ganglionic equilibrium, owing to the irritation, is the physiological form of that which, psychologically considered, is a sensation; and, logically considered, is the occurrence of a case. The explosion through the efferent nerve is the physiological form of that which psychologically is a volition, and logically the inference of a result. When we pass from the lowest to the highest forms of innervation, the physiological equivalents escape our observation; but, psychologically, we still have, first, habit—which in its highest form is understanding, and

which corresponds to the major premise of *Barbara*;
we have, second, feeling, or present consciousness,
corresponding to the minor premise of *Barbara*; and
we have, third, volition, corresponding to the conclusion
of the same mode of syllogism.[23]

Abduction leads to the stimulus that sets off an action,
that is to the "case," and induction leads to the behavior-stabiliz-
ing "rule" just as deduction does to the behavioral reaction itself,
the "result." From this point of view Peirce considers it meaningful to correlate each mode of inference with a particular element of the behavioral circuit. Abduction, which finds a suitable
rule for an unexpected result in order to infer back to a case that
explains the result, corresponds to the *sensory element*. Sense-
data merely appear to be immediate; in fact they can be identified
only through the mediation of inferential processes. Induction,
which infers from case and result to the validity of the rule that
permits deriving the prediction of the event (result) from the
initial conditions (case), corresponds to the *habitual element*.
The universal assumptions at the basis of purposive-rational action are subjected to permanent testing. They can be sedimented
as habits of behavior because and insofar as they stand a permanent test. Deduction, which infers from rule and case to the result and permits deriving conditional predictions, corresponds to
the *volitional element*. The act of purposive-rational action can
be understood as the performance of a deduction, just as the
latter, conversely, can be understood as a virtually anticipated instrumental action.[24] Thus the modes of inference attain methodological interconnection only through their function in the
behavioral system of instrumental action.

This behavioral circuit, however, is viewed not stati-
cally but as a framework for cumulatively operating processes.
True, instrumental action can be comprehended as manipulation
according to rules and under empirical conditions, in which case
it makes sense to correlate abduction with the identification of
conditions, induction with the habitualization of rules, and deduction with the exercise of manipulation. But the connection
of symbolic processes of inference and factual processes of action

becomes clear only if we understand instrumental action as the control of the external conditions of existence, which can be acquired and exercised only under the conditions of a *cumulative learning process*. Every instance of action according to technical rules is at the same time a test of these rules, every failure of a feedback-controlled action is at the same time the refutation of a hypothesis, and every reorientation of a disturbed behavioral system is at once both the extension of a previously exercised power of technical control and the result of a learning process. Inquiry is the reflected form (*Reflexionsform*) of this pre-scientific learning process that is *already posited* with instrumental action *as such*. The process of inquiry, though, satisfies three additional conditions: (1) It isolates the learning process from the life process. Therefore the performance of operations is reduced to selective feedback controls. (2) It guarantees precision and intersubjective reliability. Therefore action assumes the abstract form of experiment mediated by measurement procedures. (3) It systematizes the progression of knowledge. Therefore as many universal assumptions as possible are integrated into theoretical connections that are as simple as possible. The latter have the form of hypothetico-deductive systems of propositions.

As long as the pragmatistic framework of our learning processes remains conscious, then the formation of hypotheses, the derivation of conditional predictions, and the testing of hypotheses through such predictions are recognized as a necessary element in the self-regulating system of action and cumulative learning. Even the identification of individual events requires categories that imply general lawlike assumptions. Consequently, every event that falsifies a prediction derived from a hypothesis must be subsumed under alternative assumptions in order for us to be at all able to comprehend it *as* something. In the institutionalized process of inquiry, however, theoretical sentences and selective experiential controls become so separate that the logical structure of experience can be misunderstood. This leads to *psychologizing* the elements of the process of inquiry. That falsifications compel the abductive generation of new hypotheses and thus take on the function of determinate negation becomes unrecognizable as a logical relation. Abduction appears as a contingent process of the psychology of inquiry, once test and assumption, action and hypothesis are related to each other only externally. Only within the transcendental framework of instrumental action is it possible to see that, actually, new hypotheses must be formed according to rules of abduction and not left to the randomness of a hypothesis-creating imagination. On the other hand, in the pragmatistic system of reference it also becomes clear that the relation holding between the deduction of lawlike assumptions and their inductive confirmation is not an exclusively logical relation. From the logical point of view the outcome of an experiment can be definitive only in the case of falsification.[25] If, however, the fact of scientific progress cannot seriously be denied, then it can be explained only by the verifying power of the inductive confirmation of hypotheses. The validity of induction can, like that of abduction, be justified only through their *metalogical connection* with deduction, which is posited with the behavioral system of instrumental action as a transcendental framework for the possible stabilization of habits of behavior and the possible extension of technically exploitable knowledge.

The transcendental function of the connection of feedback-controlled action with the three modes of inference is shown in the fact that we progress through learning from problematic views to new ones capable of habitualization only if we apprehend reality under a determinate schema. This objectification of the reality of nature is grounded in the forms of inference coordinated in the behavioral circuit. Only if we attribute something like instrumental action to nature itself can we abductively discover new hypotheses, deductively derive conditional predictions from them, and confirm them through continued induction. We must act as though observable events were creations of a subject that unceasingly draws conclusions in the *modus Barbara*, under contingent initial conditions and according to a finite set of definitively valid rules, and then actually produces the deduced events in accord with the previously established predictions. This subject would be nature, which had habitualized all "laws of nature" as the rules of its behavior. Only if man in his instrumental action constitutes his natural environment from this point of view and projects himself as the opponent of an instrumentally acting nature can he hope for success with his method:

> We usually conceive Nature to be perpetually making deductions in *Barbara*. This is our natural and anthropomorphic metaphysics. We conceive that there are Laws of Nature, which are her Rules or major premises. We conceive that Cases arise under these laws; these cases consist in the predication, or occurrence, of *causes*, which are the middle terms of the syllogisms [of nature]. And, finally, we conceive that the occurrence of these causes, by virtue of the laws of Nature, results in effects which are the conclusions of the syllogisms [of nature]. Conceiving of nature in this way, we naturally conceive of science as having three tasks—(1) the discovery of Laws, which is accomplished by induction; (2) the discovery of Causes, which is accomplished by hypothetic inference; and (3) the prediction of Effects, which is accomplished by deduction.[26]

The projection of the schema of human action onto nature means that the behavioral system of instrumental action is the transcendental framework which establishes the conditions of the objectivity of possible statements about the real. On the level of processes of inquiry, this system has taken the form of the experiment. The transcendental conditions of possible experience are identical with the conditions of possible experimentation. In an experiment we bring about, by means of a controlled succession of events, a relation between at least two empirical variables. This relation satisfies two conditions. It can be expressed *grammatically* in the form of a conditional prediction that can be deduced from a general lawlike hypothesis with the aid of initial conditions; at the same time it can be exhibited *factually* in the form of an instrumental action that manipulates the initial conditions such that the success of the operation can be controlled by means of the occurrence of the effect. The relation between empirical variables underlying a "natural law" can be stated in a sentence of the form, "Whenever x, then y." At the same time it can be exhibited by an operation that produces state y by bringing about state x. The sentence can be understood as the formulation of the plan or intention that guides the operation. It is the exact form of a belief that functions as a definite rule of instrumental action (habit).

This rule is realized by an indefinite number of future operations that are characterized (if the rule is empirically true) by necessarily bringing about the same effect under exactly similar conditions. But in that case every single one of these operations must indeed "mean" more than the singular event that it "is." Every individual experiment assures us of a universal relation, which, under exactly similar conditions, must also be confirmed in all future repetitions of the same experiment:

> Indeed, it is not in an experiment, but in experimental phenomena, that rational meaning is said to consist. When an experimentalist speaks of a phenomenon, such as "Hall's phenomenon," "Zeemann's phenomenon" and its modification, "Michelson's phenomenon," or "the chessboard phenomenon," he does not mean any particular event that did happen to somebody in the dead past, but what surely will happen to everybody in the living future who shall fulfill certain conditions. The phenomenon consists in the fact that when an experimentalist shall come to act according to a certain scheme that he has in mind, then will something else happen, and shatter the doubts of sceptics, like the celestial fire upon the altar of Elijah.[27]

The effects obtained under experimental conditions are always obtained in a singular operation, yet they mean the ascertainment of a universal relation. The singular event is at the same time a general phenomenon, the reason being that it guarantees that all operations carried out in the future and repeating the initial experiment under exactly the same conditions must lead to "the same" effect. That this occurs, however, is not a result of experience, but necessary a priori: experimental action is *defined* by admitting in principle of an indefinite number of strict repetitions and compelling the repetition of results. For only on this presupposition can experiment be employed for the ends of intersubjectively compelling refutation.

Because as a general principle a *single* experiment suffices to test a specific prediction, it is possible to discover the possible boundaries of the scope of a lawlike hypothesis, which is originally formulated in universal terms, by systematically varying the initial conditions. For the specific technical rule that I follow in each individual experiment realizes only one of infinitely many predictions that I can derive from the lawlike hypothesis in question. But every one of these effects produced under experimental conditions is universal a priori, that is it must necessarily occur if the experiment is repeated under unvarying initial conditions. This a priori character is linked to the conditions of instrumental action. For experimental action is only a precise form of instrumental action in general that has been made possible by operations of measurement. The behavioral system of experimental or quasi-experimental action has the function of a transcendental framework: under conditions of experimentation, reality is objectified such that an observable reaction to the manipulation of initial conditions is with transcendental necessity a singular event that per se represents a universal effect. Peirce observes at one point that the decisive point of pragmatism is this derivation of a necessary relation between the universal and the particular: "the validity of induction depends upon the necessary relation between the general and the singular. It is precisely this which is the support of Pragmatism."[28] That singular events may be interpreted as general ones depends on the objectification of reality in the behavioral system of instrumental action under conditions that produce this necessary relation between the universal and the particular: "Whenever a man acts purposively, he acts under a belief in some experimental phenomenon."[29]

This is at the same time the answer given by a transcendental-logically structured pragmatism to the question, how is scientific progress possible on the basis of synthetic reasoning? For the validity of inductive inferences, which cannot be logically demonstrated, is thus justified methodologically through the proof that, as experimentally produced phenomena, the singular events taken as the basis for induction represent general effects.[30]

Since the transcendental conditions of possible knowledge are posited not by a consciousness as such but by a behavioral system, the transcendental concept of *possibility* acquires the meaning of a concrete program for future action. What is real are the possible results of specifiable operations, because these effects are arrived at no matter when and how often I carry out these operations as long as this occurs under the conditions specified. These experiences that are possible under the transcendental conditions of instrumental action are instructions that I learn from reality if and insofar as I intervene in it through operations. My experiences have transcendental necessity only under the factual condition of successes or failures of possible instrumental actions. But if pragmatism is viewed from a transcendental-logical perspective in this rigorous sense, then the validity of empirical statements has the following meaning: it grants an organism that operates in the behavioral system of instrumental action the power of technical control over an environment in which this organism factually occurs.

Now, if we call the relations asserted in universal propositions real,[31] in what sense can we then speak of the existence of such universals? In the context of pragmatism, Peirce once again takes up the problem of universals:

At first sight it seems no doubt a paradoxical statement that, "The object of final belief which exists only in consequence of the belief, should itself produce the belief"; ... The object of the belief exists it is true, only because the belief exists; but this is not the same as to say that it begins to exist first when the belief begins to exist. We say that a diamond is hard. And in what does the hardness consist? It consists merely in the fact that nothing will scratch it; therefore its hardness is entirely constituted by the fact of something rubbing against it with force without scratching it. And were it impossible that anything should rub against it in this way, it would be quite without meaning, to say that it was hard, just as it is entirely without meaning to say that virtue or any other abstraction is hard. But though the hardness is entirely constituted by the fact of another stone rubbing against the diamond yet we do not conceive of it as beginning to be hard when the other stone is rubbed against it; on the contrary, we say that it is really hard the whole time, and has been hard since it began to be a diamond. And yet there was no fact, no event, nothing whatever, which made it different from any other thing which is not so hard, until the other stone was rubbed against it.[32]

In another passage Peirce again uses the same example to point up the paradox of the concept of reality derived from the logic of inquiry:

> Is it not a monstrous perversion of the word and concept *real* to say that the accident of the non-arrival of the corundum prevented the hardness of the diamond from having the *reality* which it otherwise, with little doubt, would have had?[33]

From the perspective of a transcendentally elaborated pragmatism, the paradox can be easily resolved. The universal matter of fact of the "hardness" of an object called diamond has existence (if and as long as there are diamonds) independently of whether any person actually makes the attempt to rub any diamond with the aid of a sharp object. On the other hand, it is not meaningful to attribute the predicate "hardness" to an object called diamond if the statement cannot be made at least implicitly with regard to the system of reference of possible instrumental action. We do reckon with the existence of a reality that is independent of men who can act instrumentally and arrive at a consensus about statements. But what the predication of properties catches "of" this reality is a matter of fact that is *constituted only* in the perspective of possible technical control. It is in this sense that I understand the resolution of the paradox suggested by Peirce in his "Issues of Pragmaticism."

[W]e must dismiss the idea that the occult state of things (be it a relation among atoms or something else), which constitutes the reality of a diamond's hardness can possibly consist in anything but in the truth of a general conditional proposition. For to what else does the entire teaching of chemistry relate except to the "behavior" of different possible kinds of material substance? And in what does that behavior consist except that if a substance of a certain kind should be exposed to an agency of a certain kind, a certain kind of sensible result *would* ensue, according to our experiences hitherto.[34]

The concept of hardness can be explicated by a class of conditional predictions. If we take an object that satisfies the initial conditions of these predictions, then the class of all such predictions implies that the object's "hardness" *exists in itself* even independently of whether or not we perform even a single test. But this universal matter of fact is real only in relation to possible operations of this sort in general: The object called diamond *is* hard only insofar as it is constituted as an object of possible technical control and is *capable* of entering the behavioral system of instrumental action.

If Peirce had considered advocating this solution of the problem of universals in terms of the logic of inquiry, he would have had to differentiate in the concept of reality between, on the one hand, what is in fact independent of cumulative learning processes and a human world constituted by technical controllability and, on the other, what we catch "of" this reality as soon as it enters our world and becomes the correlate of true statements about reality. Marx had a conception of this difference, and Heidegger, elaborating on the work of Husserl, has explicitly formulated it: the difference between beings and Being. If the concept of reality derived from the logic of inquiry were to be developed in a pragmatistic direction, it would have to comprehend this difference. Peirce, however, limits himself to a concept of reality that is exhausted in being the correlate of all possible true statements.

This limitation of the concept of reality shows that

Peirce indeed did not pursue his pragmatistic approach along the lines of a transcendental logic of inquiry and develop it consistently. Instead he reverts to ontologizing by interpreting what is in principle a question of the logic of inquiry as one of the logic of language. If we recall his formulation of the diamond example in "The Logic of 1873," "its hardness is entirely constituted by the fact of *something* rubbing against it with force without scratching it," we see that Peirce refers to "something," not to "somebody" rubbing—in other words, not to an instrumentally acting subject. He contents himself with an objectivist construction: "that *anything* should rub against it." He abstracts from the circumstance that the initial conditions with whose aid a general effect can be predicted on the basis of a hypothesis are produced by an operation—or at least must be capable of being considered as though they had been produced by an operation. For only then is the predicted event the result of an action. In the formulation cited, Peirce leaves out of account the system of reference in which events are first constituted for us as instrumental actors.

The relation between cause and effect ("something will happen under certain circumstances"), once detached from the behavioral system of instrumental action, is immediately coordinated by Peirce with the sentence in which it is formulated. If, however, the operation through which it is simultaneously exhibited merely *supervenes* on the sentence as an accidental factor, then the problem of the existence of the universal is returned to the level of the logic of language. Universal relations exist in themselves, although as the correlate of possible true statements about reality. Peirce later attempted to eliminate the difficulties of his Scholastic realism, peculiarly modified by linguistic transcendentalism, through a bold philosophy of natural evolution. In this theory natural laws appear as the sedimented behavioral habits of a *natura naturans*, while men, to the degree that they orient their purposive-rational action according to natural laws, embody increasingly more ideas and propel the rationalization of the universe.[35] In the present context what is of interest here is the return to a contemplative concept of knowledge connected with this view.

The false ontologizing of the universals that, in their necessary relation to the particular, are first constituted within the behavioral system must have its counterpart in a corresponding mode of knowledge: one that contemplatively grasps universal matters of fact, *existing in themselves*, as such, no matter how much this mode may be mediated by processes of inference. If this is the case, however, then the motive of cognitive progress can be sought only in theoretical curiosity. Peirce speaks of the Gnostic instinct:

> It is quite true that the Gnostic Instinct is the cause
> of all purely theoretical inquiry, and that every
> discovery of science is a gratificatioñ of curiosity. But it
> is not true that pure science is or can be successfully
> pursued *for the sake* of gratifying this instinct. . . .
> Curiosity is their [the theoretical sciences'] motive;
> but the gratification of curiosity is not their aim.[36]

An objectivist conception of knowledge, which can account for theory only in terms of itself, is the counterpart of a reestablished Scholastic realism.

On the other hand, as long as he admits the transcendental connection of knowledge and instrumental action (reason and conduct), Peirce can easily set forth the meaning of the validity of corroborated empirical statements: knowledge stabilizes purposive-rational, feedback-monitored action in an environment objectified from the point of view of possible technical control. The transcendental framework of the process of inquiry establishes the necessary conditions for the possible extension of technically exploitable knowledge (*Wissen*). Since it is posited with the behavioral system of instrumental action, this framework cannot be conceived as the determination of a transcendental consciousness as such. Rather, it is dependent on the organic constitution of a species that is compelled to reproduce its life through purposive-rational action. Hence the framework that establishes a priori the meaning of the validity of empirical statements is contingent *as such*. Just as little as it can be elevated to the transempirical plane of pure noumenal determinations, however, can it be conceived as having originated under empirical conditions—at least not as long as its origins have to be conceived under the very categories that it itself first defines.

There are even some indications that allow the inference that Peirce regarded the methodological framework of inquiry together with the behavioral system of instrumental action in which it is embedded as the evolutionary substitute for lost or impaired animal steering mechanisms. Indeed, Herder had already understood culture from this perspective of compensation for deficiencies of organic equipment.

> A small dose of reasoning is necessary to connect the
> instinct with the occasion. . . . It is only a remarkable
> man or a man in a remarkable situation, who, in default
> of any applicable rule of thumb, is forced to reason
> out his plans from first principles. . . . Fortunately . . .
> man is not so happy as to be provided with a full
> stock of instincts to meet all occasions, and so is forced
> upon the adventurous business of reasoning, where
> the many meet shipwreck and the few find, not
> old-fashioned happiness, but its splendid substitute,
> success. . . . The best plan, then, on the whole, is to base
> our conduct as much as possible on Instinct, but when
> we do reason to reason with severely scientific logic.[37]

If we regard the function of knowledge in this way as a substitute for instinctive behavioral steering, then the rationality of feedback-controlled action is assessed with regard to the realization of an *interest* that can be neither a merely empirical nor a pure interest. If the cognitive process were *immediately* a life process, then the realization of this knowledge-constitutive interest would lead to the direct gratification of a need just as an instinctual movement does. The interest, however, when realized, leads not to happiness but to success. Success is assessed with regard to problem solutions that have both a life function and a cognitive function. Thus "interest" can be neither classed with those mechanisms of steering animal behavior that we can call instincts nor entirely severed from the objective context of a life process. In this at first negatively delimited sense we speak of a *knowledge-constitutive interest in possible technical control*, which defines the course of the objectification of reality necessary within the transcendental framework of processes of inquiry.

An interest of this sort, however, can be ascribed only to a subject that combines the empirical character of a species having emerged in natural history with the intelligible character of a community that constitutes the world from transcendental perspectives. This would be the subject of the process of learning and inquiry that is itself involved in a self-formative process until the point in time at which a definitive and complete knowledge of reality is attained. But it is this very subject that Peirce cannot conceive. It falls through his fingers because he applies the pragmatist criterion of meaning to the concepts of both mind and matter. Here a hidden but unyielding positivism finally prevails. Peirce subjects himself to the compulsion of taking the same constitutive structure on whose basis he justifies the demand of eliminating all concepts that cannot be operationalized, and applying it to this demand itself.

On pragmatist principles a substantial concept of matter is as inadmissible as the positivist idea of a world of facts composed of elements. Matter is at best the sum-total of all events that have occurred or will occur on the basis of all possible true predictions. Even if particles of matter are conceived as centers of force, this does not alter anything with regard to the semantic content of the concept: "Since, therefore, these forces exist only by virtue of the fact, that something will happen under certain circumstances, it follows that matter itself only exists in this way."[38] The concept of mind is also viewed in the same way. It, too, can be conceived as the center of mental forces. Like material forces, mental ones can mean nothing other than "that something will happen under certain circumstances." Particular ideas arise under particular circumstances, and the sum-total of such ideas is what we call "mind." It is remarkable that Peirce presumes that ideas or beliefs have the same status as events that fulfill conditional predictions—regardless of the fact that these predictions themselves are ideas and beliefs. Peirce does not notice this circle:

It appears then that the existence of mind
equally with that of matter according to these arguments
which have led to this view which is held by all
psychologists, as well as physicists, depends only upon
certain hypothetical conditions which may first occur in
the future, or which may not occur at all. There is
nothing extraordinary therefore in saying that the
existence of external realities depends upon the fact, that
opinion will finally settle in the belief in them. And yet
that these realities existed before the belief took rise, and
were even the cause of that belief, just as the force of
gravity is the cause of the falling of the inkstand—
although the force of gravity consists merely in the fact
that the inkstand and other objects will fall.[39]

In order to strip the concept of mind of all metaphysical illusion,
Peirce places beliefs referring to the connection of empirical
events on the same level as empirical events themselves. A belief
about a matter of fact appears as an event occurring under empirical conditions just like the very facts to which the belief refers.
This objectivism is scarcely distinguishable from Mach's doctrine
of elements. Above all, it undermines the foundation on which
the analysis of the total subject of processes of inquiry would
have to be based. This subject, the "community of investigators,"
comes into being and works under empirical conditions, and yet
at the same time it proceeds according to rules of the logic of inquiry possessing transcendental functions.

The operationalist concept of mind, patterned by Peirce
after that of matter, explains why pragmatism, which disclosed
the behavioral system of instrumental action as a constitutive
structure, also reobliterated the decisive distinction between the
facts that are constituted and the methodological framework
within which reality is objectified for the subject of inquiry. Thus
it led to a reversion to Scholastic realism interpreted according to
the logic of language. By carrying out a cumulative process of
inquiry according to rules of a logic that objectifies reality from
the point of view of possible technical control, the community of
investigators performs a synthesis. But if this synthesis falls un-

der the operationalist concept of "mind" and is dissolved objectivistically into a series of empirical events, then what remains is nothing but universal matters of fact existing in themselves and the combinations of signs through which these matters of fact are represented.

We can only conjecture why Peirce accedes to a concealed positivism and treats the pragmatist criterion of meaning in such an absolutistic manner that it destroys the foundation of pragmatism itself. Had Peirce taken seriously the communication of investigators as a transcendental subject forming itself under empirical conditions, then pragmatism would have been compelled to a self-reflection that overstepped its own boundaries. In continuing his analysis, Peirce would have had to come upon the fact that the *ground of intersubjectivity* in which investigators are always already situated when they attempt to bring about consensus about metatheoretical problems is not the ground of purposive-rational action, which is in principle solitary. True, subjects acting instrumentally make use of representational signs, and the technical rules that can be sedimented as habits must be capable of formulation in statements about relations of events. Nevertheless, as we have shown, the symbolic representation of matters of fact knowable from the transcendental perspective of possible technical control serves exclusively for the transformation of expressions in processes of reasoning. Deduction, induction, and abduction establish relations between statements that are in principle monologic. It is possible to think in syllogisms, but not to conduct a dialogue in them. I can use syllogistic reasoning to yield arguments for a discussion, but I cannot argue syllogistically with an other. Insofar as the employment of symbols is constitutive for the behavioral system of instrumental action, the use of language involved is monologic. But the communication of investigators requires the use of language that is not confined to the limits of technical control over objectified natural processes. It arises from symbolic interaction between societal subjects who reciprocally know and recognize each other as unmistakable individuals. This *communicative action* is a system of reference that cannot be reduced to the framework of *instrumental action*.

This is shown by the category of the ego or self. With admirable consistency Peirce demonstrates that as long as man grounds his identity exclusively in the success or failure of instrumental action, he can comprehend himself only privatively. He gains self-certainty only at those moments when there is a discrepancy between his own beliefs and those that are strengthened by public consensus and accepted as definitive:

> A child hears it said that the stove is hot. But it
> is not, he says; and, indeed, that central body is not
> touching it, and only what that touches is hot or cold.
> But he touches it, and finds the testimony confirmed
> in a striking way. Thus, he becomes aware of ignorance,
> and it is necessary to suppose a *self* in which this
> ignorance can inhere. So testimony gives the first
> dawning of self-consciousness.[40]

If the only matters of fact that exist are those about which true statements are possible, then individual consciousness can become visible merely as the negation of what is publicly recognized as reality. As existing consciousness the individual is subsumed without mediation under the general intellect of all true propositions:

> Thus my language is the sum total of myself. . . .
> The individual man, since his separate existence is
> manifested only by ignorance and error, so far as he is
> anything apart from his fellows, and from what he
> and they are to be, is only a negation. This is man . . .[41]

Not every communication, however, is merely the subsumption of the individual under an abstract universal, or what is in principle mute subjection to a public monologue that everyone can reproduce for himself. On the contrary, every dialogue develops on an entirely different basis, namely that of the reciprocal recognition of subjects who identify one another under the category of selfhood (*Ichheit*) and at the same time maintain themselves in their non-identity. The concept of the individual ego includes a *dialectical relation of the universal and the particular*, which cannot be conceived in the behavioral system of instrumental action.

Reflection on the community of investigators, through whose communication scientific progress is realized from the transcendental point of view of possible technical control, would necessarily burst the pragmatist framework. Precisely this self-reflection would have to show that the subject of the process of inquiry forms itself on the foundation of an intersubjectivity that as such extends beyond the transcendental framework of instrumental action. In the dialogic clarification of metatheoretical problems, the communication of investigators avails itself of a mode of knowledge linked to the framework of symbolic interaction. This cognitive mode is presupposed in the acquisition of technically exploitable knowledge (*Wissen*) but cannot itself be justified in terms of the latter's categories.

CHAPTER SEVEN

Dilthey's Theory of Understanding Expression:
Ego Identity and Linguistic Communication

The basis of mutual understanding that, at the roots of the natural sciences, is presupposed by participants in processes of inquiry, is claimed by the cultural sciences (*Geisteswissenschaften*)[1] as their authentic realm. The communication structure and community of experimenters constituted by scientists is based on cultural learning at the level of prescientific knowledge articulated in ordinary language. The strict empirical sciences move within this unquestioned horizon. That is surely why even Peirce did not find himself compelled to set off explicitly the level of symbolic interaction, on which methodical approaches and theoretical assumptions are discovered, discussed, and examined, and tentatively accepted or rejected, from the level of instrumental action. For Dilthey, on the contrary, this subcultural background of all possible processes of inquiry represents only a sector of social life-worlds. The system of the sciences is one element of a comprehensive life context, and the latter is the object of the cultural sciences. If the pragmatist self-reflection of the natural sciences had been pursued in a logically consistent manner and had not stopped at the boundaries of the tacitly presupposed communication of scientists themselves, it would have brought to consciousness the difference between *this* object domain and the level of the natural-scientific object domain. It would have had to lead to an abandonment of the monopolistic claim of positivism that identifies inquiry according to the logic of science exemplified by physics with knowledge as such. The cultural life context is formed on a level of intersubjectivity that is presupposed by the attitude of strictly empirical science but cannot be analyzed by it. If this is so, we are confronted by the question whether the cultural sciences in fact do not proceed

within a different methodological framework and are not constituted by a different cognitive interest than the natural sciences
as comprehended by pragmatism.

Dilthey undertakes to demonstrate that the cultural sciences have this special methodological position.[2] He addresses
himself to a mode of inquiry that was as familiar to him from his
own work as that of the natural sciences was to Peirce from his
own laboratory. The canon of the cultural sciences, whose foundations are associated with the names of Wolff and Humboldt,
Niebuhr, Eichhorn, Savigny, Bopp, Schleiermacher, and Grimm,
took form by about the middle of the 19th century owing especially to the research of the Historical School in Germany:

> Alongside the natural sciences, a body of knowledge
> has developed spontaneously out of the tasks of life
> itself, which is connected through the identity of its
> object. It consists of such sciences as history, economics,
> legal and political science, the study of religion, of
> literature and poetry, of art and music, of philosophical
> worldviews and systems, and finally psychology. All
> these sciences bear on the same major fact: the human
> race. They describe and narrate, judge and form
> concepts and theories in relation to this fact. . . . And
> in this way the possibility arises of defining this group
> of sciences by their common relation to the same fact,
> humanity, and of delimiting them from the natural
> sciences.[3]

Dilthey immediately raises an objection against himself, namely
that the circumscription of the object domain does not suffice for
a logically cogent delimitation of the two groups of sciences.
Physiology also treats of man and yet is a natural-scientific discipline. Different regions of facts cannot be conceived of ontologically but only epistemologically. They do not "exist"; rather,
they are constituted. The difference between the natural and cultural sciences must therefore be reduced to the orientation of the
knowing subject, to its attitude with regard to objects.[4] Dilthey
starts with a Kantian way of putting the question: "The organi-

zation of the sciences is determined by the way in which its object, nature, is given."[5]

Dilthey, however, sees the immediate transcendental-logical difference between the orientations of the natural and cultural sciences not in two different forms of objectivation but in *the degree* of objectivation itself.[6] If we mark out nature from the viewpoint of how we can gain control of it as a world of phenomena subject to general laws, we must exclude the experience of the subject:

> We gain control of this physical world through the study of its laws. These laws can only be found if the experiential character of our impressions of nature, the connection we have with it to the extent that we ourselves are nature, the lively feeling in which we enjoy nature, increasingly recede behind the abstract apprehension of it according to relations of space, time, mass, and motion. All these moments cooperate in excluding man himself in order to construct out of his impressions this great object nature as an order according to laws. It then becomes the center of reality for man.[7]

The intersubjectivity of the frame of reference within which we objectivate nature as something to be controlled according to laws is bought at the cost of neutralizing broadly complex, biographically determined and historically shaped sensibility. That is, the entire spectrum of prescientific experiences in daily life is excluded. But the knowing subject is not totally eliminated. Objectified nature is rather the correlate of an ego that intervenes in reality through instrumental action. The mode of apprehension in which "resisting" objects are first constituted according to the categories of number, space, time, and mass corresponds to an active regularization by means of operations of measurement:

> The resistance of external objects, intervening in them by hand, and their measurability make possible experimentation and the application of mathematics

for the natural scientist. Hence the uniform components of experience as discovered in observation and experiment can here be ordered in accordance with mathematical-mechanical means of construction.[8]

In contrast, the position of the subject in the cultural sciences is distinguished by unrestricted experience. Its experience is not limited by the experimental conditions of systematic observation to the area that discloses itself to the "intervention of the hand." The experiencing subject is given free access to reality. The perceptual responses of all prescientifically accumulated experiences are called into play. The larger part played by receptive faculties in the subject exposed to the entire breadth of experience has its counterpart in a lesser degree of objectivation. Reality seems to open itself up to experience from within.

The differing attitudes of the subject in the cognitive process results in different *configurations of experience and theory* in the natural and cultural sciences respectively. We have to supplement the phenomena of nature objectified within the framework of instrumental action with hypothetical "thought constructs" (*Hinzugedachtes*). The events that appear to systematic observation have immediate meaning only in association with hypotheses about the motion of bodies. Thus we must provide nature with models of possible connections in order that empirical regularities can be explained by laws. Only through constructions is it possible to solve the problem of

> thinking of objects in such a way that the flux of phenomena and the uniformities that emerge ever more clearly from this flux become comprehensible. The concepts through which this occurs are auxiliary constructions, which thought creates for this purpose. Thus nature is alien to us, transcendent to the apprehending subject, completed by means of auxiliary constructions added on to the phenomenally given. . . . Thus mathematical and mechanical constructions become means to reduce all sense phenomena, by means of hypotheses, to the motions of immutable

underpinnings of these phenomena, which take place according to immutable laws.[9]

Dilthey, looking at classical physics, sees that systematically objectified experience must be related to theories that depend on the formation of models. In the cultural sciences, to the contrary, the level of theory and the level of data are not yet divorced in this way. Concepts and theoretical designs are not so much artificial products as mimetic reconstructions. Whereas in the natural sciences knowledge terminates in theories or individual statements of laws that can be controlled through experience, in the cultural sciences theories and descriptions serve only as vehicles for the generation of a reproductive (nachbildende) experience:

> Here there are no hypothetical assumptions that support the given with something else. For understanding penetrates into alien expressions of life through a transposition from the fulness of one's own experiences.[10]

While natural-scientific procedure is distinguished by "construction," that is through the hypothetical designing of theories and subsequent experimental controls, the cultural sciences aim at "transposition," transferring mental objectivations back into reproductive experience.[11]

There is a corresponding distinction between the cognitive activities of the disciplines of the natural and cultural sciences. We can explain given events with the aid of hypotheses on the basis of established initial conditions, while symbolic structures are understood through explicative reproduction. An "explanation" requires the application of theoretical propositions to facts that are established independently through systematic observation. In contrast, "understanding" is an act in which experience and theoretical apprehension are fused. The causal-analytic method brings about a hypothetical connection of events through constructions, while the explicative method of the sciences based on understanding always finds itself moving within an objectively pregiven structure:

Now the cultural sciences differ from the natural sciences in that the latter have as their object facts that appear in consciousness as coming from without, as phenomena, and as given individually. For the former, in contrast, they appear as coming from within, as reality, and as an original, living whole. For the natural sciences this means that a connected nature is given in them through supplementary inferences and a combination of hypotheses. For the cultural sciences, on the other hand, it follows that in them the connectedness of psychic life lies at their foundations universally as something originally given. Nature we explain; psychic life we understand. For in inner experience the processes of influence (*Erwirken*) and the connection of functions as individual factors in psychic life are given as a whole. What we have at first is the experienced unity. Distinguishing its individual factors comes afterwards. This brings about a very great difference between the methods through which we study psychic life, history, and society, and those through which the knowledge of nature is achieved.[12]

Dilthey's logical analysis of the natural sciences is only slightly articulated, almost crude, in comparison with Peirce's logic of inquiry. But, on the basis of a methodologically appropriated Kantianism, there are still so many convergences, that Dilthey's suggestions do not really contradict a pragmatism elaborated as transcendental logic. Moreover, in Dilthey's scheme the natural sciences have the task only of providing a rough background against which the *logic of the cultural sciences* can be set off in relief. This is Dilthey's theme. It is centered in the relation of experience, objectivation, and understanding.

For Dilthey the category of "experience" ("*Erlebnis*") is from the very beginning a key to his theory of the cultural sciences. As the object of systematic observation and causal-analytic knowledge, mankind remains part of the natural-scientific object domain. It ceases to be a merely physical state of fact and becomes an object of the cultural sciences as soon as "human states are experienced." Here the object of inquiry is not mankind but

the world in which the historical-social life of men expresses itself. When Dilthey still believed it possible to deal with problems of the logic of science in the framework of a descriptive and
analytical psychology, he accounted for the act of understanding
expressions of life in terms of a model of feeling the psychic
states of others. Experience and the understanding of expression
are reciprocally related.

> From the fulness of our own experience, experience
> outside of us is reproduced and understood through
> transposition. And even in the most abstract sentences
> of the cultural sciences, the factual element that is
> represented in thoughts is experience and
> understanding.[13]

In understanding I transpose my own self into something external
in such a way that a past or foreign experience again becomes
present in my own. This psychology of understanding as substitute experience contains a monadological view of hermeneutics
in the cultural sciences, one that Dilthey never completely overcomes.

The impetus to a first revision of the theory of empathy
comes from the romantic tradition of hermeneutics itself. If the
congenial understanding of great works requires reproducing the
original process through which the work was produced, then it
can no longer adequately be conceived as a substitution of other
experience with one's own. What is reproduced is not a psychic
state but the generation of a product. Understanding terminates
not in empathy but in the reconstruction of a mental objectivation. It is true that the interpreter must revert from a permanently fixed expression of life "to the creative, evaluating, acting,
self-expressive, and self-objectivating" element.[14] But his understanding takes as its object not immediately psychic structures,
but symbolic ones:

> This means states, churches, institutions, mores,
> books, art works. Like man himself, such facts always
> contain the relation of an external aspect to one which
> is removed from the senses and therefore internal.[15]

In connection with hermeneutics, the romantic conceptual scheme of outer and inner is restricted to the relation of symbolic representation: the representation of an inner state through signs given in external experience. That is why Dilthey calls it an error

> to employ psychology and psychic life history for our knowledge of this inner aspect. . . . Understanding this mental content [of objective mind][16] is not psychological knowledge. It is rather a way of recurring to a mental form through its own particular structure and laws.[17]

This clear critique of psychologism is based on the insight that experience itself is organized by symbolic structures. An experience is not a subjective process of becoming conscious of fundamental organic states. Instead it is relative to *intentions* and is always mediated by an act of *understanding meaning*. Dilthey comprehends historical life as a permanent self-objectivation of mind. The objectivations in which the active mind congeals in purposes, values, and meanings represent a structure of signification that can be apprehended and analyzed independently of actual life processes, that is apart from organic, psychic, historical, and social developments. However, the objective structure of valid symbols in which we always find ourselves embedded can be understood only through experiential reconstruction such that we revert to the process in which meaning is *generated*. Every experience of any cognitive significance is poetic, if *poiesis* means the creation of meaning: that is the productive process in which the mind objectivates itself.

To replace the naive theory of empathy, Dilthey borrows from the philosophy of reflection the model that underlies the methodological connection of experience, expression, and understanding. The life of the mind consists in externalizing itself in objectivations and at the same time returning to itself in the reflection of its externalizations. The history of mankind is integrated into this self-formative process of mind. That is why the everyday existence of societal individuals moves within the same relation of experience, expression, and understanding that also constitutes the procedures of the cultural sciences. Hermeneutic understanding is only a methodically developed form of the dim reflexivity or semi-transparency with which the life of prescientifically communicating and socially interacting men takes place in any case. The

> connection of life, expression, and understanding
> [encompasses] not only the gestures, expressions, and
> words with which men communicate, or permanent
> spiritual creations . . . or the constant objectivations of
> the mind in social forms . . . : even the psychophysical
> unity of life is known to itself through the same double
> relation of experience and understanding, becoming
> aware of itself in the present and rediscovering itself
> in memory as something from the past. . . . In short,
> it is the process of understanding through which life
> becomes enlightened about itself in its depths.
> On the other hand, we understand ourselves and
> others only by inserting our own experienced life into
> every form of expression of our own and others' lives.
> So the connection of experience, expression, and
> understanding is in general the only method through
> which mankind is present for us as an object of the
> cultural sciences [even prior to any science]. The cultural
> sciences are thus grounded in this connection of life,
> expression, and understanding.[18]

It is this anchoring of skilled understanding in a prior understanding-structure of everyday life that Dilthey selects as a criterion for the delimitation of the cultural sciences: "A science belongs to the cultural sciences only if its object is accessible to us through behavior founded on the connection of life, expression, and understanding."[19] In addition, Dilthey invokes the topos of the Scholastic tradition, "verum et factum convertuntur," which was also used epistemologically by Vico against Descartes and taken up by Kant and Marx to justify the philosophy of history.[20] The act of understanding only explicitly repeats that movement which occurs in any case as a self-formative process of mind in the social life-world through mind's reflective relation to its own objectivations. Consequently the knowing subject is simultaneously part of the process in which the cultural world itself originates. Thus the subject understands scientifically the objectivations in whose production it also participates on the pre-scientific level:

> Thus the concept of cultural science is determined, according to the range of phenomena that it comprises, by the objectivation of life in the external world. *The mind only understands what it has created.* Nature, the object of natural science, encompasses that reality which is brought into being independently of the activity of the mind.[21]

In another passage this idea is expressed more emphatically:

> The first condition of the possibility of historical science is that I myself am a historical being—that he who *studies* history is the same as he who *makes* history.[22]

Vico's principle serves to justify the model on whose basis Dilthey develops the principal features of his logic of the cultural sciences. Because the knowing subject also takes part in the production of the objects of its knowledge, "universally valid synthetic judgments about history" are possible.[23] With this argument, however, Dilthey entangles himself in a vicious circle. Synthetic a priori judgments about the nature of history establish the model according to which the historical life process as such is comprehended: the model of a mind that objectivates itself and at the same time reflects its expressions of life. But Vico's principle of the identity of the knower and producer of the historical world is already based on this conception. Thus Dilthey cannot invoke it for the justification of this conception.

The relation of experience, expression, and understanding was originally introduced for methodological purposes. Reducing it to the structure of a life-world transcendentally determined by life, expression, and understanding[24] is completely unsatisfactory for a logic of the sciences. In the intellectual climate of the late 19th century, which was shaped by positivism, it is impossible for Dilthey to justify a theory of the cultural sciences through recourse to thought models of a philosophy of consciousness (or anticipations of existential analysis based exclusively on phenomenology), just as it is for Peirce to justify his ontological excursion into Scholastic realism. These patterns of interpretation borrowed from the tradition mislead both Dilthey and Peirce into objectivism. This then hinders them from logically elaborating the orientation of their critique of meaning, which is based on the logic of inquiry. Only a self-reflection of the sciences that does not prematurely transcend the realm of methodological problems can renew, at the level of positivism, the claim of a critique of knowledge that does not regress to a pre-Kantian position.

Dilthey does in fact first explicate the relation of *experience, expression, and understanding* on a strictly methodological plane. He takes the example of autobiography to unfold the implications of hermeneutics in the cultural sciences. This choice has no systematic significance. It is not supposed to predefine the interpretation of history as biographical. Autobiography presents itself for the investigation of hermeneutic procedures that are equally binding for the interpretation of world history only because it provides a graphic model of how "our consciousness (labors) to cope with life."[25] Autobiography unfolds the dim reflexivity and semi-transparency of our life history, in whose medium we have always led our lives, elevating them to an articulated form:

> The apprehension and interpretation of one's own
> life goes through a long series of stages. The most
> perfect explication is autobiography. Here the self
> apprehends the course of its life in a way that
> brings to consciousness the human substrata and
> historical relations in which it is enmeshed. Thus
> it can eventually expand its autobiography to the
> dimensions of a historical painting. And the only thing

that limits this is the same factor that gives it its
significance, namely that it is sustained by experience
and that this depth is the source from which it makes
itself and its relations to the world understandable to
itself. A person's reflection upon himself remains as
both orientation and foundation.[26]

Life history is the elementary unity of the life process that encompasses the human species. It is a system that sets its own limits. For it presents itself as a course of life limited by birth and
death. Moreover it is an experienceable unity that links the seg-
ments of this duration; the link is provided by a "meaning." Life
history constitutes itself out of life relations. Life relations exist
between an ego on the one side and things and people that enter
the ego's world on the other. A *life relation* (*Lebensbezug*) firmly
establishes the definite significance of things and people for a
subject as well as of definite modes of the subject's behavior with
regard to his environment. Life relation makes possible cognitive
apprehension only to the extent to which it simultaneously establishes both an affective attitude and action-orienting perspectives.
In the context of life relations an object is grasped theoretically
only insofar as it manifests itself within value orientations and, at
the same time, subject to rules of possible purposive activity:

> There is not a single person or thing that could be a
> mere object for me without representing pressure or
> assistance, the goal of a striving or an aim of the will,
> importance, the demand for consideration and inner
> proximity or resistance, distance, and foreignness.
> Life relation, whether restricted to the given moment
> or permanent, makes these persons and objects into
> providers of my happiness, extensions of my existence,
> augmentations of my power; or they limit the scope
> of my existence, exert pressure on me, or diminish
> my power.[27]

As reality enters the life relations of a subject, it gains relevance,
that is *significance* in a global sense, because descriptive, evalua-

tive, and prescriptive aspects are still unseparated and fused together.

> In this substratum [Dilthey continues], objectified comprehension, evaluation, and goal-positing appear as types of behavior in innumerable nuances that shade off into one another. In the course of a life they are bound up into inner connections that encompass and determine all activity and development.[28]

Life relations are integrated into an individual life history. Taken by themselves they are abstractions from a structured context whose unity is produced by cumulative life experience. In every moment all past events of a life history are subjected to the force of retrospective interpretation. The interpretive framework of each present retrospection is determined by an anticipated future. But this holds precisely to the extent that perspectives about what is expected, wanted, and hoped for depend in turn on memory, through which the past is made present reflexively:

> Owing to the nature of time I possess the singular unity of my life only by recollecting its course. When I do this, a long series of processes then acts in concert in my memory; not a single one of them is reproducible by itself. Even in my memory a selection already takes place. The principle of this selection lies in the significance that the individual experiences had for understanding the unity of the course of my life at that time in the past, that they acquired in the estimation of subsequent periods or that they obtained from a new view of the unity of my life when they were fresh in memory. Now that I think back, the only aspect of what is still reproducible for me that acquires a place in the unity of my life is what has significance for my life as I now see it. It is just through my present view of life that each part of it that is significant obtains, in the light of this view, the form in which I view it today.[29]

The unity of life history constitutes itself through the accretion of retrospective interpretations that implicitly always encompass the entire course of one's life including all earlier interpretations. Dilthey compares this cumulative life experience with induction. For each subsequent interpretation corrects the generalizations of the previous ones on the basis of negative experiences. The logical form of historical statements mirrors the peculiarity of retrospective interpretations. They are narrative statements that report on events from the perspective of later events: that is, with reference to a standpoint from which they could not have been observed and recorded.

Life experience integrates the life relations that converge in the course of a life into the unity of an individual life history. This unity is anchored in the identity of an ego and in the articulation of a meaning or significance. The identity of the ego defines itself primarily in the dimension of time as the synthesis of the manifold of receding experiences. It creates the continuity of life-historical unity in the stream of psychic events. The sustained identity seals the overcoming of what is, nevertheless, the continual present disintegration of our life. Life history realizes itself in the course of time and in the perpetuated simultaneity of a system of reference to which the parts relate as to a whole: "It is not as though objects are situated together in a room and are apprehended by someone who enters it. Their combination exists only in relation to a person."[30] Ego identity must be distinguished from the unity of the corresponding organism that can be identified as the same body from birth to death within a spatio-temporal coordinate system. For the latter an observer can register the identity of specific characteristics over a definite period of time in an intersubjectively verifiable manner. But the ego ascertains its own identity in the consciousness of the continual disintegration of life and the decay of its substrata:

> For an outside observer, the psychophysical course
> [of an individual life history] . . . constitutes a self-
> identical being through the sameness of the appearing
> body in relation to which this process takes place. At
> the same time, however, this process is characterized
> by the noteworthy matter of fact that every part

> of it is connected in consciousness with the other
> parts by an experience somehow characterized by the
> continuity, connectedness, and sameness of the
> process.[31]

This "somehow characterized" experience depends only on ego identity's constituting itself in the articulation of a meaning or significance for its life history. In general Dilthey introduces the category of significance (*Bedeutung*) in terms of the totality of a life-historical unity.

> The structure of experience in its concrete reality lies
> in the category of significance. This is the unity that
> brings together in memory the course of what has been
> experienced or reexperienced. And the significance of
> this does not consist of a point of unity lying outside
> experience. Rather, this significance is contained in
> these experiences as what constitutes their structure.[32]

The life history of an individual, held together by ego identity, is the pattern for the categorial relation of the whole to its parts. It is then from this relation that the category of significance is derived. The meaning that hermeneutic understanding takes as its object, what Dilthey emphatically calls significance, results exclusively from the role of elements in a structure whose identity includes the continual decay of identity just as much as the persistent overcoming of this corruption. It must therefore be repeatedly recreated through continually renewed, corrected, and cumulatively expanded retrospective interpretations of life history. There is "significance" only in a system of reference whose modification is of the type of a self-formative process. It must fulfill the criteria of life-historical "development":

> Mutability is as common to the objects we construct
> in the knowledge of nature as it is to life that becomes
> conscious of itself in its determinations. But in life
> alone does the present encompass the representation
> of the past in memory and of the future both in

phantasy that pursues its potentialities and in activity
that sets itself goals within these potentialities. Thus
the present is filled with pasts and bears the future
within itself. This is the meaning of the word
"development" in the cultural sciences.[33]

The significance that a person or thing acquires for a person in
an individual life relation is thus a mere derivative of the meaning of an entire developmental history of which the subject can
become aware in retrospect at any time, no matter how implicitly.
This guarantees that every specific significance is integrated into
a meaning structure that represents the inalienably individual
(and not merely singular) unity of a world centered around an
ego and of a life history held together by ego identity.

On the other hand, meanings, which must be fixed in
symbols, are never private in a rigorous sense. They always have
intersubjective validity. Thus nothing like significance could ever
constitute itself in a monadically conceived life history. Obviously
an expression of life owes its semantic content as much to its
place in a linguistic system valid for other subjects as it does to
its place in a biographical context. Otherwise the latter could not
even be expressed *symbolically*. Life experience is constructed in
communication with other life experiences:

> The individual viewpoint that clings to personal life
> experience corrects and expands itself in common life
> experience. By this I understand the sentences that
> form in any group of persons related to each other and
> that are common to them. . . . Their distinguishing
> mark is that they are creations of the common life.[34]

Dilthey introduces the concept of the "common" in a specific
sense. Being common means the intersubjectively valid and binding quality of the same symbol for a group of subjects who communicate with each other in the same language. It does not mean
the agreement of different elements in virtue of common features, i.e., elements belonging to the same logical class.

Life histories constitute themselves not only in the vertical dimension as a temporal connection of the cumulative experiences of an individual. They are also formed at every moment horizontally at the level of the intersubjectivity of communication common to different subjects:

> In the realm of this objective mind every *individual*
> *expression of life represents something common.* Each
> word, each sentence, each gesture or civility, each
> art work and each historical deed is understandable only
> because there is something common linking him who
> expresses himself in them and him who understands.
> The individual constantly experiences, thinks, and acts in
> a sphere of what is common, and only in it does he
> understand.[35]

Reflexive life experience, which brings about the continuity of life history through cumulative understanding of oneself as a stack of autobiographical interpretations, must always already be moving in the medium of mutual understanding with *other* subjects. I understand myself only in the "sphere of what is common" in which I simultaneously understand the other in his objectivations. For our two expressions of life are articulated in the same language, which for us has intersubjectively binding validity. From this point of view individual life history can even be conceived of as a product of processes that take place at the level of intersubjectivity. In a certain way the individual who has life experiences first comes into being as the result of his own self-formative process. Hence individual life history, which first offered itself as a frame of reference for analysis in the cultural sciences, can now be conceived as a function of overlapping structural connections and social systems:

> An infinite wealth of life unfolds in the individual
> existence of particular persons in virtue of their relations
> to their milieu, to other persons, and to things. But every
> single individual is at the same time a point of
> intersection for structures that permeate individuals,
> exist through them, but extend beyond their lives. These

structures possess independent existence and an
autonomous development through the content, value,
and purpose that is realized in them.[36]

Dilthey distinguishes cultural value systems from systems of the
external organization of society. But every form of interaction
and mutual understanding between individuals is mediated by an
intersubjectively valid employment of symbols that refer in the
last instance to *ordinary language*. Language is the ground of intersubjectivity, and every person must already have set foot on it
before he can objectivate himself in his first expression of life,
whether in words, attitudes, or actions. Dilthey once wrote of
language that "only in it does man's interiŏr find its complete,
exhaustive, and objectively understandable expression."[37] Language is the medium in which meanings are shared, not only in
the cognitive sense but in the comprehensive sense of significance
that encompasses affective and normative modes:

> Reciprocal understanding secures us the community
> (*Gemeinsamkeit*) that exists among individuals. . . .
> This common element is expressed in the sameness of
> reason, sympathy in emotional life, and the reciprocal
> obligation in duties and rights that is accompanied by the
> consciousness of what ought to be.[38]

The specific characteristic of this linguistically structured
community is *that individuated persons communicate in it*. On
the foundation of intersubjectivity they accord in something general in such a way that they identify with one another and reciprocally know as well as acknowledge one another as homogeneous
subjects. At the same time, however, in communication individuals can also keep a distance from one another and assert against
each other the inalienable identity of their egos. The community
that is based on the intersubjective validity of linguistic symbols
makes both possible: reciprocal *identification* and *preservation of
the non-identity* of one with another. In the dialogue relation
a dialectical relation of the general and the individual, without
which ego identity cannot be conceived, is realized. Ego iden-

tity and communication in ordinary language are complementary concepts. From different aspects they designate the conditions of interaction at the level of reciprocal recognition.

Looked at from this point of view, the identity of the ego, which secures the continuity of life-historical unity amidst the decay of momentary experiences, also presents itself as a dialogic relation. For in the retrospective interpretation of the course of its life, the ego communicates with itself as its other. Self-consciousness constitutes itself at the point of intersection of the horizontal level of intersubjective mutual understanding with others and the vertical dimension of intrasubjective "mutual" understanding with oneself. On the one hand, the ego's communication with itself can be understood as a copy, at the vertical level of cumulative life experience, of its communication with others. On the other hand, the identity of life-historical unity has incorporated the dimension of time that is lacking in linguistic communication. Conversely, therefore, in the vertical dimension of historical development the comprehensive structures that permeate individual life histories can only be conceived according to the model of the unity of a life history.[39]

Dilthey conceives of objective mind as the "community of life unities." It is characterized by a double dialectic of the whole and its parts. The first is the horizontal level of communication, marked by the relation of the totality of a linguistic community to the individuals who, within it, identify with each other to the same extent that they simultaneously assert their nonidentity against each other. The second is the vertical dimension of time, marked by the relation of the totality of a life history to the singular experiences and life relations of which it is constructed. Here the identity of the unity of life is maintained in the consciousness of the non-identity of the preceding phases of life. This "community of life unities," defined by the dialogue relation and reciprocal recognition, ego identity and the process of self-formation in life history, is postulated by Dilthey as the objective framework of the cultural sciences. He does so in the same way that Peirce postulates the entire process of inquiry pursued by the community of experimenters as the objective framework of the natural sciences. And just as Peirce was brought by

the fact of the inductive progress of the sciences to the fundamental methodological question of the necessary relation of the
universal and the particular, so Dilthey equally sees himself confronted by the *relation of the universal and the particular* through
the existence of community structured both historically and linguistically. Yet here the problem arises not just at the level of the
logic of inquiry, but at that of logic itself. Hermeneutic understanding must employ *inevitably general* categories to grasp an
inalienably *individual* meaning:[40]

> The community of life unities is the point of departure
> for all relations of the particular and the universal in the
> cultural sciences. This fundamental experience of
> community permeates the entire way of apprehending
> the world of the mind. In this experience are combined
> consciousness of a unitary self and that of similarity
> with others, the sameness of human nature and
> individuality. The experience of community is the
> presupposition of understanding. Starting with
> elementary interpretation, which requires only
> acquaintance with the meaning of words and the way
> in which they are combined in sentences according to
> rules in order to create a meaning—in other words,
> community of language and thought—the scope of
> what is common, which makes possible the process of
> understanding, continually expands.[41]

The relation between the general and the individual, recognized
by Dilthey as constitutive for life experience just as much as for
communication, returns in hermeneutic understanding. Ever new
"general truths" are necessary for analysis of the "world of the
unique":[42]

> Thus work in the cultural sciences gives rise . . . to a
> circulation of experience, understanding, and
> representation of the mental world in general concepts.
> And every stage of this work possesses an inner unity in

its conception of the mental world, as historical
knowledge of the singular develops
in a reciprocal relation to general truths.[43]

For the natural sciences, the fact of scientific progress poses the
question how a universal relation can be known, given a finite
number of established singular facts. For the cultural sciences,
the fact of a systematic expansion of the horizon of our understanding of our own as well as others' expressions of life poses a
corresponding fundamental methodological question: How can
the meaning of an individuated life structure be grasped and represented in inevitably general categories?

The Self-Reflection of the Cultural Sciences: *The Historicist Critique of Meaning*

Hermeneutic understanding is directed at a traditional context of meanings. It is distinguished from the monologic understanding of meaning required by theoretical propositions. We shall call theoretical all propositions that can be expressed in a formalized language or transformed into statements of such a language, regardless of whether they are tautological statements or propositions with empirical content. We can also say that theoretical propositions are elements of "pure" languages. Calculi, empty or interpreted, are examples of such "pure" languages. Formalized statements are purified of everything that is not on the level of symbolic relations. In the case of theories in the empirical sciences this can be seen in the requirement of the strict separation of propositions and facts: The empirical accuracy of their hypothetical deductions is subsequently controlled by means of empirical propositions that express the result of systematic observations independent of the theory. To the extent that they have empirical reference, "pure" languages demand in principle a separation between understanding logical connections and observing empirical matters of fact. Just as the monologic understanding of meaning is defined by the exclusion of factual relations, so controlled observation is defined by the exclusion of symbolic relations. It is precisely this boundary that is effaced by hermeneutic understanding.

The understanding of meaning becomes problematic from the methodological viewpoint with regard to the appropriation of traditional semantic content, as is the case in the cultural sciences. Regardless of its symbolic expression, here the "meaning" that is to be explicated has the status of a fact, an empirical given. Hermeneutic understanding can never analyze the structure of its object to the point of eliminating all contingency.

161

Otherwise it would turn into reconstruction, that is, understanding the meaning of formal relations. Formalized languages possess metalinguistic rules of constitution with whose aid we can reconstruct every statement that is possible in such a language; that is, we can reproduce it ourselves. Because we are not in possession of such rules of reconstruction for traditional meaning structures, they require a hermeneutic understanding of meaning that apprehends symbolic relations as relations of fact. Hermeneutics is both a form of experience and grammatical analysis at the same time.

Peirce showed that the application of theoretical propositions to reality is only possible within a transcendental framework that preforms experience in a specific way. Theories of the empirical sciences contain information about reality from the viewpoint of possible technical control everywhere and at all times under specifiable conditions. This has its counterpart, therefore, in a form of generalized experience that arises in the behavioral system of instrumental action. This experience abstracts from all connections with life history. Experimentally produced phenomena are based on the suppression of all aspects of life experience in favor of a general effect, i.e., one that can be randomly repeated. This specific objectification of reality serves to mold subjectively tinged concrete experience, bringing about its transcendental a priori adaptation to the universal expressions of a theoretical language in which names of individuals cannot appear. The problem of the relation of the universal and particular is that singular experiences have to be brought into agreement with abstract general categories. For hermeneutic understanding the problem is reversed. It grasps individual life experience in its entire breadth but has to adapt a set of intentions centered around an individual ego to the general categories of language. Here the problem of the relation of universal and particular does not arise owing to the inability of a concrete world of experience to meet the logic of general statements, but rather because of the inadequacy of this logic to life experience, even though the latter is always already articulated in ordinary language. The inductive progress of the empirical-analytic sciences is possible only on the basis of a transcendental a priori assimilation of possible experience to the universal expressions of theoretical languages. In contrast, the quasi-inductive course of the hermeneutic sciences is based on the specific capacity of ordinary language, which makes it possible for the function of general categories to be communicated indirectly in a concrete life context. On this foundation the language of the hermeneutic interpreter adapts itself in the course of interpretation to the life experience concentrated around individual meaning.

Ordinary language obviously has a structure that actually allows what is individual to be rendered understandable through general categories in the dialogue relation. It is this very structure that must be used in hermeneutic understanding as well, which merely makes a methodical discipline of the everyday communicative experience of understanding oneself and others. However, hermeneutics can be elaborated as an explicit procedure only if it is possible to explain that feature of the structure of ordinary language which enables it to do what the syntax of a pure language prohibits, namely to make communicable, no matter how indirectly, what is ineffably individual.

Such an explanation is suggested in Dilthey's classification of the "elementary forms of understanding."[1] Hermeneutic understanding takes as its object *three classes of life expressions*: linguistic expressions, actions, and experiential expressions.

Linguistic expressions can be completely divorced from a concrete life context. They then imply "no reference to the particularities of the life in which they originated."[2] In such cases hermeneutic interpretation is unnecessary. For there is only a virtual dialogue relation between sender and receiver:

> the judgment is identical in the one who states it and the one who understands. Like a vehicle, it goes unaltered from the possession of him who states it to the possession of him who understands it.[3]

When linguistic expressions appear in an absolute form that makes their content independent of the situation of communication, "the difference in times and persons," then understanding is monologic. It

> is oriented toward a mere content of thought that is
> identical with itself in every context. Thus understanding
> is more complete here than in relation to every other
> expression of life.[4]

In this sense, only statements of a pure language can be completely understood. On the other hand, the more that linguistic expressions remain linked to a concrete life context, the more important is their role in a specific dialogic relation: the "vehicle" is no longer external to the content of the expression. Complete understanding is impeded, because there is no longer general agreement about an unchanging meaning.

Through the penetration of heterogeneous material into the fabric of otherwise transparent logical relations, language is as it were polluted. Linguistic expression suffers the indirect admixture of "the dark background and fullness of psychic life," which cannot be incorporated in its manifest content and therefore requires interpretation for the other. Here hermeneutics enters into its own. It deciphers what at first remains alien to speaking subjects amidst their mutual understanding because this alien material can only be communicated indirectly:

> Interpretation would be impossible if the expressions of
> life were totally alien. It would be unnecessary if there
> was nothing alien in them. [Hermeneutics] thus lies
> between these two extreme opposites. It is required
> wherever there is something alien that the art of
> understanding has to assimilate.[5]

Dialogue in ordinary language moves halfway between monologue and the impossibility of linguistic communication at all. It always expresses conditions of life. Owing to their individual meaning, they are incapable of direct communication and must therefore be appropriated hermeneutically by the listener as something alien, to be understood through interpretation of the message. The dialogic use of language always requires hermeneutic understanding. This is shown by the discrepancy in principle between a life context and its linguistic objectivation. No matter how much a linguistic expression may be rooted in a situation and reveal its specific character, there always remains a gap between this expression and what is meant by it in the context of individual life relations. This gap can only be closed by interpretation.

The process of interpretation is made easier in that meanings are objectivated not only in the dimension of language but also transverbally at the level of *actions*. Actions form the second class of life expressions that understanding takes as its object. Here Dilthey is thinking of intentional action, subject to norms in relation to which the actor orients himself. Communicative action, which has the form of interaction on the basis of reciprocal expectations about behavior, "does not arise from the intention of communication"; but "the relation of action to the mental content that expresses itself in action is regular and allows probable assumptions about this content."[6] Symbolic interaction is as much a form of representation as is linguistic communication. There appear to be meanings that can be transposed from one medium into the other. This convertibility of the meaning of sentences into actions and of actions into sentences makes possible reciprocal interpretations. What was true of linguistic communication is also true of communicative action. In neither can the context of an individuated life history structured by ego identity be directly expressed. Once again, it is this gap that Dilthey emphasizes:

> Through the power of a decisive motivation the act
> proceeds from the fulness of life into finite one-sidedness.
> No matter how it may have been arrived at, it still
> expresses only a part of our essence. Potentialities that
> are contained in this essence are annihilated through the
> act. Thus the act separates itself from the background
> of a life context. And without explanation of how
> circumstances, end, means, and life context are
> connected in it, it allows no comprehensive
> determination of the inner realm in which it
> originated.[7]

Actions, too, need hermeneutic deciphering, because the unmistakable subject cannot express itself any more directly in actions that obey general norms than it can in the general categories of mutual understanding in ordinary language. Because individual conditions of life cannot be transposed completely or unaltered into either, the subject would be misunderstood if he were taken at his word and immediately identified with his manifest actions. As the art of rendering indirect communications understandable, hermeneutics corresponds exactly to the distance that the subject must *maintain* and yet at the same time *express* between itself, as the identity of its structure in life history, and its objectivations. The penalty of not doing so is being reified by those to whom the subject addresses itself.

A third class of life expressions taken by understanding as its object designates the dimension in which the relation of the ego to its linguistic and translinguistic objectivations becomes visible. Dilthey speaks of experiential expression (*Erlebnisausdruck*). Under this category he subsumes primarily psychological expressive phenomena linked to the responses of the human body, whether mimic, physiognomic, or gestural—the immediately corporeal reactions of blushing and turning pale, rigidification, nervous glance, relaxation, and even laughing and crying. Helmuth Plessner, following Dilthey, has proposed a hermeneutics of non-verbal expressions and worked out its bases in order to interpret these reactions.[8] Dilthey is not interested in a psychology of human expression but in its hermeneutics. Experiential expression is understood hermeneutically as a signal of unstated intentions and the unstatable relation of an ego to its objectivations. Thus experiential expression is not on the same level as sentences and actions. On the one hand it is closer than the symbolic expressions of ordinary language and communicative action to the spontaneous context of life. For it is unmistakably related to a specific organism in an unrepeatable situation. On the other hand experiential expression lacks a cognitive content that could be completely interpreted in sentences or actions.

> There is a peculiar relation between it, the life from which it proceeds, and the understanding that it brings about. For expression can contain more of what goes on in the mind than can be revealed by any act of

introspection. . . . At the same time, however, it is
in the nature of experiential expression that the relation
between it and the mental content it expresses can be
the basis of understanding only with reservations. It
is not judged true or false, but ungenuine or genuine
(*Unwahrhaftigkeit und Wahrhaftigkeit*). For here
dissimulation, lying, and deception interrupt the
relation between expression and the mental content
it expresses.[9]

Because it remains more intimately rooted in the context
of life and thus attains a lesser degree of objectivation than any
other symbolism, experiential expression is suited from the hermeneutic viewpoint for providing indications of the role that the
subject takes or pretends to take in any given context of its
actions and dialogues. The identity of an ego does not manifest
itself *immediately* in the general categories or general norms of
its life expressions and only communicates itself indirectly within
them. Yet this is the only way that it can take on appearance.
This is why the dimension of being and illusion or essence and
appearance belongs to symbolic representation. In relation to
manifest communications, experiential expressions can in this dimension symptomatically indicate latent meaning. They can legitimate and emphasize, deny and disavow, make ironic twists
clear, unmask dissimulations or signalize deceptions as such. In
connection with words and acts, expression serves as an indication of how seriously something is meant, whether the communicating subject is deceiving itself or others, to what degree it wants
to or may identify itself with an actual expression of its own life,
and how broad is the spectrum of connotation, concealment, or
contrary intentions.

The structure of ordinary language, however, which corresponds to the singular achievement of hermeneutic understanding, becomes comprehensible only when we take account of *the
integration of the three classes of life expressions* in everyday life
conduct. In the framework of social life-worlds, communication
in ordinary language is never isolated from habitual interactions
and attendant or intermittent experiential expressions. Mutual

understanding about linguistic symbols is subject to permanent control through the actual occurrence of the actions expected in a given context, and these in turn can be interpreted through linguistic communication if there is a disturbance of consensus. The meaning of linguistic symbols can be made clear through participation in habitual interactions. Language and action interpret each other reciprocally; this is developed in Wittgenstein's concept of the *language game*.[10] The dialectic of general and individual made possible in the intersubjectivity of talking and acting can also make use of the accompanying flow of spontaneous expressions of bodily movements and gestures and correct itself by means of them. Ego identity asserts itself against the necessary inadequacy of manifest communications by interpolating allusions and indirect communications in the form of experiential expression. Ordinary language does not obey the syntax of a pure language. It becomes complete only when enmeshed with interactions and corporeal forms of expression. The grammar of language games in the sense of a complete structure of conduct regulates not only the combination of symbols but also the interpretation of linguistic symbols through actions and expressions. A "pure" language is characterized by being exhaustively definable by metalinguistic rules of constitution, that is with exclusively symbolic means. In contrast, a natural language defies formally rigorous, in other words intralinguistic reconstruction, because it can be interpreted non-verbally.

The specific character of ordinary language is this *reflexivity*. From the viewpoint of formal language we can also say that ordinary language is its own metalanguage. It acquires this unique function in virtue of its ability to incorporate into its own dimension even the non-verbal life expressions through which it itself is interpreted. We can talk about actions and describe them. We can name expressions and even make language itself the medium of experiential expression, whether phonetically, by exploiting the expressivity of intonation, or stylistically, by representing in language itself the relation of the subject to its linguistic objectivations. All ordinary language allows reflexive allusions to what has remained unstated. Many categories of allusions of this sort have even become conventions, either in subsystems such as wit and poetry, or in stylized linguistic forms such as irony, understatement, and imitation, or in established figures of speech such as the rhetorical question, the euphemism, etc.

These cases only materialize a function that ordinary language always fulfills in principle: *interpreting itself*. And it owes this function to its complementary relation to the non-verbal forms of expression found in action and expression, which it can in turn express in the medium of language itself. Without the supplement of non-verbal objectivations, natural language remains fragmentary. But it can actualize the latent presence of missing complements; it is in this that its reflexive relation to itself consists. It can interpret itself linguistically through the detour of substituted non-verbal forms. To decipher this self-interpretation is the task of hermeneutics. In this enterprise the interpreter cannot claim demonstrative certainty. For we could only adduce "proof" for interpolations if we could return a traditional text to the life conduct of its time, in which the written and spoken word once supplemented each other in fact.

> Wolf's demand that the writer's thoughts be discovered with necessary insight through the hermeneutic art cannot be fulfilled even at the level of textual criticism and linguistic understanding. The connection of thoughts and the construction of allusions, however, depends on grasping the individual manner in which they are combined. Doing so . . . is divinatory and never yields demonstrative certainty.[11]

Nevertheless, divination, which traces out the indirect communication of language in its manifest contents, is not without control through "comparison":

> Divination and comparison are joined together and not distinguished in time. We can never dispense with a comparative procedure in relation to what is individual.[12]

In a methodological context the expression "divination" may be misleading. For it is precisely the point of the hermeneutic procedures that have been elaborated in the cultural sciences to remove the appearance of irrationality from individual meaning and the suspicion of mere arbitrariness from the appropriation of traditional meaning structures. And yet these procedures are not cogent in the same way as empirical-analytic procedures. For considered logically, they move in an inevitable circle. What corresponds in the hermeneutic sciences to the logic of inquiry designated by Peirce through the three modes of inference is a quasi-inductive development

> that starts from the apprehension of indefinite-definite parts and proceeds to the attempt to grasp the meaning of the whole, alternating with the attempt to take this meaning as a basis for defining the parts more clearly. Failure makes itself known when individual parts cannot be understood in this way. This then creates the need to redefine the meaning so that it will take account of these parts. This attempt goes on until the entire meaning has been grasped.[13]

The categorial framework within which cultural analyses proceed is also derived in each case from a process of circular concept formation:

> Each time that scientific thought undertakes to form concepts, determining the attributes that constitute the concept presupposes establishing the matters of fact that are to be brought together in the concept. And establishing and choosing these matters of fact require attributes in virtue of which their belonging to the extension of the concept can be determined. In order to define the concept of poetry I have to abstract it from the facts that constitute the extension of this concept, and to establish what works belong to poetry I must already possess an attribute through which the work can be recognized as poetic. This relation is thus the most general feature of the structure of the cultural sciences.[14]

Theoretical concepts and systems of reference are only concretizations of a strategically successful preunderstanding that is temporarily fixed for purposes of analytic comparison.

The singular dilemma of this method of the cultural sciences has been designated the *hermeneutic circle*. But, as the term suggests, if the problem is considered from the logical point of view alone, the methodological validity of this violation of form is not quite plausible. What makes the hermeneutic circle so "fruitful" and what distinguishes it from a vicious circle? The practice of interpretation and hermeneutic concept formation would be circular in the usual sense if it were a question of either exclusively linguistic or purely empirical analysis. The analysis of relations between systematically ordered symbols makes use of metalinguistic statements about an object language. If this were the entire business of hermeneutics, it scarcely would be possible to comprehend why the two levels of language were not kept separate and why a relation of circular, reciprocal definition between analytic concepts and linguistic objects should not be avoided. On the other hand, if the objects of hermeneutic understanding could be viewed not as linguistic objects but as experiential data, then the relation between the levels of theory and data would be equally unproblematic from a logical point of view. The apparent circle comes into being only because of the peculiar double status held by the objects of the cultural sciences. For the traditional semantic contents, objectivated in words or actions, that are the object of hermeneutic understanding, are likewise symbols and facts. That is why understanding must combine linguistic analysis with experience. Without the factors compelling this peculiar combination, the circular development of the interpretive process would be caught in a vicious circle.

The interpretation of a text depends on a reciprocal relation between the interpretation of "parts" through what is at first a diffusely preunderstood "whole" and the correction of this preliminary concept by means of the parts it subsumes. Obviously the "parts" can only exert a modifying force on the prejudged whole that is the background of their interpretation because they are already interpreted independently of this hermeneutic prejudgment (Vorgriff). It is true that the complex preunderstanding of the entire text has the role of a variable interpretive scheme into which individual elements are integrated in order to render them understandable. But the scheme can only make the elements it encompasses understandable to the extent that it itself can be corrected against these "data." The elements relate to the interpretive scheme neither as facts to theories nor as expressions of an object language to the interpretive expressions of a metalanguage. Both, the explicandum and the explicans, belong to the same language system. Therefore Dilthey does not assume a hierarchical relation between them (such as that between facts and theories or object language and metalanguage) but a relation of part and whole: the interpreter himself must learn to speak the language that he interprets. In so doing he can rely only on the reflexivity of ordinary language. As shown, this is based on the circumstance that the "grammar" of ordinary language does not merely lay down relations internal to language, but regulates the communicative structure of sentences, actions, and experiences as a whole—in other words, a habitual social context of life. This intermingling of language and practice explains why the hermeneutic movement based on it cannot be called circular in the logical sense. For the interpreter the connection between the interpretive scheme and the elements it encompasses presents itself as one that is immanent in language, which obeys only the rules of grammar. In itself, however, this connection is at the same time the articulation of a life context, which represents an individual meaning that cannot be wholly grasped in general categories. Thus linguistic analysis also reveals the empirical content of indirectly communicated life experience.

The symbolic structures taken by hermeneutic understanding as its object cannot be reduced to components of a pure language completely defined by metalinguistic rules of constitution. Thus their interpretation cannot take the form of analytically compelling reconstruction through the application of general rules. Nor can it be measured according to such a standard. In an open system of ordinary language that also serves as its own metalanguage, we select for the beginning of every interpretation a provisional interpretive scheme that already anticipates the result of the entire interpretive process. Insofar as interpretation is linguistic analysis, this anticipation (*Vorgriff*) has no empirical content in a rigorous sense. On the other hand, it has the status of a hypothesis and does require corroboration. This shows that interpretation *also* assumes the task of empirical analysis. Hermeneutics' roots in ordinary language, which is itself intertwined with practice, explain the double character of a method that discovers the *empirical* content of individuated conditions of life while investigating *grammatical* structures. The integration of given symbols into the chosen frame of reference, that is the process of application, both decodes the material and at the same time tests the code on the material—in other words, linguistic analysis and experiential control at once. Dilthey calls this link "the central difficulty of the entire art of interpretation":

> The entirety of a work is to be understood from the individual words and their connections, and yet the full understanding of the individual already presupposes that of the whole. This circle repeats itself in the relation of the individual work to the temperament and development of its author and returns equally in the relation of this individual work to its literary genre.[15]

If the hermeneutic circle can be resolved by demonstrating the singular integration of language and practice and the corresponding intermingling of linguistic analysis and experience, then it loses its logical doubtfulness. At the same time, however, it becomes an indication of hermeneutics' immediately *practical relation to life*. Hermeneutics is rooted in "the thought-generative work of life"[16] insofar as the survival of societal individuals is linked to the existence of a reliable intersubjectivity of mutual understanding.

> Understanding first arises in the interests of practical life. Here people are dependent on intercourse with one another. They must make themselves understandable to one another. One must know what the other wants. Thus

> the elementary forms of understanding come into being
> . . . I include the interpretation of an individual life
> expression under such an elementary form.[17]

The individual life expression is simultaneously embedded in an individual life context and spelled out in an intersubjectively valid language. The elementary forms of understanding therefore implicitly presuppose the higher ones, which aim hermeneutically at grasping a context within which an individual element first becomes understandable. The connection of hermeneutics and its knowledge-constitutive interest in actual life becomes evident in the model case of the foreign-language interpreter:

> The transition from the elementary forms of
> understanding to the higher ones is already built into the
> former. The greater the inner distance between a given
> life expression and him who understands, the more
> frequently uncertainties arise. Attempts are made to
> overcome this distance. A first transition to higher forms
> of understanding lies in the circumstance that
> understanding takes as its starting point the normal
> structure of life expression and the mental content
> expressed in it. If an internal difficulty or a contradiction
> of what is already known appears in the result of
> understanding, then he who understands is led to
> examination. He recollects cases in which the normal
> relation between life expression and the inner did not
> occur. A deviation of this sort is present in cases where
> we remove our inner states, ideas, and intentions from
> the gaze of intruders by means of an impenetrable
> attitude or silence. Here only the absence of a visible life
> expression is falsely interpreted by the observer. But in
> more than a few cases we must take into account in
> addition the existence of an intention to delude us.
> Facial expressions, gestures, and words contradict what is
> within. Thus in a number of ways the task arises of
> bringing other life expressions to bear or to recur to the

entire life context in order to arrive at a decision about our doubt.[18]

The function of understanding in the conduct of life is analogous to that demonstrated by Peirce for empirical-analytic inquiry. Both categories of investigations are embedded in systems of actions. Both are set off by disturbances of routinized intercourse whether with nature or with other persons. Both aim at the elimination of doubt and the re-establishment of unproblematic modes of behavior. The emergence of a problematic situation results from disappointed expectations. But in one case the criterion of disappointment is the failure of a feedback-controlled purposive-rational action, while in the other it is the disturbance of a consensus, that is the non-agreement of reciprocal expectations between at least two acting subjects. Accordingly, the intentions of the two orientations of inquiry differ. The first aims at replacing rules of behavior that have failed in reality with tested technical rules, whereas the second aims at interpreting expressions of life that cannot be understood and that block the mutuality of behavioral expectations. Experiment refines the everyday pragmatic controls of rules of instrumental action to a methodical form of corroboration, whereas hermeneutics is the scientific form of the interpretive activities of everyday life:

> In the course of history interpretation and criticism have developed ever-new aids to the solution of their task, just as natural-scientific inquiry has evolved ever-new refinements of the experiment.[19]

The hermeneutic interrogation of texts has one thing in common with the "interrogation of nature in the experiment." Both require duly acquired skill that proceeds according to general rules. It is true, nevertheless, that the hermeneutic art remains tied to "personal virtuosity" to a greater measure than does the mastery of operations of measurement.[20]

The hermeneutic sciences are anchored in interactions mediated by ordinary language just as are the empirical-analytic sciences in the behavioral system of instrumental action. Both are governed by *cognitive interests* rooted in the life contexts of communicative and instrumental action. Whereas empirical-analytic methods aim at disclosing and comprehending reality under the transcendental viewpoint of possible technical control, hermeneutic methods aim at maintaining the intersubjectivity of mutual understanding in ordinary-language communication and in action according to common norms. In its very structure hermeneutic understanding is designed to guarantee, within cultural traditions, the possible action-orienting self-understanding of individuals and groups as well as reciprocal understanding between different individuals and groups. It makes possible the form of unconstrained consensus and the type of open intersubjectivity on which communicative action depends. It bans the dangers of communication breakdown in both dimensions: the vertical one of one's own individual life history and the collective tradition to which one belongs, and the horizontal one of mediating between the traditions of different individuals, groups, and cultures. When these communication flows break off and the intersubjectivity of mutual understanding is either rigidified or falls apart, a condition of survival is disturbed, one that is as elementary as the complementary condition of the success of instrumental action: namely the possibility of unconstrained agreement and non-violent recognition. Because this is the presupposition of practice, *we call the knowledge-constitutive interest of the cultural sciences "practical."* It is distinguished from the technical cognitive interest in that it aims not at the comprehension of an objectified reality but at the maintenance of the intersubjectivity of mutual understanding, within whose horizon reality can first appear as something.

The practical life relation of hermeneutics can be derived not only from the structure of understanding itself. The cultural sciences also originated in categories of professional knowledge that systematized interpretation into a skill. Scientific jurisprudence proceeded from the Roman administration of justice just as the classical doctrine of politics developed out of the discussions and transactions of rhetors and citizens in the ancient city-states. The cultural disciplines did not develop out of the crafts and other professions in which technical knowledge is required, but rather out of the professionalized realms of action that require practical wisdom:

> As the professions became more numerous and specialized in society and the technical training for them developed and encompassed a growing body of theory, these technical theories, following their practical need, penetrated ever more deeply into the essence of society. ... The separating out of the individual sciences of society thus took place not through a stratagem of theoretical understanding, as though the latter had undertaken to solve the problem of the fact of the historical-social world through a methodical analysis of the object of investigation. Life itself brought about this separation.[21]

The practical cognitive interest, which dominates the history of the emergence of the cultural sciences, also determines the context of the application of hermeneutic knowledge. In the second half of the 19th century, at the latest since the canon of the cultural sciences was formed, their reaction back upon the action-orienting self-understanding of the educated public is clearly visible. Historiography and philology determine the direction in which cultural tradition is appropriated and developed in the practical consciousness of the educated bourgeois strata:

> Life and the experience of life are the continually fresh-flowing sources of the understanding of the social-historical world . . . ; only in their reaction upon life and society do the cultural sciences attain their highest significance, and this significance is in constant increase.[22]

In the practical cognitive interest, however, Dilthey also sees dangers for the scientific character of hermeneutics. Therefore he adds, "But the way to this effect must proceed through the objectivity of scientific knowledge."[23]

This last observation results from a consideration that

reveals an inconsistency of great import in Dilthey's foundation of the cultural sciences. The cultural sciences' practical relation to life, which determines both their *historical genesis* as well as the *factual context of their application*, is not merely appended externally to hermeneutic procedure. Rather, the practical cognitive interest defines the level of hermeneutics itself a priori in the same way that the technical cognitive interest defines the framework of the empirical-analytic sciences. Thus this practical relation to life cannot vitiate the objectivity of science. For it is only the knowledge-constitutive interest that lays down the conditions of the possible objectivity of knowledge. Yet in the passage mentioned, Dilthey sees two tendencies in conflict: the tendencies of "life" and "science."

> Thus, taking life as the starting point and maintaining a permanent connection with it forms the primary feature of the structure of the cultural sciences, based as they are on experience, understanding, and acquaintance with life. In the cultural sciences this immediate relation between them and life leads to a conflict between the tendencies of life and their scientific goal. Since historians, economists, political scientists, and students of religion are immersed in life, they want to influence it. They subject historical persons, mass movements, and trends to their judgment, which is conditioned by their individuality, the nation to which they belong, and the time in which they live. Even where they believe themselves to be operating free of presuppositions, they are determined by this horizon. Does not every analysis of the concepts of a previous generation show these concepts to contain components that originated in the presuppositions of the time? At the same time every science as such contains the demand for universal validity. If there are to be cultural sciences in the strict sense of science, they must adopt this goal in an ever more conscious and critical way.[24]

This contraposition of a practical relation to life and scientific objectivity reveals Dilthey to be caught in a covert positivism. He would like to free hermeneutic understanding from the interest structure in which it is embedded on the transcendental level and shift it to the contemplative dimension according to the ideal of pure description. Like Peirce, Dilthey remains in the last analysis so much subject to the force of positivism that he leaves off the self-reflection of the cultural sciences just at the point where the practical cognitive interest is comprehended as the foundation of possible hermeneutic knowledge and not as its corruption. In so doing, he falls back into objectivism.[25]

The scattered but convincing methodological investigations that took the model of autobiography as their starting point have demonstrated the asymmetry of experience, expression, and understanding. Experience and objectivation are not symmetrical in the manner of something inner that can be completely projected onto the outer plane. Only under that condition could understanding be viewed, in strict complementarity to experience, as an act that reproduces the original experience that is the basis of the given expression and thus creatively reconstructs the genesis of the objectivation. In contrast, it was shown that every objectivation is part of an intersubjectively valid symbolic structure. It is common to several subjects in that, through general symbols, they identify with one another to the same extent that they can assert themselves against one another as non-identical. Both the self and the other objectify their experience on the level of intersubjectivity, but precisely in an unmediated form. On the penalty of the loss of identity, both are forced to indirectly communicate their immediacy. Hermeneutic understanding has an oblique relation to symbolic expression precisely because the inner cannot directly emerge outward in expression. Hermeneutics must assimilate the dialectic of the general and the individual that determines the relation of objectivation and experience and comes to expression *as such* in the medium of the "common." If this is so, then understanding itself is bound to a situation in which at least two subjects communicate in a language that allows them to share, that is to make communicable through intersubjectively valid symbols, what is absolutely unsharable and individual. Hermeneutic understanding ties the interpreter to the role of a partner in dialogue. Only this *model of participation in communication learned in interaction* can explain the specific achievement of hermeneutics. Yet Dilthey never abandoned the contrary *model of empathy*, of basically solitary reproduction and re-experiencing, even in its modified form of the reconstruction of acts of meaning-creation. The theory of empathy is preserved as a fundamental concept even in his later writings:

> The position taken by higher understanding with regard to its object is determined by its task of discovering in the given a structure of life. This is possible only if the structure, which is present in one's own experience and is encountered in innumerable cases, is always present and ready with all the potentialities it contains. We call this organization, which is given in the task of understanding, empathy, whether with a person or a work. . . . This is also designated as the *transference* of one's one self into a given unity of expressions of life. It is on the basis of this empathy, this transposition, that the highest form in which the totality of psychic life operates in understanding, namely reproduction or re-experiencing, comes into being.[26]

Dilthey cannot free himself from the empathy model of understanding because, despite his Kantian orientation, he does not succeed in overcoming the contemplative concept of truth. *Re-experiencing* is in a significant sense the equivalent of *observation*. On the empirical level both fulfill the criterion of a copy theory of truth. They appear to guarantee the reproduction of an immediate given in a solitary consciousness purified of all subjective interference. The objectivity of knowledge is then defined by the elimination of such interfering influences. This condition could not be satisfied in principle by a mode of understanding that is essentially connected to a structure of communication. For in an interaction that links at least two subjects in the framework of an intersubjectivity of mutual understanding produced in ordinary language through constant meanings, the interpreter is as much a participant as the one he interprets. The relation of observing subject and object is replaced here by that of participant subject and partner. Experience is mediated by the interaction of both participants; understanding is communicative experience. Its objectivity is thus threatened from both sides: by the influence of the interpreter, whose engaged subjectivity distorts the answers, no less than by the reactions of the other, who disconcerts a participant observer. However, if we describe the threats to objectivity in this way, we have already adopted the perspective of the copy theory of truth that positivism would like to suggest to us by pointing to the model of controlled observation. The compulsion of this tradition is so strong even in Dilthey that he cannot avoid reducing the experiential realm of communication to the pattern of uninvolved observation. He who puts himself into the place of another's subjectivity and reproduces his experiences extinguishes the specificity of his own identity just like the observer of an experiment. Had Dilthey followed the logic of his own investigations, he would have seen that objectivity of understanding is possible only within the role of the reflected partner in a communication structure.

Whether dealing with contemporary objectivations or historical traditions, the interpreter cannot abstractly free himself from his hermeneutic point of departure. He cannot simply jump over the open horizon of his own life activity and just suspend the context of tradition in which his own subjectivity has been formed in order to submerge himself in a subhistorical stream of life that allows the pleasurable identification of everyone with everyone else. Nevertheless, hermeneutic understanding can arrive at objectivity to the extent that the understanding subject learns, through the communicative appropriation of alien objectivations, to comprehend itself in its own self-formative process. An interpretation can only grasp its object and penetrate it in a relation in which the interpreter reflects on the object and himself at the same time as moments of an objective structure that likewise encompasses both and makes them possible. In this sense the objectivity of understanding rests on the principle that Dilthey set forth for autobiography and that only seems to be subjectivistic: "A person's [group's, epoch's] reflection upon himself remains as both orientation and foundation."[27] Dilthey would like to consider the presumed conflict between the tendencies of life and science settled by eliminating the practical cognitive interest in favor of a selfless universality of empathy. To the contrary the reflection initiated by Dilthey himself about the impossibility of having recourse to anything behind or prior to this interest should have unmasked this conflict as an illusion. It should have been able to justify the objectivity of hermeneutic understanding in the form of knowledge based on communicative experience and irrevocably mediated by the relation of dialogue. But Dilthey remains set on the model of the "reproductive feeling of the psychic states of others":

> All of philological and historical science is based on the postulate that this reproductive understanding of the singular can be raised to objectivity. The historical consciousness built thereon makes it possible for modern man to have the entire past of humanity present within himself. He looks beyond the boundaries of his own time into past cultures. He absorbs their energy and enjoys their magic. From this he obtains a great increase in happiness. And if the systematic cultural sciences derive general lawlike relations and comprehensive connections from this objective view of the singular, the processes of understanding and interpretation still remain their foundation. Therefore the certainty of these sciences as of history depends on whether the understanding of the singular can be elevated to *universal validity*.[28]

Dilthey links the possible objectivity of knowledge in the cultural sciences to the condition of a virtual simultaneity of the interpreter with his object. Unlike surmounting "spatial distance or difference of language," this knowledge must achieve "transposition into the situation of a reader of the time and milieu of the author."[29] In the cultural sciences *simultaneity* fulfills the same function as the repeatability of experiments in the natural sciences: the interchangeability of the cognitive subject is guaranteed.

However, the methodological assumption of possible

simultaneity of the interpreter and his object has so little self-evidence that it requires a philosophy of vitalism (*Lebensphiloso-phie*) to make it plausible. Only insofar as the objectivations of the mental world represent protuberances of an omnipresent stream of life, which flows through all of time and whose unity is secured by the potential simultaneity and ubiquity of its productions, can the historical world be comprehended positivistically, that is, as the sum total of all possible experiences: For the interpreter, what can be experienced is what is the case. This world that is reproduced in the historical consciousness of modernity has its counterpart in the geniality of omni-understanding. For the reproductive experience of one who transposes himself into the original promises participation in the one omnipresent stream of life. This life itself is irrational, for the only thing that can be said about it is that it is tangible only in its objectivations. The irrationality of life justifies the interpreter in the role of uninvolved observer. For if life itself projects its objectivations onto the level of a feigned simultaneity, then the observer can "objectively" survey the "connection of the universally human with individuation, which, on the basis of the general, expands outwards into the multiplicity of spiritual existences."[30] In this way hermeneutic understanding dispenses with the specific dialectic of the general and the individual, which is grounded in communication in ordinary language. In its place it puts an unequivocal classification of phenomena according to the logic of classes. Dilthey mentions three stages of generalization. He speaks of a system of order "that leads from the regularity and structure of the universally human to the types through which understanding apprehends individuals."[31]

The basic beliefs of vitalism allow Dilthey to *transfer the natural sciences' ideal of objectivity to the cultural sciences*. This is of particular significance for the group of disciplines that Dilthey calls systematic cultural sciences and contrasts with the historical sciences, which extend from biography to world history. The latter take as their object concrete developmental structures and the self-formative processes of specifiable social subjects. The former deal with permanent structures, isolatable partial systems of social life through which historical movement proceeds. Dilthey includes these sciences in the system of independently constituted cultural sciences of man: the study of language, the economy, the state, law, religion, and art.[32] He likes to invoke the example of economics to make clear the difference between the systematic cultural sciences and the historical ones. They develop general theories about sectors of social life that are distinguished by constant structural relations and have the character of systems. A social system of this sort

> is founded primarily on the reciprocal interaction of individuals in society insofar as it is based on the same common component of human nature and has as its consequence an interlocking of activities in which this component attains gratification. . . . The lone individual is a point of intersection of a number of systems that become increasingly specialized in the course of cultural evolution. . . . Abstract science now juxtaposes these systems that are so interwoven in historical-social reality. . . . Each one . . . is the product of a component of human nature. . . . It is in human nature that this basis of the society of all periods is present, even though it attains a differentiated and internally rich development only at a higher stage of culture.[33]

Objectivism founded on vitalism encourages Dilthey to introduce general theories of social systems and subsystems on the basis of hermeneutic understanding. The identity of inexhaustible life makes it methodologically possible to realize in the present objectivations that can be recalled at any time, uninfluenced by the initial situation of the interpreter. At the same time, on the anthropological level, this identity maintains a sufficiently broad foundation for historically enduring structures and corresponding theoretical systems of reference.

However, this only passes over the difficulty that Dilthey, in a discussion of Windelband's theses, once designated as the fundamental logical problem of the systematic cultural sciences: the "*connection between the general and individuation.*"[34] The apparently circular method of a reciprocal explication of the parts in the light of a diffusely preunderstood whole and, conversely, of the whole in the reflection cast by the progressively more exactly defined parts may suffice for the interpretation of specific expressions of life and concrete developmental histories. Thus hermeneutics is the foundation of the historical cultural sciences. But it will not do to derive the systematic cultural sciences from this hermeneutics while insinuating that they miss the dialectic of the general and the individual. The methodological basis of the historical cultural sciences is obviously too narrow for the systematic ones. They do not restrict themselves to the explication of meaning structures but analyze lawlike relations between empirical variables. To the extent that they are nomological sciences, they must employ empirical-analytic procedures. Yet to the extent that they pursue the intention of the cultural sciences, they remain bound at the same time to the methodological framework of hermeneutics and do not, like the natural sciences, enter the behavioral system of instrumental action. This problem of the interlocking of *empirical-analytic procedures* with *hermeneutics* and the problem of theory formation in the systematic cultural sciences are of central significance for the logic of the social sciences, which have only fully developed in the 20th century.[35] Dilthey does not explicitly take up this problem. The reversion to an objectivism that suspends the self-reflection of hermeneutics in the cultural sciences leads to resistance against a set of problems that, if I am right, comes to light only at *one* point, at the end of Dilthey's manuscript on the "Aufbau der geschichtlichen Welt in den Geisteswissenschaften" (The Construction of the Historical World in the Cultural Sciences):

> Every cultural system forms a structure based on common features [that is, on the intersubjectivity of interaction mediated by ordinary language]. Since this structure realizes an achievement, it has a teleological character [that is, it is a structure to be analyzed from the functionalist point of view]. But here a difficulty appears that inheres in concept formation in these sciences. The individuals who co-operate in bringing about such an achievement belong to the structure only

in those processes through which they contribute to realizing the achievement. But yet they function in these processes with their whole being. Thus a self-contained area can never be constructed with regard to the goal of an achievement [as is common in the normative-analytic sciences]. For the energy directed toward achievements in the specific area is always accompanied by the other sides of human nature, whose historical changeability asserts itself. Here resides the fundamental logical problem of the science of cultural systems.[36]

The systematic cultural sciences establish general theories and yet cannot simply be cut off from the basis of world history. How can the claim to universality that is put forth for their theories be harmonized with their intention of comprehending individuated historical processes? Freud did not take up this question as a methodological question. Yet psychoanalysis, if we comprehend it as a general theory of life-historical self-formative processes, provides an answer to it.

PART THREE

Critique as the Unity of Knowledge and Interest

The reduction of theory of knowledge to philosophy of science first effected by early positivism was interrupted by a counter-tendency exemplified by Peirce and Dilthey. But the self-reflection of the natural and cultural sciences only interrupted the victorious march of positivism and did not stop it. Thus the knowledge-constitutive interests that had been discovered could be immediately misunderstood in a psychologizing manner and succumb to the critique of psychologism on whose basis modern positivism has been established in the form of logical empiricism and which has determined the scientistic self-understanding of the sciences up to the present.

The connection of knowledge and interest that we have discovered methodologically can be explained and preserved against misinterpretation through recourse to the concept of an *interest of reason*, developed by Kant and especially by Fichte. But the dimension of self-reflection cannot be rehabilitated as such by a mere return to the historical phase of the philosophy of reflection. Therefore the example of psychoanalysis will serve to demonstrate that this dimension reappears on the foundations laid by positivism. Freud developed an interpretive framework for disturbed and deviant self-formative processes that can be redirected into normal channels by therapeutically guided self-reflection. However, he viewed his theory precisely not as systematically generalized self-reflection, but as strict empirical science. Freud did not take methodological cognizance of the characteristic that distinguishes psychoanalysis from both the empirical-analytic and exclusively hermeneutic sciences. Instead, he attributed it to the peculiarity of analytic technique. Thus Freud's theory remains a scrap that the positivist logic of science since has vainly tried to digest and that the behaviorist research enterprise has tried in vain to integrate. But the hidden self-reflection that is the source of trouble cannot be conceptualized in this manner. Nietzsche is one of the few contemporaries who combine a sense for the import of methodological investigations with the ability to move light-footedly in the dimension of self-reflection. But Nietzsche, a dialectician of the Counter-Enlightenment, places the highest importance in using the form of self-reflection to deny the power of reflection. In so doing, he surrenders the knowledge-constitutive interests, of which he is well aware, to psychologism.

189

CHAPTER NINE

Reason and Interest: *Retrospect on Kant and Fichte*

Peirce and Dilthey, in the natural and cultural sciences respectively, brought the self-reflection of science to a point from which their knowledge-constitutive interests were visible. Empirical-analytic inquiry is the systematic continuation of a cumulative learning process that proceeds on the pre-scientific level within the behavioral system of instrumental action. Hermeneutic inquiry lends methodical form to a process of arriving at mutual understanding (and self-understanding) which takes place on the pre-scientific level in the tradition-bound structure of symbolic interaction. The first aims at the production of *technically exploitable* knowledge, the second at the clarification of *practically effective* knowledge. Empirical analysis discloses reality from the viewpoint of possible technical control over objectified processes of nature, while hermeneutics maintains the intersubjectivity of possible action-orienting mutual understanding (on the horizontal level of interpreting foreign cultures as well as on the vertical level of appropriating one's own traditions). The rigorously empirical sciences are subject to the transcendental conditions of instrumental action, while the hermeneutic sciences proceed on the level of communicative action.

The relations of language, action, and experience differ in principle for the two forms of science. In the behavioral system of instrumental action, reality is constituted as the totality of what can be experienced from the viewpoint of possible technical control. The reality that is objectified under these transcendental conditions has its counterpart in a specifically restricted mode of experience. The language of empirical-analytic statements about reality is formed under the same conditions. Theoretical sentences belong to an either formalized or at least formalizable language. With regard to logical form they are calculi, which we generate through the manipulation of signs according to rules which we can reconstruct at any time. Under the conditions of instrumental action pure language constitutes itself as the sum of those symbolic relations that can be produced according to rules. "Pure language" is as much the result of abstraction from the spontaneously evolved, pregiven material of ordinary languages as objectified "nature" from the spontaneously evolved, pregiven material of experience connected with ordinary language. Both restricted language and restricted experience are defined by being results of operations, whether with signs or moving bodies. Like instrumental action itself, the use of language integrated into it is monologic. It secures the cogent systematic interconnection of theoretical propositions by means of rules of inference. The transcendental role of instrumental action can be seen to be confirmed in the procedure of connecting theory and experience. That is, systematic observation has the form of an experimental (or quasi-experimental) undertaking that makes it possible to register the results of measurement operations. Operations of measurement permit the reversibly univocal correlation of operatively determined events and systematically connected signs. If the framework of empirical-analytic inquiry were that of a transcendental subject, then *measurement* would be the synthetic activity that genuinely characterizes it. Only a theory of measurement, therefore, can elucidate the conditions of the objectivity of possible knowledge for the nomological sciences.

In the context of communicative action, language and experience are not subject to the transcendental conditions of action itself. Here the role of transcendental framework is taken instead by the grammar of ordinary language, which simultaneously governs the non-verbal elements of a habitual mode of life conduct or practice. The grammar of language games links symbols, actions, and expressions. It establishes schemata of world interpretation and interaction. Grammatical rules establish the ground of an open intersubjectivity among socialized individuals. And we can only tread this ground to the extent that we internalize these rules—as socialized participants and not as impartial observers. Reality is constituted in a framework that is the form of life of communicating groups and is organized through ordinary language. What is real is that which can be experienced according to the interpretations of a prevailing symbolic system.

To this extent we can view as a limiting case the reality objectified from the viewpoint of possible technical control and its correspondingly operationalized experience. This limiting case has the following distinguishing features. Language is separated out of its embeddedness in interactions and attains monologic closure. Action is severed from communication and reduced to the solitary act of the purposive-rational utilization of means. And individuated experience is eliminated in favor of the repeatable experience of the results of instrumental action. In short, the conditions of communicative action do not apply. Accordingly, if we conceive the transcendental framework of instrumental action as an extreme variation of life-worlds constituted through ordinary language (and as the particular one in which all historically individuated life-worlds *must* abstractly agree), then it becomes clear that the pattern of communicative action does not play a transcendental role for the hermeneutic sciences in the same way that the framework of instrumental action does for the nomological sciences. For the object domain of the cultural sciences is not constituted only under the transcendental conditions of the methodology of inquiry; it is confronted as something already constituted. It is true that the rules of every interpretation are determined by the pattern of symbolic interaction in general. But once the interpreter is socialized in his mother tongue and has been instructed in interpreting as such, he does not proceed *subject* to transcendental rules, but *at the level* of transcendental structures themselves. He can decipher the experiential content of a historical text only in relation to the transcendental structure of the world to which he himself belongs. Here theory and experience are not divorced, as they are in the empirical-analytic sciences. When a disturbance occurs in a communicative experience that is reliable according to common schemata of world-interpretation and of action, the interpretation that must be made immediately is directed simultaneously at the experiences acquired in a world constituted through ordinary language and at the very grammatical rules that constitute this world. Such interpretation is linguistic analysis and experience at once. Correspondingly, it corrects its hermeneutic anticipatory interpretation against a consensus among partners, which is arrived at in accordance with grammatical rules. Here, too, experience and analytic insight converge in a singular manner.

Peirce and Dilthey evolve the methodology of the natural and cultural sciences as the logic of inquiry, and they comprehend the process of inquiry in the context of an objective human structure, of technics (*Technik*) and of practice (*Lebenspraxis*) respectively. The logic of science thereby regains the dimension of epistemology abandoned by the positivist philosophy of science. Like the transcendental logic of an earlier period, it seeks a solution to the problem of the a priori conditions of possible knowledge. However, these conditions are no longer a priori *in themselves*, but only *for the* process of inquiry. The immanent logical investigation of progress in the empirical-analytic sciences and the process of hermeneutic explication immediately comes up against limits. For neither the structural connection of the modes of inference analyzed by Peirce nor the circular movement of interpretation elucidated by Dilthey are satisfactory from the viewpoint of formal logic. How induction or the hermeneutic circle are "possible" cannot be shown logically but only epistemologically. Both cases concern rules for the logical transformation of sentences whose validity is only plausible if the transformed sentences are related a priori to determinate categories of experience within a transcendental framework, whether of instrumental action or of a life form constituted in ordinary language. These systems of reference have a transcendental function, but they determine the architectonic of processes of inquiry and not that of transcendental consciousness as such. Unlike transcendental logic, the logic of the natural and cultural sciences deals not with the properties of pure theoretical reason but with method-ological rules for the organization of processes of inquiry. These rules no longer possess the status of pure transcendental rules. They have a transcendental function but arise from actual struc-tures of human life: from structures of a species that reproduces its life both through learning processes of socially organized labor and processes of mutual understanding in interactions mediated in ordinary language. These basic conditions of life have an interest structure. The meaning of the validity of state-ments derivable within the quasi-transcendental systems of reference of processes of inquiry in the natural and cultural sciences is determined in relation to this structure. Nomological knowledge is technically exploitable in the same sense that hermeneutic knowledge is practically effective.

The reduction of the framework of nomological and hermeneutic sciences to a *structure of human life* and the corresponding derivation of the meaning of the validity of statements from cognitive interests is necessary as soon as a transcendental subject is replaced by a *species* that reproduces itself under cultural conditions, that is *that constitutes itself* in a self-formative process. Processes of inquiry (as whose subject this species interests us here) are part of a comprehensive self-formative process. The conditions of the objectivity of possible experience established by the transcendental framework of processes of inquiry, whether in the natural or cultural sciences, no longer explicate only the transcendental meaning of general finite knowledge restricted to phenomena. Instead, in accordance with the objective structure of human life that gives rise to the two orientations of inquiry, they preform the specific meaning of the methodical cognitive modes themselves. Empirical-analytic sciences disclose reality insofar as it appears within the behavioral system of instrumental action. In accordance with their immanent meaning, nomological statements about this object domain are thus designed for a specific context in which they can be applied—that is, *they grasp reality with regard to technical control that, under specified conditions, is possible everywhere and at all times.* The hermeneutic sciences do not disclose reality under a different transcendental framework. Rather, they are directed toward the transcendental structure of various actual forms of life, within each of which reality is interpreted according to a specific grammar of world-apprehension and of action. Thus, in accordance with their immanent meaning, hermeneutic statements about structures of this sort are designed for a corresponding context in which they can be applied—*they grasp interpretations of reality with regard to possible intersubjectivity of action-orienting mutual understanding specific to a given hermeneutic starting point.* Thus we speak of a technical or practical knowledge-constitutive interest insofar as the life structures of instrumental action and symbolic interaction preform the meaning of the validity of possible statements via the logic of inquiry in such a manner that, to the extent that these statements are cognitions, they have a function only in these life structures: that is to the extent that they are technically exploited or practically efficacious.

The concept of "interest" is not meant to imply a naturalistic reduction of transcendental-logical properties to empirical ones. Indeed, it is meant to prevent just such a reduction. Knowledge-constitutive interests mediate the natural history of the human species with the logic of its self-formative process (which at this point I can only assert and not demonstrate). But they cannot be employed to reduce this logic to any sort of natural basis. I term *interests* the basic orientations rooted in specific fundamental conditions of the possible reproduction and self-constitution of the human species, namely *work and interaction*. Hence these basic orientations do not aim at the gratification of immediately empirical needs but at the solution of system problems in general. The term "problem solution," however, can only be used tentatively here. For knowledge-constitutive interests may not be defined in terms of problems that can appear as problems only within a methodological framework established by these very interests. Knowledge-constitutive interests can be defined exclusively as a function of the objectively constituted problems of the preservation of life that have been solved by the cultural form of existence as such. Work and interaction by nature include processes of learning and arriving at mutual understanding. Starting at a specific stage of evolution, these processes have to be maintained in the form of methodical inquiry if the self-formative process of the species is not to be endangered. On the human level, the reproduction of life is determined culturally by work and interaction. That is why the knowledge-constitutive interests rooted in the conditions of the existence of work and interaction cannot be comprehended in the biological frame of reference of reproduction and the preservation of species. The reproduction of social life absolutely cannot be characterized adequately without recourse to the cultural conditions of reproduction, that is to a self-formative process that *already implies* knowledge in both forms. Thus knowledge-constitutive interests would be completely misunderstood if viewed as mere functions of the reproduction of social life. "Cognitive interest" is therefore a peculiar category, which conforms as little to the distinction between empirical and transcendental or factual and symbolic determinations as to that between motivation and cognition. For knowledge is neither a mere instrument of an organism's adaptation to a changing environment nor the act of a pure rational being removed from the context of life in contemplation.

Peirce and Dilthey discovered the roots in interest of scientific knowledge, but they did not reflect on it as such. They did not develop the concept of knowledge-constitutive interests or even really comprehend what it involves. True, they analyzed the foundation of the logic of inquiry in conditions of life; but they would have been able to identify the basic orientations of the empirical-analytic and the hermeneutic sciences only in a framework that was foreign to them: that is, within the conception of a *history of the species* comprehended as a *self-formative process*. The idea of a self-formative process, in which the species-subject first constitutes itself, was developed by Hegel and adopted by Marx under materialist presuppositions. On the basis of positivism, an unmediated return to this idea would have to appear as a regression to metaphysics. There is only one legitimate path between these two positions. It is the one taken by Peirce and Dilthey in reflecting on the genesis of the sciences from the perspective of an objective life structure and thus pursuing methodology in the *epistemological mode*. But neither Peirce nor Dilthey discerned what they were actually doing. Otherwise they would not have been able to preserve themselves from the experience of reflection originally developed by Hegel in the *Phenomenology*. I mean the experience of the emancipatory power of reflection, which the subject experiences in itself to the extent that it becomes transparent to itself in the history of its genesis. The experience of reflection articulates itself substantially in the concept of a self-formative process. Methodically it leads to a standpoint from which the identity of reason with the will to reason freely arises. In self-reflection, knowledge for the sake of knowledge comes to coincide with the interest in autonomy and responsibility (*Mündigkeit*).[1] For the pursuit of reflection knows itself as a movement of emancipation. Reason is at the same time subject to the interest in reason. We can say that it obeys an *emancipatory cognitive interest*, which aims at the pursuit of reflection.

Indeed, the category of cognitive interest is authenticated only by the interest innate in reason. The technical and practical cognitive interests can be comprehended unambiguously as knowledge-constitutive interests only in connection with the emancipatory cognitive interest of rational reflection. That is, only in this way can they be understood without being psychologized or falling prey to a new objectivism. Because Peirce and Dilthey do not comprehend their methodology as the self-reflection of science, which it is nonetheless, they miss the point where knowledge and interest are united.

The concept of an interest of reason already appears in Kant's transcendental philosophy. But Fichte, after subordinating theoretical to practical reason, is the first to develop this concept of an emancipatory interest inherent in acting reason.

Interest in general is the pleasure that we connect with the idea of the existence of an object or of an action. Interest aims at existence, because it expresses a relation of the object of interest to our faculty of desire. Either the interest presupposes a need (*Bedürfnis*) or it produces one.[2] Correspondingly there is a distinction between an empirical and a pure interest, introduced by Kant with regard to practical reason. Practical pleasure in the good, that is in actions that are determined by principles of reason, is a *pure interest*. As long as the will acts out of respect for the laws of practical reason, it takes an interest *in* the good, but does not act *out of* interest:

> The first signifies the *practical* interest in the action, the second the *pathological* interest in the object of the action. The first displays only the dependence of the will on principles of reason in itself, the second on the principles of reason for the benefit of inclination, since reason only provides the practical rule as to how to meet the need of inclination. In the first case I am interested

in the action, and in the second in the object of the
action (insofar as it is pleasant to me).[3]

The (pathological) interest of the senses in what is pleasant or
useful arises from need; the (practical) interest of reason in the
good awakens a need. In the former case the faculty of desire is
stimulated by inclination; in the latter it is determined by principles of reason. By analogy with sensual inclination as habitualized
desire, we may speak of an intellectual inclination free of the
senses if it is formed from a pure interest as a permanent attitude:

> Where merely a pure interest of reason must be assumed,
> it would be false to attribute to it any interest of
> inclination. Nevertheless, in order to oblige linguistic
> usage, we can concede the existence of an inclination
> even toward what can be the object only of an
> intellectual desire, that is a habitual desire from a pure
> interest of reason. But this inclination would then be not
> the cause of the latter interest but rather its effect. We
> can call it *inclination free of the senses* [*Sinnenfreie
> Neigung*] (propensio intellectualis).[4]

The systematic function of the concept of a pure practical interest of reason becomes clear in the last section of the
Foundations of the Metaphysics of Morals. Under the heading of
the "extreme limit of all practical philosophy," Kant asks the
question, how is freedom possible? The task of explaining freedom of the will is paradoxical, because freedom is defined as independence of empirical motives, whereas an explanation would be
possible only through recourse to laws of nature. Freedom could
be explained only by our designating an interest that men take in
obeying moral laws. On the other hand, obeying these laws would
not be moral action, and thus free action, if it were based on a
sensual motive. Yet moral feeling attests to something like a factual interest in the realization of moral laws—in the realization of
the "glorious ideal of a universal realm of ends in themselves (of
rational beings), to which we belong as members only if we care-

fully behave according to maxims of freedom as though they were laws of nature."[5] By definition this cannot be a sensual interest. Thus we must be dealing with a pure interest, with a subjective effect exerted on the will by the law of reason. Kant sees himself compelled to ascribe causality to reason in contrast to the natural faculty of desire. This causality must be able to affect the senses in order to become practical:

> In order to want that for which reason prescribes an ought exclusively to rational beings affected by the senses, a faculty of reason is required that can *instill a feeling of pleasure* or satisfaction in the fulfillment of duty, one that thus has causality that can determine the senses in accordance with its principles. But it is entirely impossible to comprehend, that is to make comprehensible a priori, how a mere thought that in itself contains nothing sensual can produce a sensation of pleasure or pain. For this is a special sort of causality about which, as with all causality, we cannot determine anything at all a priori, but must therefore direct our questions exclusively to experience.[6]

The task of explaining the freedom of the will imperceptibly bursts the framework of transcendental logic. For the form of the question, how is freedom possible, deceives us into not realizing that, with regard to practical reason, we are inquiring into the conditions not of possible freedom but of real freedom. The question is really, how can pure reason be practical? Therefore we must concern ourselves with an aspect of reason that, according to Kant, is really incompatible with the characteristics of freedom: an interest of reason. Of course, reason cannot become subject to the empirical conditions of sensuality. But the idea of the *affection of sensuality by reason*, in the sense of the development of an interest in action subject to moral laws, only seems to preserve reason from admixtures of experience. If the effect of this singular causality of reason, that is pure practical pleasure, is contingent and attested only by experience, then its cause must be conceived as a fact. The thought construction of an interest determined by reason alone can adequately set this interest apart from merely factual motives, but only at the price of introducing a moment of facticity into reason itself. A pure interest is conceivable only on the condition that reason, to the same degree that it instills a feeling of pleasure, follows an inclination, no matter how much this differs from immediate inclinations: in reason there is an inherent drive to realize reason. This, in turn, is inconceivable from the transcendental viewpoint. And, at the extreme limit of all practical philosophy, Kant admits nothing other than that the name of pure interest expresses this inconceivability of a causal relation between reason and sensuality, although this relation is certified by moral feeling:

> This [causality], however, cannot provide any relation of cause and effect such as that between two objects of experience. Yet here pure reason is to be the cause, by means of mere Ideas (which supply absolutely no object for experience), of an effect [that is, of pleasure in the fulfillment of duty] that occurs in experience. Thus it is entirely impossible for us humans to explain how and why the *universality of the maxim as law*, and thus morality, interests us.[7]

The concept of a pure interest has a unique function within Kant's system. It defines a fact on which we can support our certainty of the *reality* of pure practical reason. Nevertheless, this fact is not given in ordinary experience, but attested by a moral feeling that must claim the status of a transcendental experience. For our interest in obeying moral laws is produced by reason and is yet a contingent fact that cannot be comprehended a priori. To this extent, an interest based on reason also implies the thought of something that determines reason. This thought, however, leads to a non-empirical genesis of reason that is at the same time not fully severed from experience; and, according to the principles of transcendental philosophy, this is absurd. Kant is consistent in not treating this absurdity as a transcendental illusion of practical reason. He contents himself with observing that pure practical pleasure assures us *that* pure reason can be practical, without our being able to comprehend *how* this is possible. The cause of freedom is not empirical, but it is also not only intelligible; we can designate it as a fact but cannot comprehend it. The title pure interest refers us to a basis of reason that is the exclusive guarantee of the conditions for realizing reason, but that cannot itself be reduced to principles of reason. Rather, as a fact of a higher order, it underlies these principles. The *basis of reason* is attested by the interests of reason, but it eludes human knowledge, which, to attain it, would have to be not either empirical or pure but both at once. Hence Kant warns against overstepping the extreme limit of pure practical reason. For unlike the limit of applied theoretical reason, where reason surpasses experience, here the experience of moral feeling surpasses reason. "Pure interest" is a limiting concept, which articulates an experience as incomprehensible:

> How can reason, without other motives taken from elsewhere, be practical by itself? That is, how can the mere *principle of the universal validity of all its maxims as laws* . . . provide a motive for itself without any material (object) of the will in which one might take a prior interest? How can it bring about an interest that would be purely *moral*? In other words, *how can pure reason be practical?* All of human reason is entirely incapable of explaining this, and all effort and labor to find an explanation of it is in vain.[8]

It is noteworthy that Kant now transfers the concept of pure interest, which he developed from practical reason, to all faculties of the mind: "To every faculty of the mind we can ascribe an *interest*, that is a principle that contains the only condition subject to which its exercise can be promoted."[9] The reduction of interest to a principle, however, shows that the peculiar status of the concept as a violation of Kant's system has been abandoned and that the moment of facticity inhering in reason has been disregarded. It is also not clear what is added to theoretical reason by a speculative interest of reason, if the latter consists "in the *knowledge* of the object up to the level of the highest principles a priori"[10] without an identifiable experience of pleasure, unlike the case of the practical interest of reason. Indeed, it is not quite comprehensible how a pure theoretical pleasure, analogous to pure practical pleasure, should be conceived. For every interest, whether pure or empirical, determines itself in relation to the general faculty of desire and refers to possible practice. Even a speculative interest of reason would be justified as an interest only if theoretical reason were taken into the service of practical reason without thereby becoming estranged from its authentic intention of knowledge for the sake of knowledge. For a cognitive interest, what is needed is not only the promotion of the speculative employment of reason as such, but the connection of pure speculative reason with pure practical reason. In addition, it must be under the direction of practical reason:

> Pure practical reason cannot at all be expected to be
> subordinate to speculative reason and thus to reverse the
> order, because all interest is ultimately practical, and
> even that of speculative reason is only conditioned. It is
> complete only in•its practical employment.[11]

In the end Kant concedes that, strictly speaking, there can be a speculative interest of reason only if theoretical reason is connected with practical reason "in one cognition."

There is a legitimate employment of theoretical reason with practical intent. Here pure practical interest seems to assume the role of a knowledge-constitutive interest. Of the three questions in which all interest of our reason converges, the third demands such an employment of speculative reason with practical intent. The first question, What can I know? is merely speculative. The second, What ought I do? is merely practical. But the third question, What may I hope? is both practical and theoretical at the same time. Here the situation is such "that the practical serves only as a guide to answering the theoretical question and, when this is followed out, to the speculative question."[12] The principle of hope determines the practical intention for which speculative reason is engaged. As we know, in this regard knowledge leads to the immortality of the soul and the existence of God as postulates of pure practical reason. Kant is concerned with justifying this interested employment of speculative reason without simultaneously extending the empirical employment of theoretical reason. Knowledge through reason (*Vernunfterkenntnis*) with practical intent retains its own status, which is weak in contrast with knowledge that theoretical reason can assert by virtue of its own competence and without the guidance of a pure practical interest:

> If pure reason can be practical by itself and really is so, as the consciousness of the moral law proves, it is still always only one and the same reason, which judges according to principles a priori, whether with theoretical or practical intent. In the first case, its ability does not suffice to establish certain propositions as assertions. Yet it is clear that since it also does not contradict these very propositions, it must accept them as soon as they belong *inseparably to the practical interest of pure reason* —to be sure, as something supplied it from without that does not grow on its own foundation, but is nevertheless adequately certified. And it must attempt to compare and connect them with all the speculative reason it has in its power. In so doing, however, it must recognize that these are not its insights, but yet extensions of its employment with some other intention, namely the practical. And this is not at all counter to its interest in restricting speculative transgression.[13]

Kant cannot quite free the interested employment of speculative reason from ambiguity. On the one hand, he invokes the unity of reason in order that the practical involvement of theoretical reason does not appear as a remolding or supplementary instrumentalization of one rational faculty by another. On the other hand, however, theoretical and practical reason are a unity to such a slight extent that the postulates of pure practical reason remain "alien" to theoretical reason. Consequently the interested employment of theoretical reason does not lead to knowledge in the rigorous sense. Whoever were to confuse the extension of reason with practical intent with the extension of the realm of possible theoretical knowledge would make himself guilty of the speculative transgression against which the critique of pure reason, especially the entire effort of the transcendental dialectic, had been directed. The practical interest of reason could assume the role of a knowledge-constitutive interest in the narrower sense only if Kant really were to achieve the unity of theoretical and practical reason. For Kant the speculative interest of reason only aims tautologically at the exercise of the theoretical faculty for the purpose of knowledge. Only if this interest were taken seriously as a pure practical interest would theoretical reason necessarily lose its role as one that is independent of the interest of reason.

Fichte takes this step. He comprehends the act of reason, intellectual intuition, as a reflected action that returns into itself, and makes the primacy of practical reason into a principle. The accidental connection of pure speculative and pure practical reason "in one cognition" is replaced by speculative reason's dependence in principle on practical reason. The organization of reason is subordinate to the practical intention of a subject that posits itself. As Fichte's doctrine of knowledge shows, reason is immediately practical in the form of original self-reflection. By becoming transparent to itself in its self-producing, the ego frees itself from dogmatism. The moral quality of a will to emancipation is required for the ego to raise itself to intellectual intuition. The idealist "can intuit this act of the ego only in himself, and in order to be able to intuit it, he must accomplish it. He produces it within himself at will and with freedom."[14] On the other hand, a consciousness that comprehends itself as a product of the things around it, as a product of nature, is dogmatically enslaved: "The principle of the dogmatists is belief in things for their own sake: that is, indirect belief in their own self, which is dispersed, and supported only by objects."[15] In order to remove the blinders of this dogmatism, one must first have adopted the interest of reason as one's own: "The ultimate reason for the difference between the idealist and the dogmatist is thus the difference between their interests."[16] All logic presupposes the need for emancipation and an originally accomplished act of freedom, in order that man elevate himself to the idealist standpoint of autonomy and responsibility (Mündigkeit). From this standpoint it is possible to gain critical insight into the dogmatism of the natural consciousness and, consequently, into the concealed mechanism of the self-constitution of ego and world:

> The highest interest and the ground of all other interest is interest in ourselves. The same holds for the philosopher. The interest that invisibly guides all his thought is that of not losing his self in ratiocination but of preserving and asserting it.[17]

Kant, in unfolding the antinomies of pure reason, also cites interests that dogmatically guide dogmatists and empiricists, each in their own way. But in the end, Kant sees the "interest of reason in this its contradiction,"[18] an interest directed against both sides, one of which always defends the thesis and the other the antithesis—only in the abandonment of interest as such. Reason, which reflects on itself, has to "divest itself of all partisanship."[19] So speculative reason remains external to practical reason and its pure interest. In contrast, Fichte reduces the interests that intervene in the defense of philosophical systems to the fundamental antithesis between those who let themselves be moved by the interest of reason in emancipation and the self-subsistence of the ego and those who stay caught in their empirical inclinations and interests and thus remain dependent on nature.

> Now there are two stages of mankind; and before the progression of our species has attained the last one, there are two chief types of men. Some, who have not yet elevated themselves to the full feeling of their freedom and absolute self-subsistence, find themselves only in the representation of things. They have that sort of self-consciousness which is dispersed and immersed in objects and can be gleaned only from their manifold. Their image is visible to them only through things as in a mirror. When the latter are taken away from them, their self disappears at the same time. For their

own sake, they cannot abandon the belief in the
independence of things, for it is only in things that they
themselves exist. They have really become all that they
are through the external world. Whoever is indeed only
a product of things will never see himself otherwise. And
he will be right, as long as he speaks only of himself and
his kind. . . . But whoever becomes conscious of his
self-subsistence and independence of all that is outside
him—and one becomes so only by making something of
oneself independently of everything—does not require
things as the support of his self, and cannot use them,
because they abolish that self-subsistence and transform
it into empty illusion. The ego that he possesses and that
interests him annuls the belief in things; it believes in its
self-subsistence out of interest and seizes it with affect.
Its belief in itself is immediate.[20]

The affective link to the self-subsistence of the ego and the interest in freedom still reveal a connection with Kant's pure practical
pleasure. For Kant had derived the concept of the interest of reason from the feeling for the realization of the ideal of a realm of
free rational beings. Fichte, however, comprehends this pure
practical motive, the "consciousness of the categorical imperative," not as a product of practical reason, but as an act of reason
itself: as the self-reflection in which the ego makes itself transparent to itself as action that returns into itself. Fichte identifies
the work of practical reason in the activities of theoretical reason,
and terms their point of unity intellectual intuition (*intellektu-
elle Anschauung*):

The intellectual intuition dealt with by the doctrine of
knowledge is not at all a matter of being but one of
action, and Kant does not even mention it (except, if
you will, by the expression *pure apperception*). Yet even
in Kant's system it is possible to demonstrate quite
exactly the place where it should be spoken of. Since
Kant, are we not aware of the categorical imperative?
Now what sort of consciousness is this? Kant forgot to

ask himself this question, because he nowhere treats of
the foundation of *all* philosophy. Instead, in the *Critique
of Pure Reason* he treats only of theoretical philosophy,
in which the categorical imperative could not appear,
whereas in the *Critique of Practical Reason* he treats
only of practical philosophy, in which merely content
was of concern, and the question of the type of
consciousness could not arise.[21]

Because Kant secretly conceived of practical reason on the model
of theoretical reason, the problem posed for him by the transcendental experience of moral feeling, that is of the interest in obeying the moral law, was how a mere thought, which contained
nothing of the senses, could produce a sensation of pleasure or
pain. Conversely, this dilemma, together with the supplementary
construction of a special causality of reason, becomes superfluous
as soon as practical reason provides the model for theoretical reason. For then the practical interest of reason belongs to reason
itself. In the interest in the independence of the ego, reason realizes itself in the same measure as the act of reason as such produces freedom. *Self-reflection is at once intuition and emancipation, comprehension and liberation from dogmatic dependence.*
The dogmatism that reason undoes both analytically and practically is false consciousness: error and unfree existence in particular. Only the ego that apprehends itself in intellectual intuition
as the self-positing subject obtains autonomy. The dogmatist, on
the contrary, because he cannot summon up the force to carry
out self-reflection, lives in dispersal as a dependent subject that is
not only determined by objects but is itself made into a thing.
He leads an unfree existence, because he does not become conscious of his self-reflecting self-activity. Dogmatism is equally a
moral lack and a theoretical incapacity. That is why the idealist
is in danger of scorning the dogmatist instead of enlightening
him. This is the context of Fichte's famous dictum, which is often misunderstood psychologistically:

The sort of philosophy one chooses thus depends on
what sort of person one is. For a philosophical system is

not a pile of junk that could be discarded or retained at
our whim; rather, it is inspired by the soul of the man
who possesses it. A character that is lax by nature or that
has been prostrated and bent by mental servitude,
learned luxury, and vanity will never elevate itself to
idealism.[22]

In this graphic formulation Fichte is only declaring once again
the identity of theoretical and practical reason. The condition in
which we are permeated by the interest of reason, caught up by
the feeling for the independence of the ego, and advancing in the
process of self-reflection determines simultaneously the degree of
autonomy we have acquired and the standpoint of our philosophical comprehension of being and consciousness.

The development of the concept of the interest of reason
from Kant to Fichte leads from the concept of an interest in actions of free will, dictated by practical reason, to the concept of
an interest in the independence of the ego, operative in reason
itself. The identification Fichte makes of theoretical and practical
reason can be clarified in terms of this interest. As an act of freedom interest precedes self-reflection just as it realizes itself in the
emancipatory power of self-reflection. This *unity of reason and
the interested employment of reason* conflicts with the contemplative concept of knowledge. As long as the traditional meaning
of pure theory severs the cognitive process from life contexts in
principle, interest must be viewed as something foreign to theory, coming to it from without and obscuring the objectivity of
knowledge. The singular interlocking of knowledge and interest,
which we came upon in examining the methodology of the sciences, is always subject to the danger of being misunderstood
psychologistically when seen against the background of a copy
theory of pure knowledge, no matter what form such a theory
takes. We fall into the temptation of conceiving the two
knowledge-constitutive interests that have been analyzed above
as though they impinged upon an already constituted cognitive
apparatus and intervened prejudicially in a cognitive process
possessing an independent justification. This conception can still
be found in Kant's view of the employment of speculative rea-

son with practical intent, even though the interest of reason is shown to be a pure interest of (albeit practical) reason. Only in Fichte's concept of interested self-reflection does the interest embedded in reason lose its secondary character (*Nachträglichkeit*) and become constitutive likewise for knowing and acting. The concept of self-reflection as action that returns into itself, as developed by Fichte, has a systematic significance for the category of knowledge-constitutive interest. For on this level, too, interest precedes knowledge even as it only realizes itself through knowledge.

We shall not pursue the systematic intention of Fichte's *Doctrine of Knowledge*, which purports to transpose its readers, through a single act, into the central self-intuition of an absolute ego that produces both itself and the world. Hegel, with good reason, chose the complementary path of phenomenological experience. The latter does not surmount dogmatism in a single leap but traverses the stages of consciousness in its manifestations as levels of reflection. Yet it is just as impossible for us to follow the intention of the *Phenomenology of Mind*, which is supposed to lead its readers to absolute knowledge and the concept of speculative scientific knowledge. It is true that the movement of reflection that takes empirical consciousness as its starting point combines reason and interest. Since at every stage it strikes at the dogmatic character of both a worldview and a form of life, the cognitive process coincides with a self-formative process. But the life of a self-constituting species-subject cannot be conceived as the absolute movement of reflection. For the conditions under which the human species constitutes itself are not just those posited by reflection. Unlike the absolute self-positing of Fichte's ego or the absolute movement of mind, the self-formative process is not unconditioned. It depends on the contingent conditions of both subjective and objective nature: conditions of the individuating socialization of interacting individuals on the one hand, and, on the other, those of the "material exchange" of communicatively acting persons with an environment that is to be made technically controllable. Reason's interest in emancipation, which is invested in the self-formative process of the species and permeates the movement of reflection, aims at realizing these conditions of symbolic interaction and instrumental action; and, to this extent, it assumes the restricted form of the practical and technical cognitive interests. Indeed, in a certain measure, the concept of the interest of reason, introduced by idealism, needs to be reinterpreted materialistically: the emancipatory interest itself is dependent on the interests in possible intersubjective action-orientation and in possible technical control.

At this level, the interests guiding and constituting cognitive processes aim not at the existence of objects but at successful instrumental actions and interactions as such. It is in this very sense that Kant distinguished the pure interest that we take in moral actions from empirical inclinations, which are awakened merely by the existence of the objects of actions. As we have seen, however, the reason that dictates these two interests is no longer pure practical reason, but reason that combines knowledge and interest in self-reflection. Similarly, the interests directed toward communicative and instrumental action necessarily include the pertinent categories of knowledge. Of themselves, they attain the role of knowledge-constitutive interests. For these forms of action cannot be established permanently unless the pertinent categories of knowledge—that is, cumulative learning processes and permanent interpretations transmitted by tradition, are secured.

We have shown that the configuration of action, language, and experience arising in the behavioral system of instrumental action differs from that yielded by the framework of symbolic interaction. The conditions of instrumental and communicative action are also the conditions of the objectivity of possible knowledge. They establish the meaning of the validity of nomological and hermeneutic statements respectively. The embeddedness of cognitive processes in life structures calls attention to the role of knowledge-constitutive interests: a life structure is an interest structure. Like the level on which social life reproduces itself, however, this interest structure cannot be defined independently of these forms of action and the pertinent categories of knowledge. At the human level, the interest in the preservation of life is rooted in life organized through knowledge and action. Thus knowledge-constitutive interests are determined by both factors. On the one hand, they attest to the fact that cognitive processes arise from life structures and function within them. On the other hand, however, they also signify that the form of socially reproduced life cannot be characterized without recourse to the specific connection of knowing and acting.

Interest is attached to actions that both establish the conditions of possible knowledge and depend on cognitive processes, although in different configurations according to the form of action. We have made this interlocking of knowledge and interest clear through examining the category of "actions" that coincide with the "activity" of reflection, namely that of emancipatory actions. The act of self-reflection that "changes a life" is a movement of emancipation. Here the interest of reason cannot corrupt reason's cognitive power, because, as Fichte indefatigably explains, knowing and acting are fused in a *single* act. But interest is no more external to knowledge when the two moments of acting and knowing are already divorced: at the level of instrumental and communicative action.

Yet we can methodologically ascertain the knowledge-constitutive interests of the natural and cultural sciences only once we have entered the dimension of self-reflection. *It is in accomplishing self-reflection that reason grasps itself as interested.* Therefore we come upon the fundamental connection of knowledge and interest when we pursue methodology in the mode of the experience of reflection: as the critical dissolution of objectivism, that is the objectivistic self-understanding of the sciences, which suppresses the contribution of subjective activity to the preformed objects of possible knowledge. Neither Peirce nor Dilthey grasped their methodological investigations as a self-reflection of the sciences. Peirce conceived his logic of inquiry in connection with scientific progress, whose conditions it analyzes. It is an auxiliary discipline, contributing to the institutionalization and acceleration of the process of inquiry as a whole and thus to the progressive rationalization of reality. Dilthey conceived his logic of the cultural sciences in connection with the course of hermeneutics, whose conditions it analyzes. It is an auxiliary discipline, contributing to the propagation of historical consciousness and the aesthetic presentation of a ubiquitous historical life. Neither of them considered whether methodology as theory of knowledge reconstructs underlying experiences of the history of the species and thus leads to a new stage of self-reflection in the self-formative process of the species.

CHAPTER TEN

Self-Reflection as Science: *Freud's Psychoanalytic Critique of Meaning*

The end of the 19th century saw a discipline emerge, primarily as the work of a single man, that from the beginning moved in the element of self-reflection and at the same time could credibly claim legitimation as a scientific procedure in a rigorous sense. Freud was not, like Peirce and Dilthey, a philosopher of science who deals reflectively with his own experience in an established scientific discipline. To the contrary, it was by developing a new discipline that he reflected upon its presuppositions. Freud was no philosopher. Attempting to create a medical doctrine of neurosis led him to a theory of a new kind. He became involved in methodological discussions to the extent that the foundation of a science necessitates reflection about the new beginning. It was in this sense that Galileo not only created modern physics but also discussed it methodologically. Psychoanalysis is relevant to us as the only tangible example of a science incorporating methodical self-reflection. The birth of psychoanalysis opens up the possibility of arriving at the dimension that positivism closed off, and of doing so in a methodological manner that arises out of the logic of inquiry. This possibility has remained unrealized. For the scientific self-misunderstanding of psychoanalysis inaugurated by Freud himself, as the physiologist that he originally was, sealed off this possibility. However, this misunderstanding is not entirely unfounded. For psychoanalysis joins hermeneutics with operations that genuinely seemed to be reserved to the natural sciences.[1]

Initially psychoanalysis appears only as a special form of interpretation. It provides theoretical perspectives and technical rules for the interpretation of symbolic structures. Freud always patterned the interpretation of dreams after the hermeneutic model of philological research. Occasionally he compares it to the translation of a foreign author: of a text by Livy, for example.[2] But the interpretive effort of the analyst distinguishes itself from that of the philologist not only through the crystallization of a special object domain. It requires a specifically expanded hermeneutics, one that, in contrast to the usual method of interpretation in the cultural sciences, takes into account a *new dimension*. It was no accident that Dilthey took biography as the starting point of his analysis of understanding. The reconstruction of the structure of a life history that can be remembered is the model for the interpretation of symbolic structures in general. Dilthey chose biography as a model because life history seemed to have the merit of transparency. It does not resist memory through opacity. Here, in the focus of remembering life history, historical life is concentrated as "that which is known from within; it is the place of last resort."[3] For Freud, in contrast, biography is the object of analysis only as what is both known and unknown from inside, so that it is necessary to take resort to what is behind manifest memory. Dilthey directs hermeneutics toward subjective consciousness, whose meaning can be guaranteed by immediate recollection:

> Life is historical insofar as it is comprehended in its
> course of movement in time and the causal nexus that
> originates in this way. This is possible owing to the
> representation of this sequence in a memory that
> reproduces not the individual but the nexus itself in
> its various stages. What memory achieves in the
> apprehension of a life process is attained in history by
> establishing the connection between the objectivations
> of life encompassed by objective mind in its movement
> and effects.[4]

Of course Dilthey knows that beyond the horizon of life history that is present to us we cannot count on the subjective guarantee of immediate memory. That is why understanding is directed at symbolic forms and texts in which meaning structures are objectivated. In this way hermeneutics can help out the faulty memory of mankind through the critical reconstruction of these texts.

The first condition of the construction of the historical world is thus the regeneration of mankind's confused and in many ways corrupted memories of itself through critique correlated with interpretation. Therefore the basic historical science is philology in the formal sense of the scientific study of languages, in which tradition has been sedimented; the collection of the heritage of earlier men; the elimination of errors contained therein; and the chronological order and combination that put these documents in internal relation with each other. In this philology is not the historian's aid but the basis of his procedure.[5]

Like Freud, Dilthey takes account of the unreliability and the confusion of subjective memory. Both see the necessity of a critique that sets right the mutilated text of tradition. But philological criticism differs from the psychoanalytic in that it takes the intentional structure of subjective consciousness as the ultimate experiential basis in the process of appropriating objective mind. It is true that Dilthey abandoned the psychological understanding of expression in favor of the hermeneutic understanding of meaning: "the understanding of mental forms has replaced psychological subtlety."[6] But even philology, in its concern with symbolic structures, remains restricted to a language in which conscious intentions are expressed. By rendering objectivations understandable, philology actualizes their intentional content in the medium of the everyday life experience. To this extent philology only supplements the ability of life-historical memory as it would function under normal conditions. What it eliminates through the labor of criticism, in preparing texts, are only accidental flaws. The omissions and distortions removed by philological criticism have no systematic role. For the meaning structure of the texts studied by hermeneutics is always threatened only by the impact of *external conditions*. Meaning can be destroyed through the capacity and efficiency limitations of the channels of transmission, whether of memory or cultural tradition.

Psychoanalytic interpretation, in contrast, is not directed

at meaning structures in the dimension of what is consciously intended. The flaws eliminated by its critical labor are not accidental. The omissions and distortions that it rectifies have a systematic role and function. For the symbolic structures that psychoanalysis seeks to comprehend are corrupted by the impact of *internal conditions*. The mutilations have meaning *as such*. The meaning of a corrupt text of this sort can be adequately comprehended only after it has become possible to illuminate the meaning of the corruption itself. This distinguishes the peculiar task of a hermeneutics that cannot be confined to the procedures of philology but rather *unites linguistic analysis with the psychological investigation of causal connections*. In such cases an incomplete or distorted manifestation of meaning does not result from faulty transmission. For it is always a matter of the meaning of a biographical connection that has become inaccessible to the subject itself. Within the horizon of that measure of life history that can be made present, memory fails to such an extent that the disturbance of memory function as such calls hermeneutics to the scene and demands to be understood in the context of an objective meaning structure.

Dilthey had conceived life-historical memory as the condition of possible hermeneutic understanding, thus tying understanding to conscious intentions. Freud comes upon systematic disturbances of memory which, for their part, do express intentions. But the latter must then transcend the realm of what is subjectively thought. With his analysis of ordinary language, Dilthey only mentioned the limiting case of discrepancy between sentences, actions, and experiential expressions. For the psychoanalyst, however, this is the normal case.

The grammar of ordinary language governs not only the connection of symbols but also the interweaving of linguistic elements, action patterns, and expressions. In the normal case, these three categories of expressions are complementary, so that linguistic expressions "fit" interactions and both language and action "fit" experiential expressions; of course, their integration is imperfect, which makes possible the latitude necessary for indirect communications. In the limiting case, however, a language game can disintegrate to the point where the three categories of expressions no longer agree. Then actions and non-verbal expressions belie what is expressly stated. But the acting subject belies himself only for others who interact with him and observe his deviation from the grammatical rules of the language game. The acting subject himself cannot observe the discrepancy; or, if he observes it, he cannot understand it, because he both expresses and misunderstands himself in this discrepancy. His self-understanding must keep to what is consciously intended, to linguistic expression—or at least to what can be verbalized. Nonetheless, the intentional content that comes into view in discrepant actions and expressions is as much a part of the subject's life-historical structure as are subjectively intended meanings. The subject must deceive itself about these non-verbal expressions that are not coordinated with linguistic expression. And since it objectivates itself in them, it also deceives itself about itself.

Psychoanalytic interpretation is concerned with those connections of symbols in which a subject deceives itself about itself. The *depth hermeneutics* that Freud contraposes to Dilthey's philological hermeneutics deals with texts indicating *self-deceptions of the author*. Beside the manifest content (and the associated indirect but intended communications), such texts document the latent content of a portion of the author's orientations that has become inaccessible to him and alienated from him and yet belongs to him nevertheless. Freud coins the phrase "internal foreign territory"[7] to capture the character of the alienation of something that is still the subject's very own. Symbolic expressions belonging to this class of "texts" can be known according to characteristics that emerge only in the broad context of the interplay of linguistic expressions with the other forms of objectivation:

> I am certainly going beyond the conventional meaning of the word in postulating an interest in psychoanalysis on the part of the *linguist*. For language must be understood here to mean not merely the expression of thoughts in words, but also the language of gestures and every other mode of expression of psychic activity, such as writing. Then it may be pointed out that the

interpretations of psychoanalysis are primarily translations from a mode of expression that is alien to us into one with which our thought is familiar.[8]

The ongoing text of our everyday language games (speech and actions) is disturbed by apparently contingent mistakes: by omissions and distortions that can be discounted as accidents and ignored, as long as they fall within the conventional limits of tolerance. These *parapraxes* (errors), under which Freud includes cases of forgetting, slips of the tongue and of the pen, misreading, bungled actions, and so-called chance actions, indicate that the faulty text both expresses and conceals self-deceptions of the author.[9] If the mistakes in the text are more obtrusive and situated in the pathological realm, we speak of symptoms. They can be neither ignored nor understood. Nevertheless, the symptoms are part of intentional structures: the ongoing text of everyday language games is broken through not by external influences but by internal disturbances. Neuroses distort symbolic structures in all three dimensions: linguistic expression (obsessive thoughts), actions (repetition compulsions), and bodily experiential expression (hysterical body symptoms). In the case of psychosomatic disturbances, the symptom is so far removed from the original text that its symbolic character first has to be demonstrated by the work of interpretation. Neurotic symptoms in the narrower sense are located as it were between the parapraxes and psychosomatic illnesses. They cannot be belittled as accidents; at the same time their symbolic character, which identifies them as split-off parts of a symbolic structure, cannot be permanently denied. They are the scars of a corrupt text that confronts the author as incomprehensible.

The non-pathological model of such a text is the dream. The dreamer creates the dream text himself, obviously as an intentional structure. But after waking, the subject, who is still in some way identical with the author of the dream, no longer understands his creation. The dream is detached from actions and expressions; the complete language game is only imagined. Thus parapraxes and symptoms cannot manifest themselves in discrepancies between verbal and non-verbal expressions. But this isolation of dream production from behavior is simultaneously the precondition of the extreme latitude possessed by the forces that shatter the lingering text of waking consciousness (the "day's residues") and transform it into the dream text.

Thus Freud viewed the dream as the "normal model" of pathological conditions. The interpretation of dreams is always the model for the illumination of pathologically distorted meaning structures. In addition, it has a central place in the development of psychoanalysis because Freud came upon the mechanisms of defense and symptom formation through the hermeneutic decoding of dream texts:

> The transformation of the latent dream-thoughts into the manifest dream-content deserves all our attention, since it is the first instance known to us of psychical material being changed over from one mode of expression to another, from a mode of expression which is immediately intelligible to us to another which we can only come to understand with the help of guidance and effort, though it too must be recognized as a function of our mental activity.[10]

Freud obliges the analyst confronted with a dream to take the strict attitude of the interpreter. Writing of his own interpretations in the important seventh chapter of *The Interpretation of Dreams*, he admits, not without satisfaction, "we have treated as Holy Writ what previous writers have regarded as an arbitrary improvisation, hurriedly patched together in the embarrassment of the moment."[11] On the other hand, the hermeneutic view does not suffice. For dreams are among those texts that confront the author himself as alienated and incomprehensible. In his inquiry, the analyst must penetrate behind the manifest content of the dream text in order to grasp the latent dream thought which it expresses. The technique of dream interpretation goes beyond the art of hermeneutics insofar as it must grasp not only the meaning of a possibly distorted text, but the *meaning of the text distortion itself*, that is the transformation of a latent dream thought into the manifest dream. In other words, it must reconstruct what Freud called the "dream-work." The interpretation of dreams leads to a process of reflection that takes the same course as the genesis of the dream text, only in reverse. It is complementary to the dream-work. In this process the analyst can call on free association to individual elements of the dream as well as on subsequent spontaneous additions to the dream text as it was first communicated.

The uppermost dream layer that can be identified and removed in this way is the dream façade. The latter is the result of a secondary elaboration which is effected only after the dream memory has emerged as an object for the consciousness of the dreamer in his waking state. This rationalizing activity seeks to systematize confused contents, fill up gaps, and smooth over contradictions. The next dream layer can be traced back to undischarged "day's residues," that is text fragments from language games of the previous day, which were hindered and could not be carried out to the end. What remains is a depth layer with the symbolic contents that resist the work of interpretation. Freud calls them the real dream symbols, that is representations which express a latent content metaphorically or allegorically or in another systematic disguise. The next information that we obtain about these dream symbols arises from the singular experience of the *resistance* that they put up to interpretation. This resistance, which Freud explains in terms of a dream-censorship, manifests itself in lacking, hesitating, or circuitous associations as well as in the forgetting of portions of the text that are added later:

> It is impossible during our work to overlook the manifestations of this resistance. At some points the associations are given without hesitation and the first or second idea that occurs to the patient brings an explanation. At other points there is a stoppage and the patient hesitates before bringing out an association, and, if so, we often have to listen to a long chain of ideas before receiving anything that helps us to understand the dream. We are certainly right in thinking that the longer and more roundabout the chain of

associations the stronger the resistance. We can detect the same influence at work in the forgetting of dreams. It happens often enough that a patient, despite all his efforts, cannot remember one of his dreams. But after we have been able in the course of a piece of analytic work to get rid of a difficulty which had been disturbing his relation to the analysis, the forgotten dream suddenly re-emerges. Two other observations are also in place here. It very frequently comes about that, to begin with, a portion of a dream is omitted and added afterwards as an addendum. This is to be regarded as an attempt to forget that portion. Experience shows that it is that particular piece which is the most important; there was a greater resistance, we suppose, in the path of communicating it than the other parts of the dream. Furthermore, we often find that a dreamer endeavours to prevent himself from forgetting his dreams by fixing them in writing immediately after waking up. We can tell him that that is no use. . . . From all this we infer that the resistance which we come across in the work of interpreting dreams must also have had a share in their origin. We can actually distinguish between dreams that arose under a slight and under a high pressure of resistance. But this pressure varies as well from place to place within one and the same dream; it is responsible for the gaps, obscurities and confusions which may interrupt the continuity of even the finest of dreams.[12]

Later Freud also conceived dreams of punishment as a reaction of the dream-censorship to prior wishes.[13] The resistance experienced by the analyst in the attempt to free the latent dream thought from its disguise is the key to the mechanism of the dream-work. Resistance is the surest indication of a conflict:

There must be a force here which is seeking to express something and another which is striving to prevent its expression. What comes about in consequence as a manifest dream may combine all the decisions into which this struggle between two trends has been condensed. At one point one of these forces may have succeeded in putting through what it wanted to say, while at another point it is the opposing agency which has managed to blot out the intended communication completely or to replace it by something that reveals not a trace of it. The commonest and most characteristic cases of dream-construction are those in which the conflict has ended in a compromise, so that the communicating agency has, it is true, been able to say what it wanted but not in the way it wanted—only in a softened down, distorted and unrecognized form. If, then, dreams do not give a faithful picture of the dream-thoughts and if the work of interpretation is required in order to bridge the gap between them, that is the outcome of the opposing, inhibiting and restricting agency which we have inferred from our perception of the resistance while we interpret dreams.[14]

The restricting agency that controls speech and action by day slackens its domination during sleep because it can rely on the suspension of motor activity. We can assume that this agency suppresses motives of action. It hinders the realization of undesired motivations by removing from circulation the corresponding interpretations, that is representations and symbols. This circulation consists of habitualized interactions that are linked to the public realm of communication in ordinary language. The institutions of social intercourse sanction only certain motives of action. Other need dispositions, likewise attached to interpretations in ordinary language, are denied the route to manifest action, whether by the direct power of an interaction partner or the sanction of recognized social norms. These conflicts, at first external, are perpetuated intrapsychically; insofar as they are not manifested consciously, this perpetuation takes place as a permanent conflict between a defensive agency representing social repression and unrealizable motives of action. The psychically most effective way to render undesired need dispositions harmless is to *exclude from public communication* the interpretations to which they are attached—in other words, *repression*. Freud calls the excluded symbols and the motives that are excluded through them unconscious wishes. Through the mechanism of repression, conscious motivations present in the public use of language are transformed into unconscious, as it were delinguisticized, motives. In sleep, when the censorship can be slackened owing to the suspension of motor activity, repressed motives find a language through connection with the publicly allowed symbols of the day's residues. But this language is *privatized:* "for dreams are not in themselves social utterances, not a means of giving information."[15]

The text of the dream can be conceived as a compromise, one that is concluded between a substitute social censorship contained in the self and unconscious motives excluded from communication. Because, under the exceptional conditions of sleep, unconscious motives push forward into the material of the preconscious, which can be publicly communicated, the compromise language of the dream text is marked by a peculiar combination of public and privatized language. The succession of visual scenes is no longer ordered by syntactic rules. For the differentiating linguistic means for expressing logical relations are lacking. Even the elementary rules of logic are put out of commission. In the degrammaticized language of the dream, connections are produced through the blending and compression of material; Freud speaks of "condensation." These compressed images of the primitive language of the dream are suited for shifting semantic emphases, thereby displacing the original meanings. The mechanism of "displacement" serves the censorship agency in distorting the original meaning. The other mechanism is the eradication of offensive passages in the text. The structure of dream language, with its loosely related compressions, fosters these omissions.

Dream analysis recognizes omission and displacement as two different strategies of defense: repression in the narrower sense, which is directed against one's own self, and disguise, which can also be the basis for a projective redirection of the self toward the outside. In the present context it is interesting that Freud first discovered these defensive strategies in the mutilations and distortions of the dream text. For defense is directed immediately against the interpretations of motives of action. These are made harmless through the disappearance from public communication of the symbols linked to need dispositions. Thus the term "censorship" is meant literally: both psychological and official censorship suppress linguistic material and the meanings articulated in it. Both forms of censorship make use of the same defense mechanisms: the procedures of prohibiting and rewriting a text correspond to the psychic mechanisms of omission (repression) and displacement.[16]

Finally, the latent content generally disclosed by dream analysis sheds light on the role and function of dream production as such. For it always consists of the repetition of conflict-charged scenes from childhood: "Dreaming is a piece of infantile mental life that has been superseded."[17] These infantile scenes allow the inference that the most productive unconscious wishes stem from relatively early repressions. That is, they are derived from conflicts in which the immature and dependent person of the child was permanently subjected to the authority of the first reference persons and the social demands that they represent. Thus, as early as 1900, Freud could summarize the psychology of the dream processes in the thesis that "a normal train of thought is only submitted to abnormal psychical treatment of the sort we have been describing [which is typical of dreams] if an unconscious wish, derived from infancy and in a state of repression, has been transferred onto it."[18] Dream analysis is therefore allotted a specific task: "to lift the veil of amnesia which hides the earliest years of childhood and to bring to conscious memory the manifestations of early infantile sexual life which are contained in them."[19]

The nocturnal regression of psychic life to the infantile stage renders understandable the peculiarly timeless character of unconscious motives. As soon as split-off symbols and repressed motives of action can oppose the censorship and gain access to preconscious material, as in the dream, or to the realm of public communication and habitual interaction, as in the symptoms of the various neuroses, they tie the present to configurations from the past.

Freud transfers the traits that he has derived from the normal model of the dream text to those phenomena of waking life whose symbolism is mutilated and distorted in a way comparable to the degrammaticized language of the dream. The clinical pictures of conversion hysteria, compulsion neurosis, and the various phobias appear only as the pathological limiting cases of a scale of misbehavior, which in part falls within the realm of normality and in part actually sets the standards of what counts as normal. In the methodically rigorous sense, "wrong" behavior means every *deviation from the model of the language game of communicative action*, in which motives of action and linguistically expressed intentions coincide. In this model, split-off symbols and the need dispositions connected with them are not allowed. It is assumed either that they do not exist or, if they do, that they are without consequences on the level of public communication, habitual interaction, and observable expression. This model, however, could be generally applicable only under the conditions of a non-repressive society. Therefore deviations from it are the normal case under all known social conditions.

The object domain of depth hermeneutics comprises all the places where, owing to internal disturbances, the text of our everyday language games are interrupted by incomprehensible symbols. These symbols cannot be understood because they do not obey the grammatical rules of ordinary language, norms of action, and culturally learned patterns of expression. They are either ignored and glossed over, rationalized through secondary elaboration (if they are not already the product of rationalizations), or reduced to external, somatic disturbances. Freud uses the medical term "symptom" to cover such deviant symbol formations, which he studied in the dream as an exemplar. Symptoms are persistent and normally disappear only if replaced by functional equivalents. The persistence of symptoms expresses a fixation of ideas and modes of behavior in constant and compelling patterns. They restrict the flexibility margin of speech and communicative action. They can depreciate the reality content of perceptions and thought processes, unbalance the emotional economy, ritualize behavior, and immediately impair bodily functions. Symptoms can be regarded as the result of a compromise between repressed wishes of infantile origin and socially imposed prohibitions of wish-fulfillment. That is why they mainly display both elements, although in varying quantities. For they have the character of substitute formations for a denied gratification and also express the sanction with which the defensive agency threatens the unconscious wish. Finally, symptoms are signs of a specific self-alienation of the subject who has them. The breaks in the text are places where an interpretation has forcibly prevailed that is ego-alien even though it is produced by the self. Because the symbols that interpret suppressed needs are excluded from public communication, *the speaking and acting subject's communication with himself is interrupted.* The privatized language of unconscious motives is rendered inaccessible to the ego, even though internally it has considerable repercussions upon that use of language and those motivations of action that the ego controls. The result is that the ego necessarily deceives itself about its identity in the symbolic structures that it consciously produces.

Usually an interpreter has the task of mediating communication between two partners speaking different languages. He translates from one language into the other, brings about the intersubjectivity of the validity of linguistic symbols and rules, and overcomes difficulties of mutual understanding between partners who are separated by historical, social, or cultural boundaries. This model of hermeneutics from the cultural sciences does not hold for the work of psychoanalytic interpretation. For, even in the pathological limiting case of neurosis, the patient's ability to maintain mutual understanding with his role or conversational partners is not restricted directly, but only indirectly through the repercussions of the symptoms. What happens is that the neurotic, even under conditions of repression, takes care to maintain the intersubjectivity of mutual understanding in everyday life and accords with sanctioned expectations. But for this undisturbed communication under conditions of denial, he pays the price of *communication disturbance within himself*. The institution of power relations necessarily restricts public communication. If this restriction is not to affect the appearance of intersubjectivity, then the limits to communication must be established in the interior of subjects themselves. Thus *the privatized portion of excommunicated language*, along with the undesired motives of action, are silenced in the neurotic and made inaccessible to him. This disturbance of communication does not require an interpreter who mediates between partners of divergent languages but rather one who teaches one and the same subject to comprehend his own language. The analyst instructs the patient in reading his own texts, which he himself has mutilated and distorted, and in translating symbols from a mode of expression deformed as a private language into the mode of expression of public communication. This translation reveals the genetically important phases of life history to a memory that was previously blocked, and brings to consciousness the person's own self-formative process. Thus psychoanalytic hermeneutics, unlike the cultural sciences, aims not at the understanding of symbolic structures in general. Rather, *the act of understanding* to which it leads is *self-reflection*.

The thesis that psychoanalytic knowledge belongs to the category of self-reflection can be easily demonstrated on the basis of Freud's papers on analytic technique.[20] For analytic treatment cannot be defined without recourse to the experience of reflection. Hermeneutics derives its function in the process of the genesis of self-consciousness. It does not suffice to talk of the translation of a text; the translation itself is reflection: "the translation of what is unconscious into what is conscious."[21] Repressions can be eliminated only by virtue of reflection:

> The task which the psycho-analytic method seeks to perform may be formulated in different ways, which are, however, in their essence equivalent. It may, for instance, be stated thus: the task of the treatment is to remove the amnesias. When all gaps in memory have been filled in, all the enigmatic products of mental life elucidated, the continuance and even a renewal of the

morbid condition are made impossible. Or the formula
may be expressed in this fashion: all repressions must
be undone. The mental condition is then the same
as one in which all amnesias have been removed.
Another formulation reaches further: the task consists
in making the unconscious accessible to consciousness,
which is done by overcoming the resistances.[22]

The starting point of psychoanalytic theory is the experience of resistance, that is the blocking force that stands in
the way of the free and public communication of repressed contents. The analytic process of making conscious reveals itself as
a process of reflection in that it is not only a process on the cognitive level but also dissolves resistances on the affective level.
The dogmatic limitation of false consciousness consists not only
in the lack of specific information but in its specific inaccessi-
bility. It is not only a cognitive deficiency; for the deficiency is
fixated by habitualized standards on the basis of affective attitudes. That is why the mere communication of information and
the labelling of resistances have no therapeutic effect:

It is a long superseded idea, and one derived
from superficial appearances, that the patient suffers
from a sort of ignorance, and that if one removes this
ignorance by giving him information (about the causal
connection of his illness with his life, about his
experiences in childhood, and so on) he is bound to
recover. The pathological factor is not his ignorance in
itself, but the root of this ignorance in his *inner
resistances*; it was they that first called this ignorance
into being, and they still maintain it now. The task of
the treatment lies in combating these resistances.
Informing the patient of what he does not know because
he has repressed it is only one of the necessary
preliminaries to the treatment. If knowledge about the
unconscious were as important for the patient as people
inexperienced in psychoanalysis imagine, listening to
lectures or reading books would be enough to cure him.

Such measures, however, have as much influence on the symptoms of nervous illness as a distribution of menu-cards in a time of famine has upon hunger. The analogy goes even further than its immediate application; for informing the patient of his unconscious regularly results in an intensification of the conflict in him and an exacerbation of his troubles.[23]

At first glance the work of the analyst seems to coincide with that of the historian or, better, with that of the archaeologist. For it consists in reconstructing the patient's early history. At the end of analysis it should be possible to present narratively those events of the forgotten years of life that are relevant to the patient's case history and that neither the physician nor patient knew at the beginning of analysis. The intellectual work is shared by physician and patient in the following way: The former *reconstructs* what has been forgotten from the faulty texts of the latter, from his dreams, associations, and repetitions, while the latter, animated by the constructions suggested by the physician as hypotheses, *remembers*. The interpreting analyst's work of construction accords considerably with the method of reconstruction used by the archaeologist with regard to the sites of archaeological finds. But whereas the goal of the archaeologist is the historical representation of a forgotten process or a "history," the "path that starts from the analyst's construction ought to end in the patient's [present] recollection."[24] Only the patient's recollection decides the accuracy of the construction. If it applies, then it must also "restore" to the patient a portion of lost life history: that is it must be able to elicit a self-reflection.

At the beginning of a step of analytic work, the knowledge of the physician making the construction does not differ from that of the patient who is putting up resistance. The construction being entertained as a hypothesis takes the scattered elements of a mutilated and distorted text and fills them out to make a comprehensible pattern. Seen from the analyst's perspective, it remains mere knowledge "for us," until its communication turns into enlightenment—that is, into knowledge "for it," for the patient's consciousness: "On that particular matter our knowledge will then have become his knowledge as well."[25] Freud calls the common endeavor that overcomes this gap between communication and enlightenment "working-through." Working-through designates the dynamic component of a cognitive activity that leads to recognition only against resistances.

The analyst can initiate the process of enlightenment to the degree that he succeeds in altering the function of the dynamic of repression in such a way that it works toward the critical dissolution of resistance instead of its stabilization:

> The unconscious impulses do not·want to be remembered in the way the treatment desires them to be, but endeavour to reproduce themselves in accordance with the timelessness of the unconscious and its capacity for hallucination. Just as happens in dreams, the patient regards the products of the awakening of his unconscious impulses as contemporaneous and real; he seeks to put his passions into action without taking any account of the real situation. The doctor tries to compel him to fit these emotional impulses into the nexus of the treatment and of his life-history, to submit them to intellectual consideration and to understand them in the light of their psychical value. This struggle between the doctor and the patient, between intellect and instinctual life, between understanding and seeking to act, is played out almost exclusively in the phenomena of transference.[26]

The patient is subject to the compulsion to repeat his original conflict under the conditions of censorship. He acts within the constraints of the pathological attitudes and substitute formations that became fixed in childhood as compromises between wish-fulfillment and defense. The physician confronts the process that he is to reconstruct not as a historical matter but as a power operating in the present. The analytic situation, as the design of an experiment, has two main components. First, it weakens defense mechanisms through the reduction of conscious controls (by relaxation, free association, and unreserved communication), thus reinforcing the need to act. At the same time, however, it makes these repetitive reactions run idle in the presence of a reserved partner who suspends the pressure of life. Thus these reactions react back upon the patient himself. In this way the common neurosis is transformed into a *transference neurosis*. Under the controlled conditions of an artificial illness, the pathological repetition compulsion can be refashioned into a "motive to remember." The physician uses the opportunity to provide the symptoms with a new transference meaning and to "bring it about that something that the patient wishes to discharge in action is disposed of through the work of remembering."[27] The as it were experimental control of "repetition" under the conditions of the analytic situation offers the physician the opportunity for both knowledge and treatment. Acting in the transference situation (and in comparable situations in everyday life during the period of treatment) leads to scenes that offer clues to the reconstruction of the original scene of childhood conflict. But the physician's constructions can be changed into actual recollections of the patient only to the degree that the latter, confronted with the results of his action in transference with its suspension of the pressure of life, sees himself through the eyes of another and learns to reflect on his symptoms as offshoots of his own actions.

We started with the assertion that the process of knowledge induced in the patient by the physician is to be comprehended as self-reflection. This assertion is supported by the logic of the transference situation and the division of labor in communication between the physician, who elaborates constructions, and the patient, who transforms action into recollection. Analytic insight complements a miscarried self-formative process, owing to a *compensatory learning process, which undoes processes of splitting-off*. These processes detach symbols from public linguistic usage and distort the prevailing rules of communication through private language in order to render harmless the motives of action connected with the excluded symbols. The virtual totality that is sundered by splitting-off is represented by the model of pure communicative action. According to this model all habitual interactions and all interpretations relevant to life conduct are accessible at all times. This is possible on the basis of internalizing the apparatus of unrestricted ordinary language of uncompelled and public communication, so that the transparency of recollected life history is preserved. Self-formative processes that deviate from this model (and Freud leaves no doubt that, under the conditions of a sexual development with two peaks and a forced latency period, *all* such socialization processes must take an *anomalous* course) are the result of suppression by social institutions. This external impact is replaced by the intrapsychic defense of an internally established agency and made permanent. It leads to long-term compromises with the demands of the split-off portion of the self, which come into being at the price of pathological compulsion and self-deception. This is the foundation of symptom formation, through which the text of everyday language games is characteristically affected and thus is made into the object of possible analytic treatment.

Analysis has immediate therapeutic results because the critical overcoming of blocks to consciousness and the penetration of false objectivations initiates the appropriation of a lost portion of life history; it thus reverses the process of splitting-off. That is why analytic knowledge is self-reflection. And that is why Freud rejects the comparison of psychoanalysis with chemical analysis. The analysis and decomposition of complexes into their simple components do not yield a manifold of elements which could then be recombined syntactically. Freud calls the expression "psychosynthesis" an intellectually empty phrase, because it misses the specific achievement of self-reflection, in which analytic decomposition *as such* is synthesis, the re-establishment of a corrupted unity:

> In actual fact, indeed, the neurotic patient presents us with a torn mind, divided by resistances. As we analyze it and remove the resistances, it grows together; the great unity which we call his ego fits into itself all the instinctual impulses which before had been split off and held apart from it.[28]

Three additional peculiarities demonstrate that analytic

knowledge is self-reflection. First, it includes two moments equally: the cognitive, and the affective and motivational. It is critique in the sense that the analytic power to dissolve dogmatic attitudes inheres in analytic insight. Critique terminates in a transformation of the affective-motivational basis, just as it begins with the need for practical transformation. Critique would not have the power to break up false consciousness if it were not impelled by a *passion for critique*. At the beginning there is the experience of suffering and desperation and the interest in overcoming this burdensome condition. The patient seeks out the physician because he suffers from his symptoms and would like to recover from them; psychoanalysis can rely on this just like medicine in general. But in distinction from usual medical treatment, the pressure of suffering and the interest in gaining health are not only the *occasion* for the inauguration of therapy but the *presupposition* of the success of the therapy itself.

> It is possible to observe during the treatment
> that every improvement in his condition reduces the
> rate at which he recovers and diminishes the instinctual
> force impelling him towards recovery. But this
> instinctual force is indispensable; reduction of it
> endangers our aim—the patient's restoration to health.
> What, then, is the conclusion that forces itself inevitably
> upon us? Cruel though it may sound, we must see to
> it that the patient's suffering, to a degree that is in
> some way or other effective, does not come to an end
> prematurely. If, owing to the symptoms having been
> taken apart and having lost their value, his suffering
> becomes mitigated, we must re-instate it elsewhere in the
> form of some appreciable privation; otherwise we run
> the danger of never achieving any improvements except
> quite insignificant and transitory ones.[29]

Freud demands that analytic cure be carried out under conditions of abstinence. He would like to prevent the patient from prematurely replacing his symptoms with painless substitute-gratification during the course of treatment. In customary medical practice this demand would appear absurd. It is meaningful in psychoanalytic therapy because the latter's success depends not on the physician's technically successful influence on a sick organism but rather on the course of the sick person's self-reflection. And the latter proceeds only as long as analytic knowledge is impelled onward against motivational resistances by the *interest in self-knowledge*.

A second peculiarity is connected with this. Freud always emphasized that a patient who enters analytic treatment may not relate to his illness as to a somatic disease. He must be brought to regard the phenomena of his illness as part of his self. Instead of treating his symptoms and their causes as external, the patient must be prepared, so to speak, to assume responsibility for his illness. Freud discussed this problem in respect to the analogous case of responsibility for the content of dreams:

> Obviously one must hold oneself responsible for the evil impulses of one's dreams. What else is one to do with them? Unless the content of the dream (rightly understood) is inspired by alien spirits, it is a part of my own being. If I seek to classify the impulses that are present in me according to social standards into good and bad, I must assume responsibility for both sorts; and if, in defence, I say that what is unknown, unconscious and repressed in me is not my "ego," then I shall not be basing my position upon psycho-analysis, I shall not have accepted its conclusions—and I shall perhaps be taught better by the criticisms of my fellow-men, by the disturbances in my actions and the confusion of my feelings. I shall perhaps learn that what I am disavowing not only "is" in me but sometimes "acts" from out of me as well.[30]

Because analysis expects the patient to undergo the experience of self-reflection, it demands "moral responsibility for the content" of the illness. For the insight to which analysis is to lead is indeed only this: that the ego[31] of the patient recognize itself in its other, represented by its illness, as in *its own* alienated *self* and identify with it. As in Hegel's dialectic of the moral life, the criminal recognizes in his victim his own annihilated essence; in this self-reflection the abstractly divorced parties recognize the destroyed moral totality as their common basis *and thereby* return to it. Analytic knowledge is also moral insight, because in the movement of self-reflection the unity of theoretical and practical reason has not yet been undone.

The last peculiarity of analysis confirms this character. The demand that no one may practice analysis if he has not first undergone a training analysis seems to accord with the usual requirements of medical qualification. One must have learned the profession that one would like to practice. But the demand aiming to prevent the dangers of "wild" analysis postulates more than an adequate training. Rather, the analyst is required to undergo analysis in the role of patient in order to free himself from the very illnesses that he is later to treat as an analyst. This is extraordinary:

> After all, nobody maintains that a physician is incapable
> of treating internal diseases if his own internal organs
> are not sound; on the contrary, it may be argued
> that there are certain advantages in a man who is himself
> threatened with tuberculosis specializing in the
> treatment of persons suffering from that disease.[32]

Obviously, however, the analytic situation contains dangers that are not typical of the rest of medical practice—"sources of error from personal comparison." The physician is inhibited in his work of psychoanalytic interpretation and misses the right constructions, if, under the compulsion of unconscious motives, he also projects his own anxieties onto his partner or does not perceive certain of the patient's modes of behavior:

> So long as he is capable of practising at all, a doctor
> suffering from disease of the lungs or heart is not
> handicapped either in diagnosing or treating internal
> complaints; whereas the special conditions of analytic
> work do actually cause the analyst's own defects to

interfere with his making a correct assessment of the state of things in his patient and reacting to them in a useful way.[33]

At another point Freud attributes this to "a special aspect of the object, since psychology does not treat of objects like those of physics, which can arouse only a cool scientific interest."[34] In the transference situation the physician does not behave contemplatively. Rather, he derives his interpretation to the degree that he methodically assumes the role of interaction partner, converting the neurotic repetition compulsion into a transference identification, preserving ambivalent transferences while suspending them, and, at the right moment, dissolving the patient's attachment to him. In doing all this, the physician makes himself the instrument of knowledge: not, however, by bracketing his subjectivity, but precisely by *its controlled employment*.[35]

In a later phase of his development Freud fit the basic assumptions of psychoanalysis into a *structural model*.[36] The interplay of the three agencies, ego, id, and super-ego, represents the functional structure of the psychic apparatus. The names of the three agencies do not quite accord with Freud's basic mechanistic view of the structure of psychic life, although they are supposed to serve as an explanation of the mode of operation of the psychic apparatus. It is no accident that the conceptual constructions ego, id, and super-ego owe their names to the experience of *reflection*. Only subsequently were they transposed into an objectivistic frame of reference and re-interpreted. Freud discovered the functions of the ego, in connection with the two other agencies, the id and the super-ego, in the interpretation of dreams and in analytic dialogue, that is in the interpretation of specifically mutilated and distorted texts. He emphasizes that "the whole theory of psychoanalysis is . . . in fact built up on the perception of the resistance offered to us by the patient when we attempt to make his unconscious conscious to him."[37] Resistance is the manifestation of a singular defensive achievement, which must be comprehended both with regard to the defensive agency and the material which is defended against and repressed.

Resistance means keeping from consciousness. We assume a sphere of the conscious and, given within the horizon of consciousness, preconscious, which can be evoked at any time. This sphere is attached to linguistic communication and actions. It satisfies the criterion of publicness, which means communicability, whether in words or actions. In contrast, what is *unconscious is removed from public communication*. Insofar as it expresses itself in symbols or actions anyway, it manifests itself as a symptom, that is as a mutilation and distortion of the text of everyday habitual language games. In complementary ways the experience of resistance and the specific distortion of symbolic structures have the same reference: the unconscious, which is "suppressed," that is kept from free communication, but which creeps into public speech and observable actions through detours, and thus "urges" toward consciousness. Repression comprises both submergence and active emergence.

Starting with the experiences of the physician's communication with his patient, Freud derived the concept of the unconscious from a specific form of disturbance of communication in ordinary language. For this he would really have needed a theory of language, which did not exist at the time and whose outlines are only just beginning to take form today. Nonetheless, several fruitful observations are to be found in Freud's works. The human species is distinguished from animals by a

> complication through which internal processes in the ego may also acquire the quality of consciousness. This is the work of the function of speech, which brings material in the ego into a firm connection with mnemic residues of visual, but more particularly of auditory, perceptions. Thenceforward the perceptual periphery of the cortical layer can be excited to a much greater extent from inside as well, internal events such as passages of ideas and thought-processes can become conscious, and a special device is called for in order to distinguish between the two possibilities—a device known as *reality-testing*. The equation "perception = reality (external world)" no longer holds. Errors, which can now easily arise and do so regularly in dreams, are called *hallucinations*.[38]

The function of language, on which Freud focusses here, is a stabilization of processes of consciousness in such a way that the "internal" is fastened to symbols and obtains "external" existence. On the basis of this function, the boundary of animal intelligence could be crossed and adaptive behavior transformed into instrumental action. Freud shares the pragmatist concept of thought as "experimental action, a motor palpating, with small expenditure of discharge."[39] Through linguistic symbols, alternative chains of action can be followed through experimentally, in other words calculated. That is why language is the basis of ego functions, on which the capacity for reality-testing depends. On the other hand, reality-testing in the rigorous sense is necessary only after needs can be connected in hallucinations with linguistic anticipations of gratifications and thereby channelled as culturally defined needs. Only in the medium of language is the heritage of man's natural history articulated in the form of *interpreted needs*: the heritage of a plastic impulse potential,[40] which, while pre-oriented in libidinal and aggressive directions, is otherwise undefined, owing to its uncoupling from inherited motor activity. On the human level, instinctual demands are represented by interpretations, that is by hallucinatory wish-fulfillments. Since surplus[41] libidinal and aggressive demands are dysfunctional for individuals as for the species, they clash with reality. The reality-testing agency of the ego makes these conflicts foreseeable. It comes to know which instinctual impulses, by motivating actions, would bring about dangerous situations and make external conflicts inevitable. The ego comes to know such impulses themselves as indirect dangers. It reacts with anxiety and techniques of defending against anxiety. In those cases in which conflict between wish and reality cannot be solved through intervening in reality, only flight remains. If, however, given a constant excess of wishful fantasy over real possibilities of gratification, the normal situation offers no opportunities for flight, then the technique of defense against anxiety turns away from reality as the immediate source of danger and directs itself against the instinctual demands, which have been identified as the indirect source of danger. "It will then be clear that the [intrapsychic] defensive process is analogous to the flight by means of which the ego removes itself from a danger that threatens it from outside. The defensive process is an attempt at flight from an instinctual danger."[42] This attempt to conceive the internal defensive process on the model of flight leads to formulations that accord surprisingly with the hermeneutic insights of psychoanalysis. The fleeing ego, which can no longer remove itself from an external reality, must hide from itself. The text in which the ego understands itself in its situation is thus purged of representatives of the undesired instinctual demands: in other words, it is censored. The self's identity with this defended-against part of the psyche is denied; the latter is reified, for the ego, into a neuter, an id (it). The same holds for the representatives of the id at the level of the purged symbolic structure, that is for symptoms:

> For the mental process which has been turned into a symptom owing to repression now maintains its existence outside the organization of the ego and independently of it. Indeed, it is not that process alone but all its derivatives which enjoy, as it were, this same privilege of extra-territoriality; and whenever they come into associative contact with a part of the ego-organization, it is not at all certain that they will not draw that part over to themselves and thus enlarge themselves at the expense of the ego. An analogy with which we have long been familiar compared a symptom to a foreign body which was keeping up a constant succession of stimuli and reactions in the tissue in which it was embedded. It does sometimes happen that the defensive struggle against an unwelcome instinctual impulse is brought to an end with the formation of a symptom. As far as can be seen, this is most often possible in hysterical conversion. But usually the outcome is different. The initial act of repression is followed by a tedious or interminable sequel in which the struggle against the instinctual impulse is prolonged into a struggle against the symptom.[43]

The secondary defensive struggle against symptoms shows that the process of internal flight, with which the ego hides from itself, substitutes for an external enemy the derivatives of the id, which have been neutralized to foreign bodies.

The ego's flight from itself is an operation that is carried out in and with language. Otherwise it would not be possible to reverse the defensive process hermeneutically, via the analysis of language. In a linguistic framework, Freud attempted to render the act of repression comprehensible as a severance from language as such of ideas representing the instincts. In so doing he assumed that

> ... the real difference between a Ucs. and a
> Pcs. idea (thought) consists in this: that the former is
> carried out on some material which remains unknown,
> whereas the latter (the Pcs.) is in addition brought into
> connection with word-presentations. ... The question,
> "How does a thing become conscious?" would thus be
> more advantageously stated: "How does a thing become
> preconscious?" And the answer would be: "Through
> becoming connected with the word-presentations
> corresponding to it."[44]

Now the distinction between word-presentations and asymbolic ideas is problematic, and the assumption of a non-linguistic substratum, in which these ideas severed from language are "carried out," is unsatisfactory. In addition, it is not clear according to what rules (other than *grammatical* rules) unconscious ideas could be connected with verbal residues. At this point the absence of a developed theory of language makes itself felt. It seems to me more plausible to conceive the act of repression as a banishment of need interpretations themselves. The degrammaticized and imagistically compressed language of the dream provides some clues to an *excommunication model* of this sort. This process would be the intrapsychic imitation of a specific category of punishment, whose efficacy was striking especially in archaic times: the expulsion, ostracism, and isolation of the criminal from the social group whose language he shares. The *splitting-off of individual symbols from public communication* would mean at the same time the *privatization of their semantic content*.[45] Nevertheless, some logical connection of deformed and public language remains, to the degree that translation from the private-language dialect remains possible—it is in this that the therapist's activity of linguistic analysis consists.

The conceptual constructions of the ego and the id arose from an interpretation of the analyst's experiences with the patient's "resistance." Freud conceived the defensive process as the reversal of reflection, that is as the process, analogous to flight, through which the ego conceals itself from itself. "Id" is then the name for the part of the self that is externalized through defense, while "ego" is the agency that fulfills the task of reality-testing and censorship of instinctual impulses. The topological distinction of unconscious and conscious (or preconscious) seemed to coincide with this structural differentiation. If making conscious the unconscious may be called reflection, then the process that runs counter to reflection must transform the conscious into the unconscious. But the same clinical experience on which the constructions of the ego and the id were based shows that the activity of the defensive agency is by no means always conscious. Rather, it mainly proceeds unconsciously. This required introducing the category of the super-ego:

> The objective sign of this resistance is that his
> associations fail or depart widely from the topic that
> is being dealt with. He may also recognize the resistance
> *subjectively* by the fact that he has distressing feelings
> when he approaches the topic. But this last sign may
> also be absent. We then say to the patient that we infer
> from his behaviour that he is now in a state of resistance;
> and he replies that he knows nothing of that, and is only
> aware that his associations have become more difficult.
> It turns out that we were right; but in that case his
> resistance was unconscious too, just as unconscious as the
> repressed, at the lifting of which we were working. We
> should long ago have asked the question: from what part
> of his mind does an unconscious resistance like this
> arise? The beginner in psychoanalysis will be ready at

once with the answer: it is, of course, the resistance of the unconscious. An ambiguous and unserviceable answer! If it means that the resistance arises from the repressed, we must rejoin: certainly not! We must rather attribute to the repressed a strong upward drive, an impulsion to break through into consciousness. The resistance can only be a manifestation of the ego, which originally put the repression into force and now wishes to maintain it. That, moreover, is the view we always took. Since we have come to assume a special agency in the ego, the super-ego, which represents demands of a restrictive and rejecting character, we may say that repression is the work of this super-ego and that it is carried out either by itself or by the ego in obedience to its orders.[46]

Intelligent adaptation to external reality, which enables the ego to test reality, has its counterpart in the *appropriation of social roles* through *identification with other subjects,* who confront the child with socially sanctioned expectations. The super-ego is formed through the internalization of these expectations on the basis of introjection, the establishment of abandoned love objects in the ego. The residues of abandoned object-choices give rise to the agency of conscience, which anchors in the personality structure itself the repressive demands of society against "surplus" instinctual aims. The latter occasion conflict and are identified as "dangerous" because of their "excessive" character. The super-ego is the intrapsychic extension of social authority. The ego then exercises the function of censoring the instincts under the supervision of the super-ego. As long as it acts as the executive organ of the super-ego, the defensive process remains unconscious. It is in this way that it is distinguished from the conscious mastery of instincts. The dependent ego of the child is obviously too weak to carry out defensive operations from moment to moment in an effective way based on its own powers. Thus is established in the self that agency which compels the ego to flee from itself with the same objective force that lets the offshoots of the id confront the ego objectively as the result of repression.

It seems as though the internalization of prohibitive norms is a process of the same type as defense against undesirable motives.[47] This is the basis of the affinity between the super-ego and the id, both of which remain unconscious. But the processes of internalization and defense are complementary. Whereas in the latter socially undesired motivations of action, which first belong to the ego as wishful fantasies, are suppressed, in the former socially desired motivations of action are impressed upon a resistant ego from without. Internalization may be compared to the defensive process in that it, too, removes from discussion precepts that are first articulated in language. But this blocking is not associated with a deformation of ordinary language into private language. In this connection Freud emphasizes that

> it is . . . impossible for the super-ego . . . to disclaim its origin from things heard; for it is a part of the ego and remains accessible to consciousness by way of these word-presentations (concepts, abstractions). But the cathectic energy does not reach these contents of the super-ego from auditory perception (instruction or reading) but from sources in the id.[48]

Apparently a sort of sanctification of certain propositions comes into being through their connection with repressed libidinal motives of action. Thus the symbols expressed in the commands of the super-ego are not excluded from public communication as such; but, as libidinally bound basic propositions, they are immunized against critical objections. This is the basis of the weakness of the reality-testing ego in relation to the authority-wielding super-ego, although they remain within a common, unmutilated language.

The *derivation of the structural model from experiences of the analytic situation* links the three categories ego, id, and super-ego to the specific meaning of a form of communication into which physician and patient enter with the aim of setting in motion a process of enlightenment and bringing the patient to self-reflection. In explicating the ego, id, and super-ego, we must refer back to this context; thus it is not meaningful to describe it in terms of the structural model derived from it. Nevertheless, this is what Freud does. He construes the interpretive work of the physician in the theoretical expressions of the structural model. In this way, the form of communication that was first described from the perspective of analytic technique seems to be theoretically accounted for. In truth, this theoretical exposition does not contain a single element that goes beyond the previous description of technique. *The language of the theory is narrower than the language in which the technique was described.* This holds precisely for those expressions that refer to the specific meaning of analysis. According to the language of psychoanalytic technique, what has become unconscious is transformed into consciousness and re-appropriated by the ego, repressed impulses are detected and criticized, the divided self can no longer bring about synthesis, etc.[49] In the structural model, however, the ego agency is precisely not endowed with the capacity that these expressions invoke. The ego exercises the functions of intelligent adaptation and censorship of the instincts, but the specific activity of which defensive activity is only the negative side is lacking: self-reflection.

Freud makes a careful distinction between displacement, as a primary process, and sublimation, which is a displacement under the control of the ego. Analogously, he distinguishes between defense as an unconscious reaction and the rational mastery of instincts, which is a defense not only by means of the ego, but under the ego's control. But what does not appear among ego functions on the metapsychological level is the movement of reflection, which transforms one state into another—which transforms the pathological state of compulsion and self-deception into the state of superseded conflict and reconciliation with excommunicated language. Strangely enough, the structural model denies the origins of its own categories in a process of enlightenment.

The Scientistic Self-Misunderstanding of Metapsychology: On the Logic of General Interpretation

In his "Autobiographical Study," Freud confesses that even in his early years his scientific interest was directed "at human relations rather than natural objects." Neither then nor later did he experience a predilection for the position and activity of a doctor. Yet as a student he first found "calm and full gratification" in physiology. In Ernst Brücke's laboratory he worked for six years on problems of the histology of the nervous system.[1] This dichotomy in his interest may have contributed to Freud's founding what is in fact a new *science of man* while always considering it a *natural science*. Moreover, it was from neurophysiology, where he had learned to treat questions of human relevance according to medical and natural-scientific methods, that Freud borrowed the models that served him in theory formation. Freud never doubted that psychology is a natural science.[2] Psychic processes can be made the objects of research in the same way as observable natural events.[3] Conceptual constructions do not have a different role in psychology from that in a natural science. The physicist, for example, does not provide information about the essence of electricity, but instead uses "electricity" as a theoretical concept, just as the psychologist uses "instinct."[4] However, only psychoanalysis made psychology into a science:

> The hypothesis we have adopted of a psychical apparatus extended in space, expediently put together, developed by the exigencies of life, which gives rise to the phenomena of consciousness only at one particular point and under certain conditions—this hypothesis has put us in a position to establish psychology on foundations similar to those of any other science, such, for instance, as physics.[5]

Freud does not evade the consequences of this identification of psychoanalysis with the natural sciences. He considers it possible in principle that some day the therapeutic employment of psychoanalysis will be replaced by the pharmacological employment of biochemistry. The self-understanding of psychoanalysis as a natural science suggests the model of the technical utilization of scientific information. If analysis only *seems* to appear as an interpretation of texts and *actually* leads to making possible technical control of the psychic apparatus, then there is nothing unusual about the idea that psychological influence could at some point be replaced with greater effect by somatic techniques of treatment:

> The future may teach us to exercise a direct influence, by means of particular chemical substances, on the amounts of energy and their distribution in the mental apparatus. . . . But for the moment we have nothing better at our disposal than the technique of psycho-analysis. . . .[6]

This passage reveals that a technological understanding of analysis accords only with a theory that has cut itself loose from the categorial framework of self-reflection and replaced a structural model suitable for self-formative processes with an *energy-distribution model*. As long as the theory derives its meaning in relation to the reconstruction of a lost fragment of life history and, therefore, to self-reflection, its application is necessarily *practical*. It effects the reorganization of the action-orienting self-understanding of socialized individuals, which is structured in ordinary language. In this role, however, psychoanalysis can never be replaced by technologies derived from other theories of the empirical sciences in the rigorous sense. For psychopharmacology only brings about alterations of consciousness to the extent that it controls functions of the human organism as objectified natural processes. In contrast, the experience of reflection induced by enlightenment is precisely the act through which the subject frees itself from a state in which it had become an object for itself. This specific activity must be accomplished by the subject itself. There can be no substitute for it, including a technology, unless technology is to serve to unburden the subject of its own achievements.

Starting from models of the pathlike flow of energy between neurons, current in contemporary neurophysiology, Freud in his early years outlined a psychology from which he then immediately distanced himself.[7] At that time Freud hoped to be able to provide psychology with an *immediate* foundation as a natural science, namely as a special part of the physiology of the brain, which was itself patterned after mechanics. This psychology was to represent "psychical processes as quantitatively determined states of specifiable material particles."[8] Categories such as tension, discharge, stimulation, and inhibition were applied to the distribution of energy in the nervous system and the paths of conduction connecting neurons, conceived of in accordance with the mechanics of solids. Freud abandoned this physicalist program in favor of a psychological approach in the narrower sense. This approach, in turn, retains the neurophysiological language of the original but makes its basic predicates accessible to a tacit *mentalist reinterpretation*. Energy becomes instinctual energy, about whose physical substratum no statements can be made. The inhibition and discharge of energy supplies and the mechanism of their distribution are supposed to operate after the pattern of a spatially extended system, whose localization, however, is henceforth eliminated:

> What is presented to us in these words is the
> idea of *psychical locality*. I shall entirely disregard
> the fact that the mental apparatus with which we are
> here concerned is also known to us in the form of an
> anatomical preparation, and I shall carefully avoid
> the temptation to determine psychical locality in any
> anatomical fashion. I shall remain upon psychological
> ground, and I propose simply to follow the suggestion
> that we should picture the instrument which carries out
> our mental functions as resembling a compound
> microscope or a photographic apparatus, or something
> of the kind. On that basis, psychical locality will

correspond to a point inside the apparatus at which one of the preliminary stages of an image comes into being. In the microscope and telescope, as we know, these occur in part at ideal points, regions in which no tangible component of the apparatus is situated. I see no necessity to apologize for the imperfections of this or of any similar imagery. Analogies of this kind are only intended to assist us in our attempt to make the complications of mental functioning intelligible by dissecting the function and assigning its different constituents to different component parts of the apparatus.[9]

"Accordingly, we will picture the mental apparatus as a compound instrument, to the components of which we will give the name of "agencies," or (for the sake of greater clarity) "systems." It is to be anticipated, in the next place, that these systems may perhaps stand in a regular spatial relation to one another, in the same kind of way in which the various systems of lenses in a telescope are arranged behind one another. Strictly speaking, there is no need for the hypothesis that the psychical systems are actually arranged in a *spatial* order. It would be sufficient if a fixed order were established by the fact that in a given psychical process the excitation passes through the systems in a particular *temporal* sequence."[10]

Freud sets up several elementary correlations between subjective experiences on the one hand and energy currents, conceived of as objective, on the other.[11] Pain (*Unlust*) results from the accumulation of stimulation, with the intensity of the stimulation proportional to an energy quantum. Inversely, pleasure originates in the discharge of dammed-up energy, in other words through a decrease of stimulation. The motions of the apparatus are regulated by the tendency to avoid the accumulation of stimulation. This correlation of mentalistic expressions (such as impulse, stimulation, pain, pleasure, wish) and physical processes (such as energy quanta, energy tension and discharge, and, as a system property, the tendency toward the efflux of energy) suffices to sever the categories of the conscious and the unconscious, which were primarily derived from communication between physician and patient, from the frame of reference of self-reflection and transfer them to the energy-distribution model:

> The first wishing seems to have been a hallucinatory cathecting of the memory of satisfaction. Such hallucinations, however, if they were not to be maintained to the point of exhaustion, proved to be inadequate to bring about the cessation of the need or, accordingly, the pleasure attaching to satisfaction. A second activity—or, as we put it, the activity of a second system—became necessary, which would not allow the mnemic cathexis to proceed as far as perception and from there to bind the psychical forces; instead, it diverted the excitation arising from the need along a roundabout path which ultimately, by means of voluntary movement, altered the external world in such a way that it became possible to arrive at a real perception of the object of satisfaction. We have already outlined our schematic picture of the psychical apparatus up to this point; the two systems are the germ of what, in the fully developed apparatus, we have described as the Ucs. and Pcs.[12]

In 1895, together with Breuer, Freud had published *Studies on Hysteria*, where pathological phenomena were already explained according to the model developed later. Under hypnosis Breuer's patient had revealed that her symptoms were connected with past scenes of her life history in which she had to suppress strong stimuli. These affects could be interpreted as displaceable quantities of energy for which the normal paths of discharge were closed off and which therefore had to be used abnormally. Considered psychologically, the symptom comes into being through the damming up of an affect. In the model this can also be represented as a result of the conversion of a quantity of energy that is impeded in flowing out. The therapeutic procedure practiced by Breuer was supposed to have the aim of providing "that the quota of affect used for maintaining the symptom, which had got on to the wrong lines and had, as it were, become strangulated there, should be directed on to the normal path along which it could obtain discharge (or *abreaction*)."[13] Freud soon recognized the disadvantages of hypnosis and introduced instead the technique of free association. The "basic rule of analysis" formulates the conditions of a reserve free from repression in which the "serious situation" (*Ernstsituation*), that is the pressure of social sanctions, can be suspended as credibly as possible for the duration of the communication between doctor and patient.

The transition from the old to the new technique is essential. It results not only from considerations of therapeutic utility but from insight into a principle: that for the patient's remembering to be therapeutically successful, it must lead to the *conscious* appropriation of a suppressed fragment of life history. Because the hypnotic release of the unconscious only manipulates processes of consciousness and does not entrust them *to the subject itself*, it cannot definitively penetrate the barrier to memory. Freud rejected Breuer's technique because analysis is not a *steered natural process* but rather, on the level of intersubjectivity in ordinary language between doctor and patient, a *movement of self-reflection*. Freud elaborated this especially in the abovementioned paper on "Remembering, Repeating, and Working-Through." And yet, at the end of the same paper, he still conceives this movement of self-reflection, induced under conditions of the basic rule of analysis, according to the old model of Breuer—that is, of remembering as abreacting:

> This working-through of the resistances may in practice turn out to be an arduous task for the subject of the analysis and a trial of patience for the analyst. Nevertheless it is a part of the work which effects the greatest changes in the patient and which distinguishes analytic treatment from any kind of treatment by suggestion. From a theoretical point of view one may correlate it with the "abreacting" of the quotas of affect strangulated by repression—an abreaction without which hypnotic treatment remained ineffective.[14]

Because Freud was caught from the very beginning in a scientistic self-understanding, he succumbed to an objectivism that regresses immediately from the level of self-reflection to contemporary positivism in the manner of Mach and that therefore takes on a particularly crude form. Independently of the evolution of his work, the way in which Freud went astray methodologically can be reconstructed approximately as follows. The basic categories of the new discipline, the conceptual constructions, the assumptions about the functional structures of the psychic apparatus and about mechanisms of both the genesis of symptoms and the dissolution of pathological compulsions—this metapsychological framework was first derived from experiences of the analytic situation and the interpretation of dreams. The meaning of this observation bears on methodology and not only the psychology of research. For these metapsychological categories and connections were not only *discovered* under determinate conditions of specifically sheltered communication, they cannot even be *explicated* independently of this context. The conditions of this communication are thus the conditions of the possibility of analytic knowledge for both partners, doctor and patient, likewise. Perhaps Freud was thinking of this implication when he wrote that the claim to fame of analytic work was that "in its execution research and treatment coincide."[15] We have shown on the basis of the structural model that, with regard to the logic of science, the categorial framework of psychoanalysis is tied to the presuppositions of the interpretation of muted and distorted texts by means of which their authors deceive themselves. If this is so, however, then psychoanalytic theory formation is embedded in the context of self-reflection.

An alternative is the attempt to reformulate psychoanalytic assumptions in the categorial framework of a strict empirical science. Some have been newly formulated in the framework of behavioristically oriented learning psychology and then subjected to the usual procedures of verification. More sophisticated is the attempt to take the personality model developed by ego psychology but rooted in instinct theory and reformulate it as a self-regulating system in terms of modern functionalism. In both cases the new theoretical framework makes possible the operationalization of concepts; in both cases it requires verification of the derived hypotheses under experimental conditions. Freud surely assumed tacitly that his metapsychology, which severs the structural model from the basis of communication between doctor and patient and instead attaches it to the energy-distribution model by means of definitions, represented an empirically rigorous scientific formulation of this sort.

However, his relation to metapsychology, of which he occasionally spoke as a "witch" in order to resist its terribly speculative character, was not free of ambivalence.[16] This ambivalence may imply a mild doubt of the status of this science, which he nevertheless defended so emphatically. Freud erred in not realizing that psychology, insofar as it understands itself as a strict empirical science, cannot content itself with a model that keeps to a physicalistic use of language without seriously leading to operationalizable assumptions. The energy-distribution model only creates the semblance that psychoanalytic statements are about measurable transformations of energy. Not a single statement about quantitative relations derived from the conception of instinctual economics has ever been tested experimentally. The model of the psychic apparatus is so constructed that metapsychological statements imply the observability of the events they are about. But these events are never observed—nor can they be observed.

It may be that Freud did not become aware of the methodological import of this limitation because he considered the analytic situation of dialogue quasi-experimental in character and therefore viewed the clinical basis of experience as a sufficient substitute for experimental verification. He countered the reproach that psychoanalysis did not admit of experimental verification by referring to astronomy, which also does not experiment with its heavenly bodies but is limited to their observation.[17] The real difference between astronomical observation and analytic dialogue, however, is that in the former the quasi-experimental selection of initial conditions permits the controlled observation of predicted events, while in the latter the level of control of the results of instrumental action[18] is completely missing and replaced by the level of the intersubjectivity of mutual understanding about the meaning of incomprehensible symbols. Despite his assertion, Freud unswervingly retained analytic dialogue as the sole empirical basis not only for the development of metapsychology but for the validity of psychoanalytic theory as well, and this betrays consciousness of the real status of the science. Freud surely surmised that the consistent realization of the program of a "natural-scientific" or even rigorously behavioristic psychology would have had to sacrifice the *one intention* to which psychoanalysis owes its existence: the intention of enlightenment, according to which ego should develop out of id. But he did not abandon this program, he did not comprehend metapsychology as the only thing it can be in the system of reference of self-reflection: a *general interpretation of self-formative processes.*

It would be reasonable to reserve the name metapsychology for the fundamental assumptions about the pathological connection between ordinary language and interaction that can be set forth in a structural model based on the theory of language. Here we are dealing not with an empirical theory but a metatheory or, better, *metahermeneutics,* which explicates the conditions of the possibility of psychoanalytic knowledge. Metapsychology unfolds *the logic of interpretation in the analytic situation of dialogue.* In this respect it is on the same level as the methodology of the natural and cultural sciences. It, too, reflects on the transcendental framework of analytic knowledge as an objective structure of organized processes of inquiry, which here include processes of self-knowledge. However, in contrast to the logic of the natural and cultural sciences, methodology cannot exist detached from material content at the level of self-reflection. For here the structure of the cognitive situation is identical with the object of knowledge. To comprehend the transference situation as the condition of possible knowledge means at the same time comprehending a pathological situation. Because of this material content, the theoretical propositions that we should like to allocate to metapsychology are not recognized as metatheoretical propositions. This is why they are scarcely distinguished from empirically substantive interpretations of deviant self-formative processes themselves. Yet there remains a distinction on the methodological level. For like theories in the empirical sciences, no matter how different their empirical basis, general interpretations are directly accessible to empirical corroboration. In contrast, basic metahermeneutical assumptions about communicative action, language deformation, and behavioral pathology derive from subsequent reflection on the conditions of possible psychoanalytic knowledge. They can be confirmed or rejected only indirectly, with regard to the outcome of, so to speak, an entire category of processes of inquiry.

At the level of its self-reflection, the methodology of the natural sciences takes cognizance of a specific connection between language and instrumental action, comprehends it as an objective structure, and defines its transcendental role. The same holds for the methodology of the cultural sciences with regard to the connection between language and interaction. Metapsychology deals with just as fundamental a connection: the connection between *language deformation* and *behavioral pathology*. In so doing, it presupposes a theory of ordinary language having two tasks: first, to account for the intersubjective validity of symbols and the linguistic mediation of interactions on the basis of reciprocal recognition; second, to render comprehensible socialization—that is, initiation into the grammar of language games—as a process of individuation. Since, according to this theory, the structure of language determines likewise both language and conduct, motives of action are also comprehended as linguistically interpreted needs. Thus motivations are not impulses that operate from behind subjectivity but subjectively guiding, symbolically mediated, and reciprocally interrelated intentions.

It is the task of metapsychology to demonstrate this normal case as the limiting case of a motivational structure that depends simultaneously on publicly communicated and repressed and privatized need interpretations. Split-off symbols and defended-against motives unfold their force over the heads of subjects, compelling substitute-gratifications and symbolizations. In this way they distort the text of everyday language games and make themselves noticeable as disturbances of habitual interactions: as compulsion, lies, and the inability to correspond to expectations that have been made socially obligatory. In contrast to conscious motivations, the unconscious ones hereby acquire the driving, instinctual character of something that uncontrollably compels consciousness from outside it. Impulse potential, whether incorporated in social systems of collective self-preservation or suppressed instead of absorbed, clearly reveals libidinal and aggressive tendencies. This is why an instinct theory is necessary. But the latter must preserve itself from false objectivism. Even the concept of instinct that is applied to animal behavior is derived privately from the preunderstanding of a linguistically interpreted, albeit reduced human world: in short, from situations of hunger, love, and hate. The concept of instinct, when transferred back from animals to men, is still rooted in meaning structures of the life-world, no matter how elementary they may be. They are twisted and diverted intentions that have turned from conscious motives into causes and subjected communicative action to the causality of "natural" conditions. This is the causality of fate, and not of nature, because it prevails through the symbolic means of the mind. Only for this reason can it be compelled by the power of reflection.

The work of Alfred Lorenzer, which conceives the analysis of processes of instinctual dynamics as linguistic analysis in the sense of depth hermeneutics,[19] has rendered us capable of grasping more precisely the crucial mechanisms of linguistic pathology, the deformation of internal structures of language and action, and their analytic elimination. Linguistic analysis takes symptoms and deciphers unconscious motives present in them just as a meaning suppressed by censorship can be reconstructed from corrupt passages and gaps in a text. In so doing, it transcends the dimension of the subjectively intended meaning of intentional action. It steps back from language as a means of communication and penetrates the symbolic level in which subjects *deceive themselves* about themselves through language and simultaneously give themselves away in it. As soon as language is excluded from public communication by repression, it reacts with a complementary compulsion, to which consciousness and communicative action bend as to the force of a second nature. Analysis attends to causal connections that come into being in this way. The terms of this relation are usually traumatic experiences of a childhood scene on the one hand and falsifications of reality and abnormal modes of behavior, both perpetuated owing to the repetition compulsion, on the other. The original defensive process takes place in a childhood conflict situation as flight from a superior partner. It removes from public communication the linguistic interpretation of the motive of action that is being defended against. In this way the grammatical structure of public language remains intact, but portions of its semantic content are privatized. Symptom formation is a substitute for a symbol whose function has been altered. The split-off symbol has not simply lost all connection with public language. But this grammatical connection has as it were gone underground. It derives its force from confusing the logic of the public usage of language by means of semantically false identifications. At the level of the public text, the suppressed symbol is objectively understandable through rules *resulting* from contingent circumstances of the individual's life history, but not connected with it according to intersubjectively *recognized* rules. That is why the symptomatic concealment of meaning and corresponding disturbance of interaction cannot at first be understood either by others or by the subject himself. They can only become understandable at the level of an intersubjectivity that must be created between the subject as ego and the subject as id. This occurs as physician and patient together reflectively break through the barrier to communication. This is facilitated by the transference situation; for the analyst does not participate in the patient's unconscious actions. The repeated conflict returns upon the patient and, with the interpretive assistance of the analyst, can be recognized in its compulsiveness, brought into connection with repetitive scenes outside the analysis, and ultimately be traced back to the scene in which it originated. This reconstruction undoes false identifications of common linguistic expressions with their meanings in private language and renders comprehensible the hidden grammatical connection between the split-off symbol and the symptomatically distorted public text. The essentially *grammatical* connection between linguistic symbols appears as a *causal* connection between empirical events and rigidified personality traits.[20] Self-reflection dissolves this connection, bringing about the disappearance of the deformation of private language as well as the symptomatic substitute-gratification of repressed motives of action, which have now become accessible to conscious control.

The model of the three mental agencies, id, ego, and super-ego, permits a systematic presentation of the structure of language deformation and behavioral pathology. Metahermeneutic statements can be organized in terms of it. They elucidate the methodological framework in which empirically substantive interpretations of self-formative processes can be developed. These general interpretations, however, must be distinguished from the metapsychological framework. They are interpretations of early childhood development (the origins of basic motivational patterns and the parallel formation of ego functions) and serve as narrative forms that must be used in each case as an interpretive scheme for an individual's life history in order to find the original scene of his unmastered conflict. The learning mechanisms described by Freud (object choice, identification with an ideal, introjection of abandoned love objects) make understandable the dynamics of the genesis of ego structures at the level of symbolic interaction. The defense mechanisms intervene in this process when and where social norms, incorporated in the expectations of primary reference persons, confront the infantile ego with an unbearable force, requiring it to take flight from itself and objectivate itself in the id. The child's development is defined by problems whose solution determines whether and to what extent further socialization is burdened with the weight of unsolved conflicts and restricted ego functions, creating the predisposition to an accumulation of disillusionments, compulsions, and denials (as well as failure)—or whether the socialization process makes possible a relative development of ego identity.

Freud's general interpretations contain assumptions about interaction patterns of the child and his primary reference persons, about corresponding conflicts and forms of conflict mastery, and about the personality structures that result at the end of the process of early childhood socialization, with their potential for subsequent life history. These personality structures even make possible conditional predictions. Since learning processes take place in the course of communicative action, theory can take the form of a narrative that depicts the psychodynamic development of the child as a course of action: with typical role assignments, successively appearing basic conflicts, recurrent patterns of interaction, dangers, crises, solutions, triumphs, and defeats. On the other hand, conflicts are comprehended metapsychologically from the viewpoint of defense, as are personality structures in terms of the relations between ego, id, and superego. Consequently this history is represented schematically as a self-formative process that goes through various stages of self-objectivation and that has its telos in the self-consciousness of a reflectively appropriated life history.

Only the metapsychology that is presupposed allows the *systematic generalization* of what otherwise would remain pure *history*. It provides a set of categories and basic assumptions that apply to the connections between language deformation and behavioral pathology in general. The general interpretations developed in this framework are the result of numerous and repeated clinical experiences. They have been derived according to the elastic procedure of hermeneutic anticipations (*Vorgriffe*),[21] with their circular corroboration. But these experiences were already subject to the *general anticipation of the schema of disturbed self-formative processes*. In addition, an interpretation, once it claims the status of "generality," is removed from the hermeneutic procedure of continually correcting one's preunderstanding on the basis of the text. In contrast to the hermeneutic anticipation of the philologist, general interpretation is "fixed" and, like a general theory, must prove itself through predictions deduced from it. If psychoanalysis offers a narrative background against which interrupted self-formative processes can be filled out and become a complete history, the predictions that have been obtained with its help serve the reconstruction of the past. But they, too, are hypotheses that can prove wrong.

A general interpretation defines self-formative processes as lawlike successions of states of a system: Each succession varies in accordance with its initial conditions. Therefore the relevant variables of developmental history can be analyzed in their dependence on the system as a whole. However, the objective-intentional structure of life history, which is accessible only through self-reflection, is not functionalistic in the normal sense of this term. The elementary events are processes in a drama, they do not appear within the instrumentalist viewpoint of the purposive-rational organization of means or of adaptive behavior. The functional structure is interpreted in accordance with a dramatic model. That is, the elementary processes appear as parts of a structure of interactions through which a "meaning" is realized. We cannot equate this meaning with ends that are realized through means, on the model of the craftsman. What is at issue is not a category of meaning that is taken from the behavioral system of instrumental action, such as the maintenance of the state of a system under changing external conditions. It is a question, rather, of a meaning that, even if it is not intended as such, takes form in the course of communicative action and articulates itself reflectively as the experience of life history. This is the way in which "meaning" discloses itself in the course of a drama. But in our own self-formative process, we are at once both actor and critic. In the final instance, the meaning of the process itself must be capable of becoming part of our consciousness in a critical manner, entangled as we are in the drama of life history. The subject must be able to relate his own history and have comprehended the inhibitions that blocked the path of self-reflection. For the final state of a self-formative process is attained only if the subject remembers its identifications and alienations, the objectivations forced upon it and the reflections it arrived at, as the path upon which it constituted itself.

Only the *metapsychologically founded and systematically generalized history* of infantile development with its typical developmental variants puts the physician in the position of so combining the fragmentary information obtained in analytic dialogue that he can reconstruct the gaps of memory and hypothetically anticipate the experience of reflection of which the patient is at first incapable. He makes interpretive suggestions for a story that the patient cannot tell. Yet they can be verified in fact only if the patient adopts them and tells his own story with their aid. The interpretation of the case is corroborated only by the successful continuation of an interrupted self-formative process.

General interpretations occupy a singular position between the inquiring subject and the object domain being investigated. Whereas in other areas theories contain statements about an object domain to which they remain external *as statements*, the validity of general interpretations depends directly on statements about the object domain being applied by the "objects," that is the persons concerned, to *themselves*. Information in the empirical sciences usually has meaning only for participants in the process of inquiry and, subsequently, for those who use this information. In both cases, the validity of information is measured only by the standards of cogency and empirical accuracy. This information represents cognitions that have been tested on objects through application to reality; but it is valid only for subjects. To the contrary, analytic insights possess validity for the analyst only after they have been accepted as knowledge by the analysand himself. For the empirical accuracy of general interpretations depends not on controlled observation and subsequent communication among investigators but rather on the accomplishment of self-reflection and subsequent communication between the investigator and his "object."

It may be objected that, just as with general theories, the empirical validity of general interpretations is determined by repeated applications to real initial conditions and that, once demonstrated, it is binding for all subjects who have any access to knowledge. Although correct in its way, this formulation conceals the specific difference between general theories and general interpretations. In the case of testing theories through observation (that is in the behavioral system of instrumental action), the application of assumptions to reality is a matter for the inquiring subject. In the case of testing general interpretations through self-reflection (that is in the framework of communication between physician and patient), this application becomes *self-application* by the object of inquiry, who participates in the process of inquiry. The process of inquiry can lead to valid information only via a transformation in the patient's self-inquiry. When valid, theories hold for all who can adopt the position of the inquiring subject. When valid, general interpretations hold for the inquiring subject and all who can adopt its position only to the degree that those who are made the object of individual interpretations *know and recognize themselves* in these interpretations. The subject cannot obtain knowledge of the object unless it becomes knowledge for the object—and unless the latter thereby emancipates itself by becoming a subject.

This is not as odd as it may sound. Every accurate interpretation, including those in the cultural sciences, is possible only in a language *common* to the interpreter and his object, owing to the fact that interpretation restores an intersubjectivity of mutual understanding that had been disturbed. Therefore it must hold likewise for both subject and object. But this function of thought has consequences for general interpretations of self-formative processes that do not occur in the case of interpretations in the cultural sciences. For general interpretations share with general theories the additional claim of allowing causal explanations and conditional predictions. In distinction from the strict empirical sciences, however, psychoanalysis cannot make good this claim on the basis of a methodologically clear separation of the object domain from the level of theoretical statements. This has implications (1) for the construction of the language of interpretation, (2) for the conditions of empirical verification, and (3) for the logic of explanation itself.

Like all interpretations, (1) general interpretations also remain rooted in the dimension of ordinary language. Although they are systematically generalized narratives, they remain historical. Historical representation makes use of narrative statements. They are narrative because they represent events as elements of histories.[22] We explain an event narratively if we show how a subject is involved in a history. In every history, individual names appear, because a history is always concerned with changes in the state of a subject or of a group of subjects who consider themselves as belonging together. The unity of the history is provided by the identity of the horizon of expectations that can be ascribed to them. The narrative tells of the influence of subjectively experienced events that change the state of the subject or group of subjects by intervening in a life-world and attaining significance for acting subjects. In such histories, the subjects must be able to understand both themselves and their world. The historical significance of events always refers implicitly to the meaning structure of a life history unified by ego identity or of a collective history defined by group identity. That is why narrative representation is tied to ordinary language. For only the peculiar reflexivity of ordinary language makes possible communicating what is individual in inevitably general expressions.[23]

By representing an individuated temporal structure, every history is a particular history. Every historical representation implies the claim of *uniqueness*. A *general* interpretation, on the contrary, must break this spell of the historical without departing from the level of narrative representation. It has the form of a narrative, because it is to aid subjects in reconstructing their own life history in narrative form. But it can serve as the background of many such narrations only because it does not hold merely for an individual case. It is a *systematically generalized history*, because it provides a scheme for many histories with foreseeable alternative courses. Yet, at the same time, each of these histories must then be able to appear with the claim of being the autobiographical narrative of something individuated. How is such a generalization possible? In every history, no matter how contingent, there is something general, for someone else can find something exemplary in it. Histories are understood as examples in direct proportion to the typicality of their content. Here the concept of type designates a quality of translatability: a history or story is typical in a given situation and for a specific public, if the "action" can be easily taken out of its context and transferred to other life situations that are just as individuated. We can apply the "typical" case to our own. It is we ourselves who undertake the application, abstract the comparable from the differences, and concretize the derived model under the specific life circumstances of our own case.

So the physician, too, proceeds when reconstructing the life history of a patient on the basis of given material. So the patient proceeds himself when, on the basis of the scheme offered him, he recounts his life history even in its previously forgotten phases. Both physician and patient orient themselves not toward an *example* but, indeed; toward a *scheme*. In a general interpretation, the individual features of an example are missing; the step of abstraction has already been taken. Physician and patient have only to take the further step of application. What characterizes systematic generalization, therefore, is that in hermeneutic experiences, which are relatively a priori to application, the abstraction from many typical histories with regard to many individual cases has already taken place. A general interpretation contains no names of individuals but only anonymous roles. It contains no contingent circumstances, but recurring configurations and patterns of action. It contains no idiomatic use of language, but only a standardized vocabulary. It does not represent a typical process, but describes in type-concepts the scheme of an action with conditional variants. This is how Freud presents the Oedipal conflict and its solutions: by means of structural concepts such as ego, id, and super-ego (derived from the experience of analytic dialogue); by means of roles, persons, and patterns of interaction (arising from the structure of the family); and by means of mechanisms of action and communication (such as object-choice, identification, and internalization). The terminological use of ordinary language is not just an attribute of an accidental stage in the development of psychoanalysis. Rather, all attempts to provide metapsychology with a more rigorous form have failed, because the conditions of the application of general interpretations exclude the formalization of ordinary language. For the terms used in it serve the structuring of narratives. It is their presence in the patient's ordinary language which the analyst and the patient make use of in completing an analytic narrative scheme by making it into a history. By putting individual names in the place of anonymous roles and filling out interaction patterns as experienced scenes, they develop ad hoc a new language, in which the language of general interpretation is brought into accord with the patient's own language.

This step reveals application to be a translation. This remains concealed as long as, owing to the common social background of bourgeois origins and college education, the terminological ordinary language of the theory meets the patient's language halfway. The problem of translation becomes explicit as such when the linguistic distance increases on account of social distance. Freud is aware of this. This is shown in his discussion of the possibility that in the future psychoanalysis might be propagated on a mass basis:

> We shall then be faced by the task of adapting our technique to the new conditions. I have no doubt that the validity of our psychological assumptions will make its impression on the uneducated too, but we shall need to look for the simplest and most easily intelligible ways of expressing our theoretical doctrines.[24]

The problems of application that arise with theories in the empirical sciences only seem to be analogous. In the application of lawlike hypotheses to initial conditions, it is true that the singular events expressed in existential statements ("this stone") have to be brought into relation to the universal expressions of theoretical statements. But this subsumption is unproblematic, since the singular events only come into consideration insofar as they satisfy the criteria of general predicates ("this stone" is considered, for example, as "mass"). Thus it suffices to establish whether the singular event corresponds to the operational definition through which the theoretical expression is determined. This operational application necessarily proceeds within the framework of instrumental action. Consequently it does not suffice for the application of the theoretical expressions of general interpretations. The material to which the latter are applied consists not of singular events but of symbolic expressions of a fragmentary life history, that is of components of a structure that is individuated in a specific way. In this case it depends on the hermeneutic understanding of the person providing the material whether an element of his life history is adequately interpreted by a suggested theoretical expression. This hermeneutic application necessarily proceeds in the framework of communication in ordinary language. It does not do the same job as operational application. In the latter case, the deciding factor is whether given empirical conditions may count as a case for the application of the theory, leaving untouched the theoretical deductions as such. In contrast, hermeneutic application is concerned with *completing* the narrative background of a general interpretation by creating a narrative, that is the narrative presentation of an individual history. The conditions of application define a *realization* of the interpretation, which was precluded on the level of general interpretation itself. Although theoretical deductions are mediated by communication with the physician, they must be made by the patient himself.

This is the context of (2) the methodological peculiarity that general interpretations do not obey the same criteria of refutation as general theories. If a conditional prediction deduced from a lawlike hypothesis and initial conditions is falsified, then the hypothesis may be considered refuted. A general interpretation can be tested analogously if we derive a construction from one of its implications and the communications of a patient. We can give this construction the form of a conditional prediction. If it is correct, the patient will be moved to produce certain memories, reflect on a specific portion of forgotten life history, and overcome disturbances of both communication and behavior. But here the method of falsification is not the same as for general theories. For if the patient rejects a construction, the interpretation from which it has been derived cannot yet be considered refuted at all. For psychoanalytic assumptions refer to conditions in which the very experience in which they must corroborate themselves is suspended: the experience of reflection is the only criterion for the corroboration or failure of hypotheses. If it does not come about, there is still an alternative: either the interpretation is false (that is, the theory or its application to a given case) or, to the contrary, the resistances, which have been correctly diagnosed, are too strong. The criterion in virtue of which false constructions fail does not coincide with either controlled observation or communicative experience. The interpretation of a case is corroborated only by the successful *continuation of a self-formative process*, that is by the completion of self-reflection, and not in any unmistakable way by what the patient says or how he *behaves*. Here success and failure cannot be intersubjectively established, as is possible in the framework of instrumental action or that of communicative action, each in its way. Even the disappearance of symptoms does not allow a compelling conclusion. For they may have been replaced by other symptoms that at first are inaccessible to observation or the experience of interaction. For the symptom, too, is bound in principle to the meaning that it has *for* the subject engaged in defense. It is incorporated in the structure of self-objectivation and self-reflection and has no falsifying or verifying power independent of it. Freud is conscious of this methodological difficulty. He knows that the "no" of the analysand rejecting a suggested construction is ambiguous:

> In some rare cases it turns out to be the expression of a legitimate dissent. Far more frequently it expresses a resistance which may have been evoked by the subject-matter of the construction that has been put forward but which may just as easily have arisen from some other factor in the complex analytic situation. Thus, a patient's "No" is no evidence of the correctness of a construction, though it is perfectly compatible with it. Since every such construction is an incomplete one, since it covers only a small fragment of the forgotten events, we are free to suppose that the patient is not in fact disputing what has been said to him but is basing his contradiction upon the part that has not yet been uncovered. As a rule he will not give his assent until he has learnt the whole truth—which often covers a very great deal of ground. So that the only safe interpretation of his "No" is that it points to incompleteness; there can be no doubt that the construction has not told him everything.
>
> It appears, therefore, that the direct utterances of the patient after he has been offered a construction afford very little evidence upon the question whether we have been right or wrong. It is of all the greater interest that there are indirect forms of confirmation which are in every respect trustworthy.[25]

Freud is thinking of the confirming associations of the dreamer, who brings up previously forgotten text fragments or produces new dreams. On the other hand, doubt then arises whether the dreams have not been influenced by suggestion on the part of the physician:

> If a dream brings up situations that can be interpreted as referring to scenes from the dreamer's past, it seems especially important to ask whether the physician's influence can also play a part in such contents of the dream as these. And this question is most urgent of all in the case of what are called "corroborative" dreams, dreams which, as it were, "tag along behind" the analysis. With some patients these are the only dreams that one obtains. Such patients reproduce the forgotten experiences of their childhood only after one has constructed them from their symptoms, associations and other signs and has propounded these constructions to them. Then follow the corroborative dreams, concerning which, however, the doubt arises whether they may not be entirely without evidential value, since they may have been imagined in compliance with the physician's words instead of having been brought to light from the dreamer's unconscious. This ambiguous position cannot be escaped in the analysis, since with these patients unless one interprets, constructs and propounds, one never obtains access to what is repressed in them.[26]

Freud is convinced that the physician's suggestion finds its limit in the mechanism of dream formation, which cannot be influenced. Still, the analytic situation attributes a special significance not only to the patient's "No" but to his "Yes" as well. For even the patient's confirmations cannot be taken at face value. Some critics charge that the analyst merely induces a modification of a previous interpretation of life history by talking the patient into a new terminology.[27] Freud counters that the patient's confirmation does not have a different implication for the verification of a construction than for its denial:

> It is true that we do not accept the "No" of a person

under analysis at its face value; but neither do we allow his "Yes" to pass. There is no justification for accusing us of invariably twisting his remarks into a confirmation. In reality things are not so simple and we do not make it so easy for ourselves to come to a conclusion.

A plain "Yes" from a patient is by no means unambiguous. It can indeed signify that he recognizes the correctness of the construction that has been presented to him; but it can also be meaningless, or can even deserve to be described as "hypocritical," since it may be convenient for his resistance to make use of an assent in such circumstances in order to prolong the concealment of a truth that has not been discovered. The "Yes" has no value unless it is followed by indirect confirmations, unless the patient, immediately after his "Yes," produces new memories which complete and extend the construction. Only in such an event do we consider that the "Yes" has dealt completely with the subject under discussion.[28]

Even indirect confirmation by association only has a relative value when considered in isolation. Freud is right in insisting that only the further course of analysis can decide a construction's usefulness or lack of it. Only the context of the self-formative process as a whole has confirming and falsifying power.[29]

As with the other forms of knowledge, the testing of hypotheses in the case of general interpretations can follow only those rules that are appropriate to the test situation. Only they guarantee the rigorous objectivity of validity. Whoever demands, to the contrary, that general interpretations be treated like the philological interpretation of texts or like general theories and subjected to externally imposed standards, whether of a functioning language game or of controlled observation, places himself from the very beginning outside the dimension of self-reflection, which is the only context in which psychoanalytic statements can have meaning.

A final peculiarity of the logic of general interpretations results (3) from the combination of hermeneutic understanding with causal explanation: understanding itself obtains explanatory power. The fact that, with regard to symptoms, constructions can assume the form of explanatory hypotheses, shows their affinity with the causal-analytic method. At the same time, the fact that a construction is itself an interpretation and that the standard of verification is the patient's act of recollection and agreement demonstrates its difference from the causal-analytic procedure and a certain kinship with the hermeneutic-interpretive method. Freud takes up this question in a medical form by inquiring whether psychoanalysis may seriously be called a causal therapy. His answer is conflicting; the question itself seems to be wrongly posed:

> In so far as analytic therapy does not make it its first
> task to remove the symptoms, it is behaving like a
> causal therapy. In another respect, you may say, it is
> not. For we long ago traced the causal chain back
> through the repressions to the instinctual dispositions,
> their relative intensities in the constitution and the
> deviations in the course of their development. Supposing,
> now, that it was possible, by some chemical means,
> perhaps, to interfere in this mechanism, to increase or
> diminish the quantity of libido present at a given time or
> to strengthen one instinct at the cost of another—this
> then would be a causal therapy in the true sense of the
> word, for which our analysis would have carried out the
> indispensable preliminary work of reconnaissance. At
> present, as you know, there is no question of any such
> method of influencing libidinal processes; with our
> psychical therapy we attack at a different point in the
> combination—not exactly at what we know are the roots
> of the phenomena, but nevertheless far enough away
> from the symptoms, at a point which has been made
> accessible to us by some very remarkable circumstances.[30]

The comparison of psychoanalysis with biochemical

analysis shows that its hypotheses do not extend to causal connections between observable empirical events. For if they did, then scientific information would put us in a position, as in biochemistry, to manipulatively transform a given situation. Psychoanalysis does not grant us a power of technical control over the sick psyche comparable to that of biochemistry over a sick organism. And yet it achieves more than a mere treatment of symptoms, because it certainly does grasp causal connections, although not at the level of physical events—at a point "which has been made accessible to us by some very remarkable circumstances." This is precisely the point where language and behavior are pathologically deformed by the causality of split-off symbols and repressed motives. Following Hegel we can call this the causality of fate, in contrast to the causality of nature. For the causal connection between the original scene, defense, and symptom is not anchored in the invariance of nature according to natural laws but only in the spontaneously generated invariance of life history, represented by the repetition compulsion, which can nevertheless be dissolved by the power of reflection.

The hypotheses we derive from general interpretations do not, like general theories, refer to nature, but rather to the sphere that has become second nature through self-objectivation: the "unconscious." This term designates the class of all motivational compulsions that have become independent of their context, that proceed from need dispositions that are not sanctioned by society, and that are demonstrable in the causal connection between the situation of original denial on the one hand and abnormal modes of speech and behavior on the other. The importance of causal motivations of action having this origin is a measure of the disturbance and deviance of the self-formative process. In technical control over nature we get nature to work for us through our knowledge of causal connections. Analytic insight, however, affects the causality of the unconscious as such. Psychoanalytic therapy is not based, like somatic medicine, which is "causal" in the narrower sense, on making use of known causal connections. Rather, it owes its efficacy to overcoming causal connections themselves. Metapsychology does, indeed, contain assumptions about the mechanisms of defense, the splitting-off of symbols, the suppression of motives, and about the complementary mode of operation of self-reflection: assumptions that thus "explain" the origin and elimination of the causality of fate. The analogue to the lawlike hypotheses of general theories would thus be these metapsychological basic assumptions about linguistic structure and action. But they are elaborated on the metatheoretical level and therefore do not have the status of normal lawlike hypotheses.

The concept of a causality of the unconscious also renders comprehensible the therapeutic effect of "analysis," a word in which critique as knowledge and critique as transformation are not accidentally combined. The immediate practical consequences of critique are obtained by causal analysis only because the *empirical* structure that it penetrates is at the same time an *intentional* structure that can be reconstructed and understood according to grammatical rules. We can at first view a construction offered to the patient by the physician as an explanatory hypothesis derived from a general interpretation and supplementary conditions. For the assumed causal connection exists between a past conflict situation and compulsively repeated reactions in the present (symptoms). Substantively, however, the hypothesis refers to a meaning structure determined by the conflict, the defense against the wish that sets off the conflict, the splitting-off of the wish symbol, the substitute gratification of the censored wish, symptom formation, and secondary defense. A causal connection is formulated hypothetically as a hermeneutically understandable meaning structure. This formulation satisfies simultaneously the conditions of a causal hypothesis and of an interpretation (with regard to a text distorted by symptoms). Depth-hermeneutic understanding takes over the function of explanation. It proves its explanatory power in self-reflection, in which an objectivation that is both understood and explained is also overcome. This is the critical accomplishment of what Hegel had called comprehending (*Begreifen*).

In its logical form, however, explanatory understanding differs in one decisive way from explanation rigorously formulated in terms of the empirical sciences. Both of them have recourse to causal statements that can be derived from universal propositions by means of supplementary conditions: that is, from derivative interpretations (conditional variants) or lawlike hypotheses. Now the content of theoretical propositions remains unaffected by operational application to reality. In this case we can base explanations on context-free laws. In the case of hermeneutic application, however, theoretical propositions are translated into the narrative presentation of an individual history in such a way that a causal statement does not come into being without this context. General interpretations can abstractly assert their claim to universal validity because their derivatives are additionally determined by context. Narrative explanations differ from strictly deductive ones in that the events or states of which they assert a causal relation is further defined by their application. Therefore general interpretations do not make possible context-free explanations.[31]

CHAPTER TWELVE

Psychoanalysis and Social Theory: *Nietzsche's Reduction of Cognitive Interests*

Freud conceived of sociology as applied psychology.[1] In his writings on the theory of civilization (*Kultur*)[2] he tried his hand at sociology, led to the area of social theory by problems of psychoanalysis.

The analyst makes use of a preliminary conception of normality and deviance when he regards certain disturbances of communication, behavior, and organic function as "symptoms." But this conception is obviously culturally determined and cannot be defined in terms of a clearly established matter of fact: "We have seen that it is not scientifically feasible to draw a line of demarcation between what is psychically normal and abnormal; so that that distinction, in spite of its practical importance, possesses only a conventional value."[3] If, however, what counts as a normal or deviant self-formative process can be defined only in accordance with the institutional framework of a society, then this society as a whole could itself be in a pathological state when compared with other cultures, even though it sets the standard of normality for the individual cases it subsumes:

> [I]n an individual neurosis we take as our starting point the contrast that distinguishes the patient from his environment, which is assumed to be "normal." For a group all of whose members are affected by one and the same disorder no such background could exist; it would have to be found elsewhere.[4]

What Freud calls the diagnosis of communal neuroses requires an investigation that goes beyond the criteria of a given institutional framework and takes into account the history of the cultural evolution of the human species, the "process of civilization."

274

This evolutionary perspective is suggested as well by another consideration arising from psychoanalysis.

The central fact of defense against undesirable instinctual impulses points to a fundamental conflict between functions of self-preservation, which must be secured under the constraint of external nature through the collective effort of societal individuals, and the transcending potential of internal nature of libidinal and aggressive needs. Furthermore the superego, constructed on the basis of substitutive identifications with the expectations of primary reference persons, ensures that there is no immediate confrontation between an ego governed by wishes and the reality of external nature. The reality which the ego comes up against and which makes the instinctual impulses leading to conflict appear as a source of danger is the system of self-preservation, that is, society, whose institutional demands upon the emergent individual are represented by the parents. Consequently, the external authority whose intrapsychic extension is the superego has an *economic* foundation:

> The motive of human society is in the last resort an
> economic one; since it does not possess enough provisions
> to keep its members alive unless they work, it must
> restrict the number of its members and divert their
> energies from sexual activity to work. It is faced, in
> short, by the eternal, primaeval exigencies of life,
> which are with us to this day.[5]

But if the basic conflict is defined by the conditions of material labor and economic scarcity, i.e., the shortage of goods, then the renunciations it imposes are a historically variable factor. The pressure of reality and the corresponding degree of societal repression then depend on the degree of technical control over natural forces as well as on the organization of their exploitation and the distribution of the goods produced. The more the power of technical control is extended and the pressure of reality decreased, the weaker becomes the prohibition of instincts compelled by the system of self-preservation: The organization of the ego becomes correspondingly stronger, along with the capacity to master denial rationally. This suggests a comparison of the world-historical process of social organization with the socialization process of the individual. As long as the pressure of reality is over-powering and ego organization is weak, so that instinctual re-nunciation can only be brought about by the forces of affect, the species finds collective solutions for the problem of defense, which resemble neurotic solutions at the individual level. The same configurations that drive the individual to neurosis move society to establish institutions. What characterizes institutions is at the same time what constitutes their similarity with patho-logical forms. Like the repetition compulsion from within, insti-tutional compulsion from without brings about a relatively rigid reproduction of uniform behavior that is removed from criticism:

> Knowledge of the neurotic afflictions of individuals
> has well served the understanding of the major social
> institutions, for the neuroses ultimately reveal
> themselves as attempts to solve on an individual basis
> the problems of wish compensation that ought to be
> solved socially by institutions.[6]

This also provides a perspective for the deciphering of cultural tradition. In tradition, the projective contents of wish fantasies expressing defended-against intentions have been deposited. They can be viewed as sublimations that represent suspended gratifi-cations and guarantee publicly sanctioned compensation for nec-essary cultural renunciation. "All of the history of civilization shows only the paths men have taken to bind their unsatisfied wishes under the varying conditions of fulfillment and denial by reality, which are changed by technical progress."[7]

This is the psychoanalytic key to a social theory that con-verges in a surprising manner with Marx's reconstruction of the history of the species while in another regard advancing specif-ically new perspectives. Freud comprehends "civilization," as Marx does society, as the means by which the human species elevates itself above animal conditions of existence. It is a sys-tem of self-preservation that serves two functions in particular: self-assertion against nature and the organization of men's interrelations.[8] Like Marx, although in different terms, Freud distinguishes the forces of production, which indicate the level of technical control over natural processes, from the relations of production:

> Human civilization, by which I mean all those respects in which human life has raised itself above its animal status and differs from the life of beasts—and I scorn to distinguish between culture and civilization—presents, as we know, two aspects to the observer. It includes on the one hand all the knowledge and capacity that men have acquired in order to control the forces of nature and extract its wealth for the satisfaction of human needs, and, on the other hand, all the regulations necessary in order to adjust the relations of men to one another and especially the distribution of the available wealth. The two trends of civilization are not independent of each other: firstly, because the mutual relations of men are profoundly influenced by the amount of instinctual satisfaction which the existing wealth makes possible; secondly, because an individual man can himself come to function as wealth in relation to another one, in so far as the other person makes use of his capacity for work, or chooses him as a sexual object; and thirdly, moreover, because every individual is virtually an enemy of civilization, though civilization is supposed to be an object of universal human interest.[9]

The last assertion, that everyone is virtually an enemy of civilization, already points up the difference between Freud and Marx. Marx conceives the institutional framework as an ordering of interests that are immediate functions of the system of social labor according to the relation of social rewards and imposed obligations. Institutions derive their force from perpetuating a distribution of rewards and obligations that is rooted in force and distorted according to class structure. Freud, on the contrary, conceives the institutional framework in connection with the repression of instinctual impulses. In the system of self-preservation this repression must be universally imposed, independent of a class-specific distribution of goods and misfortune (as long as an economy of scarcity stamps every satisfaction with the compulsory character of a reward):

> It is remarkable that, little as men are able to exist in isolation, they should nevertheless feel as a heavy burden the sacrifices which civilization expects of them in order to make a communal life possible. Thus civilization has to be defended against the individual, and its regulations, institutions and commands are directed to that task. They aim not only at effecting a certain distribution of wealth but at maintaining that distribution; indeed, they have to protect everything that contributes to the conquest of nature and the production of wealth against men's hostile impulses. Human creations are easily destroyed, and science and technology, which have built them up, can also be used for their annihilation.[10]

Freud defines institutions in a different context than that of instrumental action. What requires ordering is not labor but the compulsion of *socially divided* labor:

> . . . With the recognition that every civilization rests on a compulsion to work and a renunciation of instinct and therefore inevitably provokes opposition from those affected by these demands, it has become clear that civilization cannot consist principally or solely in wealth itself and the means of acquiring it and the arrangements for its distribution; for these things are threatened by the rebelliousness and destructive mania of the participants in civilization. Alongside of wealth we now come upon the means by which civilization can be defended—measures of coercion and other measures that are intended to reconcile men to it and to recompense them for their sacrifices. These latter may be described as the mental assets of civilization.[11]

The institutional framework of the system of social labor serves the organization of labor in co-operation and the division of labor and in the distribution of goods, that is in *embedding purposive-rational action in an interaction structure*. Although this web of communicative action also serves functional needs of the system of social labor, at the same time it must be institutionally stabilized. For, under the pressure of reality, not all interpreted needs find gratification, and socially transcendent motives of action cannot all be defended against with consciousness, but only with the aid of affective forces. Thus the institutional framework consists of compulsory norms, which not only sanction linguistically interpreted needs but also redirect, transform, and suppress them.

The power of social norms is based on a defense which enforces substitute-gratifications and produces symptoms as long as it is a result of unconscious mechanisms and not of conscious control. These norms obtain their institutionally fixed and opaque character precisely from the collective neurotic, hidden compulsion that replaces the manifest compulsion of open sanctions. At the same time, a part of the substitute-gratifications can be refashioned into legitimations for prevailing norms. Collective fantasies compensate for the renunciations imposed by civilization. Since they are not private, but instead, on the level of public communication itself, lead a split-off existence that is removed from criticism, they are elaborated into interpretations of the world and taken into service as rationalizations of authority. Freud calls this the "mental assets of civilization": religious worldviews and rites, ideals and value systems, styles and products of art, the world of projective formations and objective appearances—in short, "illusions."

Nevertheless, Freud is not so careless as to reduce the cultural superstructure to pathological phenomena. An illusion that has taken objective form at the level of cultural tradition, such as the Judaeo-Christian religion, is not a delusion:

> What is characteristic of illusions is that they are
> derived from human wishes. In this respect they come
> near to psychiatric delusions. But they differ from them,
> too, apart from the more complicated structure of

delusions. In the case of delusions, we emphasize as essential their being in contradiction with reality. Illusions need not necessarily be false—that is to say, unrealizable or in contradiction to reality.[12]

For the individual, the institutional framework of the established society is an immovable reality. Wishes that are incompatible with this reality cannot be realized. Therefore they retain the character of fantasies, after being transformed into symptoms by the defensive process and shunted into the path of substitute-gratification. But for the species as a whole, the boundaries of reality are in fact movable. The degree of socially necessary repression can be measured by the variable extent of the power of technical control over natural processes. With the development of technology, the institutional framework, which regulates the distribution of obligations and rewards and stabilizes a power structure that maintains cultural renunciation, can be loosened. Increasingly, parts of cultural tradition that at first have only projective content can be changed into reality. That is, virtual gratification can be transposed into institutionally recognized gratification. "Illusions" are not merely false consciousness. Like what Marx called ideology, they too harbor utopia. If technical progress opens up the objective possibility of reducing socially necessary repression below the level of institutionally demanded repression, this utopian content can be freed from its fusion with the delusory, ideological components of culture that have been fashioned into legitimations of authority and be converted into a critique of power structures that have become historically obsolete.

It is in this context that class struggle has its place. The system of power maintains general repressions, which are imposed likewise on all members of society. As long as it is administered by a social class, then class-specific privations and denials are linked to the general ones. The traditions that legitimate authority also must compensate the mass of the population for these specific renunciations that go beyond the general privations. That is why the oppressed masses are the first to be incapable of integration by legitimations that have become fragile. It is they who first critically turn the utopian content of tradition against the established civilization:

If we turn to those restrictions that apply only to certain classes of society, we meet with a state of things which is flagrant and which has always been recognized. It is to be expected that these underprivileged classes will envy the favoured ones their privileges and will do all they can to free themselves from their own surplus of privation. Where this is not possible, a permanent measure of discontent will persist within the culture concerned and this can lead to dangerous revolts. If, however, a culture has not got beyond a point at which the satisfaction of one portion of its participants depends upon the suppression of another, and perhaps larger, portion—and this is the case in all present-day cultures—it is understandable that the suppressed people should develop an intense hostility towards a culture whose existence they make possible by their work, but in whose wealth they have too small a share. . . . It goes without saying that a civilization which leaves so large a number of its participants unsatisfied and drives them into revolt neither has nor deserves the prospect of a lasting existence.[13]

Marx had developed the idea of the self-constitution of the human species in natural history in two dimensions: as a process of self-production, which is impelled forward by the productive activity of those who perform social labor and stored in the forces of production, and as a self-formative process, which is impelled forward by the critical-revolutionary activity of classes and which is stored in experiences of reflection. On the other hand, Marx was not able to provide an account of the status of the science that, as critique, was supposed to reconstruct the self-constitution of the species; for his materialist concept of the synthesis of man and nature remained restricted to the categorial framework of instrumental action.[14] This framework could account for productive knowledge but not reflective knowledge. Nor was the model of productive activity suited for the reconstruction of power and ideology. In contrast, Freud has acquired in metapsychology a framework for distorted communicative action that allows the conceptualization of the origins of institutions and the role and function of illusions, that is of power and ideology. Freud's theory can represent a structure that Marx did not fathom.

Freud comprehends institutions as a power that has exchanged acute external force for the permanent internal compulsion of distorted and self-limiting communication. Correspondingly he understands cultural tradition as the collective unconscious, censored in varying measure and turned outwards, where motives that have been split off from communication are driven incessantly about and are directed by the excluded symbols into channels of substitute gratification. These motives, rather than external danger and immediate sanction, are now the forces that hold sway over consciousness by legitimating power. These are the same forces from which ideologically imprisoned consciousness can free itself through self-reflection when a new potential for the mastery of nature makes old legitimations lack credibility.

Marx was not able to see that power and ideology are distorted communication, because he made the assumption that men distinguished themselves from animals when they began to produce their means of subsistence. Marx was convinced that at one time the human species elevated itself above animal conditions of existence by transcending the limits of animal intelligence and being able to transform adaptive behavior into instrumental action. Thus what interests him as the natural basis of history is the physical organization specific to the human species under the category of possible labor: the tool-making animal. Freud's focus, in contrast, was not the system of social labor but the family. He made the assumption that men distinguished themselves from animals when they succeeded in inventing an agency of socialization for their biologically endangered offspring subject to extended childhood dependency. Freud was convinced that at one time the human species elevated itself above animal conditions of existence by transcending the limits of animal society and being able to transform instinct-governed behavior into communicative action. Thus what interests him as the natural basis of history is the physical organization specific to the human species under the category of surplus impulses and their canalization: the drive-inhibited and at the same time fantasizing animal. The two-stage development of human sexuality, which is interrupted by a latency period owing to Oedipal repression, and the role of aggression in the establishment of the super-ego make man's basic problem not the organization of labor but the evolution of institutions that permanently solve the conflict between surplus impulses and the constraint of reality. Hence Freud does not investigate primarily those ego functions that develop on the cognitive level within the framework of instrumental action. He concentrates on the origins of the motivational foundation of communicative action. What interests him is the destiny of the primary impulse potentials in the course of the growing child's interaction with an environment, determined by his family structure, on which he remains dependent during a long period of upbringing.

But if the natural basis of the human species is essentially determined by surplus impulses and extended childhood dependency, and if the emergence of institutions from structures of distorted communication can be comprehended on this basis, then power and ideology acquire a different and more substantial role than they do for Marx. In this way the logic of the movement of reflection directed against power and ideology, which derives its thrust from developments in the system of social labor (technology and science), becomes graspable. It is the logic of trial and error, but transposed to the level of world history. Within the premises of Freudian theory, the natural basis neither offers a promise that the development of the productive forces will ever create the objective possibility for completely freeing the institutional framework from repressiveness, nor can it discourage such a hope. Freud clearly set out the direction of the history of the species, determined simultaneously by a process of self-production under categories of work and a self-formative process under conditions of distorted communication. At every stage, development of the forces of production produces the objective possibility of mitigating the force of the institutional framework and "(replacing) the affective basis of (man's) obedience to civilization by a rational one."[15] Every step on the road to realizing an idea beset by the contradiction of violently distorted communication is marked by a transformation of the institutional framework and the destruction of an ideology. The goal is "providing a rational basis for the precepts of civilization": in other words, an organization of social relations according to the principle that the validity of every norm of political consequence be made dependent on a consensus arrived at in communication free from domination.[16] But Freud insists that every effort to incorporate this idea into action and to promote enlightenment in a critical-revolutionary way be strictly committed to the determinate negation of unequivocally identifiable suffering—and committed equally to the practical-hypothetical consciousness of carrying out an experiment that can *fail.*

The ideas of the Enlightenment stem from the store of historically transmitted illusions. Hence we must comprehend the actions of the Enlightenment as the attempt to test the limit of the realizability of the utopian content of cultural tradition under given conditions. But at the level of practical reason the logic of trial and error requires restrictions that can be dispensed with by the logic of control in the empirical sciences. In a test that is to try out the conditions of a possible "reduction of suffering," the risk of increased suffering may not be made part of the design of the experiment itself. It is this consideration that led to Freud's cautiously expressed reserve with regard to the "great experiment in civilization that is now in progress in the vast country that stretches between Europe and Asia."[17] Cognitive progress in the dimensions of both the sciences and critique justifies the hope that "it is possible for scientific work to gain some knowledge about the reality of the world, by means of which we can increase our power and in accordance with which we can arrange our life." It is this rational hope that fundamentally divides the intention of enlightenment from dogmatic traditions, doubtful as this may presently seem: ". . . My illusions are not, like religious ones, incapable of correction. They have not the character of a delusion. If experience should show . . . that we have been mistaken, we will give up our expectations. Take my attempt for what it is . . ."—that is, as one that *can* be refuted in practice. This caution does not inhibit critical-revolutionary activity. But it does prohibit the totalitarian *certainty* that the idea which this activity justly takes as its orientation can be realized under all circumstances. Freud assigns power and ideology too profound a role to have been able to promise assurance instead of a logic of justified hope and controlled experiment.[18]

This is the merit of a theory that incorporates into the natural basis of history the heritage of natural history, however flexible, consisting in an impulse potential that is both libidinal and aggressive and that exceeds the opportunities for gratification. Paradoxically, however, the same viewpoint can err into an objectivistic construction of history in which Freud reverts to a lower stage of reflection than that attained by Marx. This impedes the development of the basic insight of psychoanalysis at the level of social theory.[19] Since Marx tied the self-constitution of the species to the mechanism of social labor, he was never tempted to sever the dynamic of developmental history from the activity of the species as a subject and conceive it in categories of natural evolution. Freud, on the other hand, even on the metapsychological level, introduced an energy model of instinctual dynamics with an objectivist turn. Thus he sees even the species' process of civilization as linked to a dynamic of the instincts. The libidinal and aggressive instinctual forces, the prehistorical forces of evolution, permeate the species subject and determine its history. But the biological scheme of the philosophy of history is only the silhouette of a theological model; the two are equally precritical. The conception of the instincts as the prime mover of history and of civilization as the result of their struggle forgets that we have only derived the concept of impulse privatively from language deformation and behavioral pathology. At the human level we never encounter any needs that are not already interpreted linguistically and symbolically affixed to potential actions. The heritage of natural history, consisting of unspecialized impulse potentials, determines the initial conditions of the reproduction of the human species. But, from the very beginning, the means of this social reproduction give the preservation of the species the quality of self-preservation. We must immediately add, however, that the experience of collective self-preservation establishes the preunderstanding in terms of which we privatively infer something like preservation of the species for the animal prehistory of the human species. In any case, a reconstruction of the history of the species that does not depart from the basis of critique must remain heedful of the basis of its experience. It must comprehend the species, from the "moment" when it can reproduce its life only under cultural conditions, as a *subject*, albeit as one that first produces itself as a subject.

Marx in the idealist tradition tacitly retained synthesis as a point of reference: the synthesis of a portion of subjective nature with nature that is objective for it, while the contingent conditions of synthesis point to a nature in itself that has been disclosed. "Nature in itself" is a construction. It designates a *natura naturans* that has created both subjective nature and what confronts it as objective nature. But it does so in such a way that we, as knowing subjects, in principle cannot take up a position outside of or "beneath" the cleavage of "nature in itself" into a subjective and objective nature. The reconstructed impulse potentials belong as such to an unknowable nature in itself. Yet they are accessible to knowledge insofar as they define the initial situation of the conflict through which the species has been struggling. In contrast, the forms in which the conflict is carried out, namely work, language, and power, depend on the cultural conditions of our existence. We have ascertained the structures of work, language and power not naively but through the *self-reflection of knowledge*, beginning with the philosophy of science, entering the transcendental dimension, and finally becoming aware of its objective context.

The process of inquiry in the natural sciences is organized in the transcendental framework of instrumental action, so that nature necessarily becomes the object of knowledge from the viewpoint of possible technical control. The process of inquiry in the cultural sciences moves at the transcendental level of communication, so that the explication of meaning structures is necessarily subject to the viewpoint of the possible maintenance of the intersubjectivity of mutual understanding. Because they mirror structures of work and interaction, in other words, structures of life, we have conceived of these two transcendental viewpoints as the cognitive expression of knowledge-constitutive interests. But it is only through the self-reflection of sciences falling within the category of critique that the connection of knowledge and interest emerges cogently. We have chosen psychoanalysis as an example. Here the process of inquiry, which is at the same time a process of self-inquiry, is bound to the conditions of analytic dialogue. These conditions are transcendental insofar as they establish the meaning of the validity of psychoanalytic interpretations. Yet at the same time they are objective insofar as they make possible the factual treatment of pathological phenomena. The *reduction* of a transcendental viewpoint to an objective structure and a corresponding cognitive interest is superfluous, because the analytic resolution of distorted communication that determines behavioral compulsion and false consciousness is at once both theory and therapy.

In the case of an objectivation whose power is based only on the subject not recognizing itself in it as its other, knowing it in the act of self-reflection is immediately identical with the interest in knowledge, namely in emancipation from that power. The analytic situation makes real the unity of intuition and emancipation, of insight and liberation from dogmatic dependence, and of reason and the interested employment of reason developed by Fichte in the concept of self-reflection. Only self-reflection is no longer the act of an absolute ego but takes place under the conditions of communication between physician and patient forced into being by pathology. Given materialist presuppositions, the interest of reason therefore can no longer be conceived as an autarchic self-explication of reason. The proposition that interest inheres in reason has an adequate meaning only within idealism, that is only as long as we are convinced that reason can become transparent to itself by providing its own foundation. But if we comprehend the cognitive capacity and critical power of reason as deriving from the self-constitution of the human species under contingent natural conditions, then it is *reason that inheres in interest*. Freud encounters this unity of reason and interest in the situation in which the physician's Socratic questioning can aid a sick person's self-reflection only under pathological compulsion and the corresponding interest in abolishing this compulsion.

Meditating on the historical relativity of the standards

for what counts as pathological led Freud from pathological compulsion at the individual level to the pathology of society as a whole. Freud conceives institutions of authority and cultural traditions as temporary solutions of a basic conflict between surplus impulse potentials and the conditions of collective self-preservation. These solutions are temporary because, on the affective basis of repression, they produce the compulsion of pathological substitute solutions. But just as in the clinical situation, so in society, pathological compulsion itself is accompanied by the interest in its abolition. Both the pathology of social institutions and that of individual consciousness reside in the medium of language and of communicative action and assume the form of a structural deformation of communication. That is why for the social system, too, the interest inherent in the pressure of suffering is also immediately an interest in enlightenment; and reflection is the only possible dynamic through which it realizes itself. The interest of reason inclines toward the progressive, critical-revolutionary, but *tentative* realization of the major illusions of humanity, in which repressed motives have been elaborated into fantasies of hope.

The interest of self-preservation proceeds in accordance with the interest of reason. But the interest of self-preservation is indirect. It is neither an empirical need nor the system property of an organism. For the interest of self-preservation absolutely cannot be defined independently of the cultural conditions represented by work, language, and power. The interest of self-preservation cannot aim at the reproduction of the life of the species automatically and without thought, because under the conditions of the existence of culture this species must first interpret what it counts as life. These interpretations, in turn, orient themselves according to ideas of the good life. The "good" is neither a convention nor an essence, but rather the result of fantasy. But it must be fantasied so exactly that it corresponds to and articulates a fundamental interest: the interest in that measure of emancipation that historically is objectively possible under given and manipulable conditions. As long as human beings must sustain their life through work and interaction subject to instinctual renunciation, in other words under the pathological compulsion of deformed communication, the interest of self-preservation necessarily takes the form of the interest of reason, which only develops through critique and confirms itself through the practical consequences of critique.

Only when the unity of knowledge and interest has become transparent through analysis of the category of critical science can the correlation of the transcendental perspectives of inquiry and knowledge-constitutive interests also be comprehended as necessary. Since the reproduction of social life is linked to the cultural conditions of work and interaction, the interest of self-preservation is directed not immediately at the gratification of empirical needs but at the functional conditions of work and interaction: it extends equally to the pertinent categories of knowledge, namely cumulative learning processes and permanent interpretations transmitted by tradition. As soon as this everyday knowledge is secured and expanded in a methodical form, the corresponding processes of inquiry become subject to the internal requirements of this interest.

As long as the interest of self-preservation is misunderstood in terms of naturalism, it is difficult to see how it could take the form of a knowledge-constitutive interest without remaining external to the function of knowledge. Now we have shown through one example of critical science that the interest of self-preservation can be logically conceived only as an interest that operates through reason itself. If, however, knowledge and interest are one in the movement of self-reflection, then even the dependence of the transcendental conditions of the natural and cultural sciences on technical and practical cognitive interests does not imply the heteronomy of knowledge. What this means is that the knowledge-constitutive interests that determine the conditions of objectivity of the validity of statements are rational *themselves*, so that the meaning of knowledge, and thus the criterion of its autonomy as well, cannot be accounted for without recourse to a connection with interest in general. Freud recognized this connection of knowledge and interest, which is constitutive for knowledge *as such*. He defended it against the psychologistic misunderstanding according to which this connection entails a subjectivistic devaluation of knowledge:

. . . An attempt has been made to discredit scientific endeavour in a radical way, on the ground that, being bound to the conditions of our own organization, it can yield nothing else that subjective results, whilst the real nature of things outside ourselves remains inaccessible. But this is to disregard several factors which are of decisive importance for the understanding of scientific work. In the first place, our organization—that is, our mental apparatus—has been developed precisely in the attempt to explore the external world, and it must therefore have realized in its structure some degree of expediency (Zweckmässigkeit); in the second place, it is itself a constituent part of the world which we set out to investigate, and it readily admits of such an investigation; thirdly, the task of science is fully covered if we limit it to showing how the world must appear to us in consequence of the particular character of our organization; fourthly, the ultimate findings of science, precisely because of the way in which they are acquired, are determined not only by our organization but by the things which have affected that organization; finally, the problem of the nature of the world without regard to our percipient mental apparatus is an empty abstraction, devoid of practical interest. No, our science is no illusion.[20]

Nietzsche attempted to demonstrate precisely the contrary. He saw the connection of knowledge and interest, but psychologized it, thus making it the basis of a metacritical dissolution of knowledge as such. Nietzsche carried to its end the self-abolition of epistemology inaugurated by Hegel and continued by Marx, arriving at the self-denial of reflection.

Nietzsche's thoughts on the theory of knowledge (in the broad sense) tacitly take two basic positivist assumptions as their starting point. First, Nietzsche was convinced that the traditional critique of knowledge, from Kant to Schopenhauer, advocated an unfulfillable claim, that is, the knowing subject's reflection on itself. Thus it called for a metacritique. The modern form of skepticism can be unmasked as a veiled dogmatism:

Deeply mistrustful of epistemological dogmas, I loved
to look first out of one window and then out of another,
keeping myself from immuring myself in them, for I
considered this harmful—and finally, is it likely that a
tool can criticize its own fitness?—What I paid
attention to, rather, was that no epistemological
skepticism or dogmatism ever came into being without
ulterior motives, and that these doctrines decline in
value as soon as one considers what really forced them
into this position. Basic insight: Kant as well as Hegel
or Schopenhauer—the skeptical-epochistic as well as
historicizing or pessimistic—are of moral origin.[21]

Nietzsche invokes the argument used by Hegel against Kant in
order to close off entry into the theory of knowledge. Nevertheless, he does not draw the conclusion of restricting epistemology
to methodology. He actually pursues the self-reflection of the
sciences, but with the goal of circumventing both critique and
science in a paradoxical fashion.

Second, Nietzsche shares the positivist conception of science. Only that information which meets the criteria of empirical-
scientific results counts as knowledge in a rigorous sense. In this
way a standard is erected in relation to which tradition as a whole
descends to the level of mythology. With each step of scientific
development, archaic worldviews, religious outlooks, and philosophical interpretations lose ground. Cosmologies, as well as all
pre-scientific interpretations of the world that make possible
action-orientation and the justification of norms, lose their credibility to the degree that an objectified nature becomes known in
its causal connections and subjected to the power of technical
control:

To the degree that the sense of causality increases, the
scope of the realm of morality decreases. For every
time that men comprehend necessary effects and learn
to think in abstraction from chance, from all irregular
subsequent happenings (post hoc), they destroy a
host of fantastic causalities, which were previously
believed in as the foundations of morals. The real

world is much smaller than the world of fantasy. And
each time, an element of fear and compulsion has
disappeared from the world, as well as an element of
respect for the authority of morals: morality at large
has lost. Whoever, on the contrary, wants to increase it,
must know how to prevent results from becoming
controllable.[22]

Like Comte before him, Nietzsche conceives the critical
consequences of scientific-technical progress as overcoming metaphysics. Like Max Weber after him, he conceives the practical
consequences of this process as a rationalization of action and
a subjectivization of action-orienting belief systems. Scientific
theories can disempower the claim to validity asserted by traditional interpretations, which were always related to practice, even
if implicitly. To this extent, they are *critical*. But they must leave
open the place of the refuted interpretations, because they cannot generate a relation to practice. To this extent they are *de-
structive*. Scientific theories give rise to technically exploitable
knowledge, but not to normative or action-orienting knowledge:

Science explains the course of nature, but can never
give man *commands*. Inclination, love, pleasure, pain,
exaltation, exhaustion—science knows nothing of all
this. What man lives and experiences he must *interpret*,
and thus evaluate, on some basis.[23]

The process of enlightenment made possible by the sciences is
critical, but the critical dissolution of dogmas produces not liberation but indifference. It is not emancipatory but nihilistic.
Outside the connection of theory and practice, which the sciences dissolve and cannot adequately replace by a new connection, information has no "meaning." At first Nietzsche follows
the immanent constraint of the positivist enlightenment. But
what separates him from positivism is the consciousness of the
abandoned intention that used to be connected with knowledge.
As the philosopher that he can no longer be, Nietzsche cannot
rid himself of the memory "that it was always assumed that

man's salvation must depend on insight into the origin of things." At the same time, he sees

> that now, on the contrary, the farther we penetrate into the origin, the less our interests are involved. Indeed, all the valuations and petty interests that we attached to things begin to lose their meaning the further back we go with our knowledge and the more we arrive at the things themselves.[24]

In Nietzsche's reception of it, the positivist concept of science becomes peculiarly ambivalent. On the one hand, modern science is conceded a monopoly of knowledge, which is confirmed by the devaluation of metaphysical knowledge. On the other hand, the knowledge thus monopolized is itself devalued by necessarily dispensing with metaphysics' innate connection with practice and thus losing our interest. According to positivism, there cannot be any knowledge that transcends the methodical knowledge of the empirical sciences. But Nietzsche, who accepts this, cannot bring himself to let it retain the title of knowledge. For, through the same methodology that guarantees certainty to its cognitions, science is alienated from the interests that could be their only source of meaning. With regard to the objects that attract an interest going beyond technical control,

> science puts forth a *sovereign ignorance*, a feeling that "knowing" does not even occur, that it would be a sort of arrogance to dream of it—even more, that we are not left with the most minute concept for considering "knowing" as even a *possibility*.[25]

In the second of his *Thoughts Out of Season*, Nietzsche had already expressed an objection to history analogous to that bearing on the "meaninglessness" of the natural sciences. The cultural sciences are also alienated from the context of life as soon as they obey the criteria of scientific method. Historical consciousness serves life conduct only as long as a cultural tradition is critically appropriated and continued within the horizon of the present. Living history takes what is past and foreign and makes it into a component of an ongoing self-formative process in the present. Historical education is the standard of the "plastic power" with which a person or culture becomes transparent to itself in making present what is past or foreign. Those who think historically

> believe that the meaning of existence will come to life increasingly in the course of its process. They look backwards only in order to understand the present by considering the previous process and to learn to desire the future more energetically. They do not know at all how unhistorically they think and act despite all of their history, or how their concern with history is in the service not of pure knowledge but of life.[26]

The reason that Nietzsche presumes to find a moment of the unhistorical in this reflection, which is employed by life conduct, proceeds from it, and returns to it, is that this "configuration of life and history"[27] changes as soon as history becomes a science. When the material of world history is objectivated in the fictitious simultaneity of a consciousness that merely contemplates and enjoys it, and is enclosed in a museum, the objects of history lose their consequences for the knowing subject. The methodically objectified tradition is neutralized precisely as tradition and therefore can no longer become part of the present self-formative process: "Knowledge . . . now no longer operates as a motive of transformation directed outwards, and remains concealed in a certain chaotic inner world."[28]

Nietzsche's polemic against the spoiled leisure of the virtuosi of contemporary historicism is based on a critique of the scientization of history. Nietzsche does not yet perceive that objectivism is a false scientific self-understanding. Instead he accepts it as the necessary implication of historical science itself. Hence Nietzsche believes that a history "in the service of life" requires a pre-scientific attachment to the unhistorical and transhistorical.[29] This confrontation would no longer have been possible if he had incorporated into his critique of the cultural sciences his concept of "interpretation," developed two years earlier in his essay "On Truth and Lying in an Amoral Sense." For then the category of interpretation would have had to appear as the concealed foundation of the philological-historical method, just as objectivism would have emerged as the false consciousness of a method inevitably linked to the self-formative process of the knowing subject.

Nietzsche's embarrassment is the same with regard to the cultural sciences as to the natural sciences. He cannot abandon the claim of the positivist concept of science, while being unable to cast off the more attractive concept of a form of theory that has meaning for life. In respect to history he contents himself with the demand that it should throw off its methodological strait jacket even at the cost of losing possible objectivity. And he would like to pacify himself with the reflection that "It is not the victory of *science* that distinguishes our nineteenth century but the victory of the scientific *method* over science."[30] But this formula was not applicable to the natural sciences: For them the analogous suggestion to break out of methodical thought would have condemned itself. Here, if he wanted to combine the incompatible properties of positivism and classical philosophy, Nietzsche would have had to criticize the objectivism of science immanently, in order to lay bare science's hidden connection with life conduct.

Nietzsche's "theory of knowledge," although formulated in aphoristic aperçus, consists in the attempt to comprehend the categorial framework of the natural sciences (space, time, event), the concept of law (causality), the operational basis of experience (measurement), and the rules of logic and calculation as the *relative a priori* of a world of objective illusion that has been produced for the purposes of mastering nature and thus of preserving existence:

> The entire cognitive apparatus is an apparatus for abstraction and simplification—not directed at knowledge but at the *control* of things: "end" and "means" are as far from the essence as are "concepts." With "end" and "means" we control the process (—we

> invent a process that is comprehensible), with
> "concepts" we control the "things" which make the
> process occur.[31]

Nietzsche conceives science as the activity through which we turn "nature" into concepts for the purpose of mastering nature. The compulsion to logical correctness and empirical accuracy exemplifies the constraint of the interest in possible technical control over objectified natural processes and, thereby, the compulsion of preserving existence:

> How much our *intellect*, too, is a result of conditions of
> existence: we would not have it, if we did not *need* to
> have it, and we would not have it *as it is*, if we did
> not need to have it *as it is*, if we could live
> *otherwise*. . . .[32] This *compulsion* to form concepts,
> genera, forms, ends, and laws (*"one world of identical
> cases"*) should not be understood as though we were
> capable through them of ascertaining the *true* world,
> but rather as the compulsion to adapt to ourselves a
> world in which *our existence* is made possible. Thereby
> we create a world that is calculable, simplified,
> understandable, etc., for us.[33]

This sentence could be understood along the lines of a transcendental-logically conceived pragmatism. The knowledge-constitutive interest in mastering nature would establish the conditions of the possible objectivity of natural knowledge. Far from eliminating the difference between illusion and knowledge, it would itself determine the framework in which reality is objectively knowable for us. This would maintain the critical claim of scientific knowledge in opposition to metaphysics, but also call into question the monopolistic claim of modern science. For there could be other knowledge-constitutive and knowledge-legitimating interests beside the technical. This is obviously not Nietzsche's view. The methodological reduction of science to an interest in self-preservation serves not for the transcendental-logical definition of possible knowledge but for the negation of the possibility of knowledge as such: "Our cognitive apparatus is not organized for 'knowledge.' "[34] Reflection on the new standard developed by modern science remains the occasion for a critique of traditional interpretations of the world, but this same critique is now extended to science itself. Both metaphysics and science have produced the fiction of a calculable world of identical cases, although the fiction of the scientific a priori has at least proved tenable. The objectivist "aberration" that Nietzsche, motivated by the positivist self-understanding of science, points out in philosophy is the same as the one to which science necessarily succumbs:

> The aberration of philosophy comes from this: instead of seeing logic and the categories of reason as means to the adaptation of the world to ends of utility (that is, "in principle," for a useful *falsification*), men believe to possess in them the criterion of truth or *reality*. The "criterion of truth" was in fact merely *the biological utility of such a system of principled falsification*. And since an animal species knows nothing more important than preserving itself, one may in fact speak of "truth" here. The naïveté was only to take this anthropocentric idiosyncrasy as the *measure of things*, as the judge of "real" and "unreal"—in short, to make absolute what is conditioned.[35]

The basis of knowledge in interest affects the possibility of knowledge as such. Since the gratification of all needs is congruent with the interest in self-preservation, any illusion at random can put forth the same claim to validity, as long as some need interprets the world through it. The connection of knowledge and interest, conceived naturalistically, may dispel objectivist illusion in every form, but only to re-justify it subjectivistically.

> As long as the word "knowledge" has any meaning at all, the world is knowable. But it can be *interpreted* differently; it does not have a meaning behind it, but

> innumerable meanings.—"Perspectivism." It is our
> needs *that interpret the world*; our instincts and their
> pro and con.[36]

From this Nietzsche draws the conclusion[37] that the theory of knowledge now has to be replaced by a doctrine of perspectives based on the affects. Nevertheless, it is easy to see that Nietzsche would never have arrived at perspectivism if from the very beginning he had not rejected epistemology as impossible.

Because Nietzsche was always so caught in positivism that he could not acknowledge to himself that his critique of the objectivist self-understanding of science was critique of knowledge, he necessarily misunderstood in naturalistic terms the knowledge-constitutive interest that he discovered. Only if interest and instinct are immediately identical can the subjective conditions of the objectivity of possible knowledge affect the meaning of the distinction between illusion and knowledge as such. Nothing, however, compels adoption of an empiricist interpretation of knowledge-constitutive interests, as long as the self-reflection of science, which becomes conscious of the interest basis of knowledge, is not positivistically misunderstood itself, that is rejected as critique. It is precisely this to which Nietzsche sees himself constrained. He always comes up with the same argument against the theory of knowledge:

> One would have to *know* . . . what *certainty* is, what *knowledge* is, and so forth. But since we do *not* know this, a critique of the cognitive faculty is absurd. How could the instrument criticize itself, if it can use only *itself* for this critique? It cannot even define itself.[38]

Hegel had used this argument against Kant in order to impel the critique of knowledge to a critique of its own premises and thus further an interrupted self-reflection. Nietzsche, on the contrary, borrows the argument in order to make sure of the impossibility of self-reflection as such.

Nietzsche shares the blindness of a positivist age in respect of the experience of reflection. He denies the status of knowledge to the critical recollection of self-generated illusion that has become independent and opposed to the subject—that is, to the self-reflection of false consciousness: "We know that the destruction of an illusion does not by itself yield truth, but only one more *piece of ignorance*, an extension of our 'empty space,' a growth in our 'solitude.' "[39] Unlike his positivistically disposed contemporaries, however, with Nietzsche this denial of reflection does not result from the enchantment of the scientist by the objectivist illusion of science, which must be pursued *intentione recta*. Nietzsche—and this puts him above all others— denies the critical power of reflection with and only with *the means of reflection itself*. His critique of Western philosophy, his critique of science, and his critique of prevailing morality constitute a single testimonial to knowledge striven after on the path of self-reflection and only on this path. Nietzsche knows this: "From the beginning we are unlogical and therefore unjust beings and *can know this*: this is one of the greatest and most insoluble disharmonies of existence."[40] Yet Nietzsche is so rooted in basic positivist beliefs that he cannot systematically take cognizance of the cognitive function of self-reflection from which he lives as a philosophical writer. The ironic contradiction of a self-denial of reflection, however, is so stubborn that it cannot be dissolved by arguments but only appeased by invocations. Reflection that annihilates itself cannot rely on the aid of beneficent regression. It requires auto-suggestion to conceal from itself what it unceasingly accomplishes, namely critique:

> We psychologists of the future—we have little good will for self-observation: we take it almost as a sign of degeneration if an instrument seeks "to know itself." We are instruments of knowledge and would like to have the entire naïveté and precision of an instrument. Consequently we may not analyze ourselves, "know" ourselves.[41]

The history of the dissolution of the theory of knowledge into methodology is the prehistory of modern positivism. Nietzsche wrote its last chapter. As a virtuoso of reflection that denies itself, he simultaneously developed and misinterpreted in an empiricist manner the connection of knowledge and interest. For the new phase of positivism, Nietzsche seemed to have furnished the proof that the self-reflection of the sciences only leads to the psychologizing of matters that, like matters of logic and methodology, may not be placed on the same level as empirical relations. The "self-reflection" of the sciences could appear as a further example of the naturalistic fallacy, which in the history of modern philosophy was so often repeated and with so many consequences. Accordingly, it was believed that all that was necessary was a restoration of the separation in principle of questions of validity from those of genesis. In the process, epistemology, including the theory of knowledge developed immanently out of the logic of the natural and cultural sciences, could be surrendered to the psychology of research. On this basis modern positivism then erected a pure methodology, purged, however, of the really interesting problems.

APPENDIX

Knowledge and Human Interests: A *General* *Perspective*

I

In 1802, during the summer semester at Jena, Schelling gave his Lectures on the Method of Academic Study. In the language of German Idealism he emphatically renewed the concept of theory that has defined the tradition of great philosophy since its beginnings.

> The fear of speculation, the ostensible rush from the theoretical to the practical, brings about the same shallowness in action that it does in knowledge. It is by studying a strictly theoretical philosophy that we become most immediately acquainted with Ideas, and only Ideas provide action with energy and ethical significance.[1]

The *only* knowledge that can truly orient action is knowledge that frees itself from mere human interests and is based on Ideas —in other words, knowledge that has taken a theoretical attitude.

The word "theory" has religious origins. The *theoros* was the representative sent by Greek cities to public celebrations.[2] Through *theoria*, that is through looking on, he abandoned himself to the sacred events. In philosophical language, *theoria* was transferred to contemplation of the cosmos. In this form, theory already presupposed the demarcation between Being and time that is the foundation of ontology. This separation is first found in the poem of Parmenides and returns in Plato's *Timaeus*. It reserves to *logos* a realm of Being purged of inconstancy and uncertainty and leaves to *doxa* the realm of the mutable and perishable. When the philosopher views the immortal order, he cannot help bringing himself into accord with the proportions of the cosmos and reproducing them internally. He manifests these proportions, which he sees in the motions of nature and the harmonic series of music, within himself; he forms himself through mimesis. Through the soul's likening itself to the ordered motion of the cosmos, theory enters the conduct of life. In *ethos* theory molds life to its form and is reflected in the conduct of those who subject themselves to its discipline.

This concept of theory and of life in theory has defined philosophy since its beginnings. The distinction between theory in this traditional sense and theory in the sense of critique was the object of one of Max Horkheimer's most important studies.[3] Today, a generation later, I should like to reexamine this theme,[4] starting with Husserl's *The Crisis of the European Sciences*, which appeared at about the same time as Horkheimer's.[5] Husserl used as his frame of reference the very concept of theory that Horkheimer was countering with that of critical theory. Husserl was concerned with crisis: not with crises in the sciences, but with their crisis as science. For "in our vital state of need this science has nothing to say to us." Like almost all philosophers before him, Husserl, without second thought, took as the norm of his critique an idea of knowledge that preserves the Platonic connection of pure theory with the conduct of life. What ultimately produces a scientific culture is not the information content of theories but the formation among theorists themselves of a thoughtful and enlightened mode of life. The evolution of the European mind seemed to be aiming at the creation of a scientific culture of this sort. After 1933, however, Husserl saw this historical tendency endangered. He was convinced that the danger was threatening not from without but from within. He attributed the crisis to the circumstance that the most advanced disciplines, especially physics, had degenerated from the status of true theory.

II

Let us consider this thesis. There is a real connection between the positivistic self-understanding of the sciences and traditional ontology. The *empirical-analytic* sciences develop their theories in a self-understanding that automatically generates continuity with the beginnings of philosophical thought. For both are committed to a theoretical attitude that frees those who take it from dogmatic association with the natural interests of life and their irritating influence; and both share the cosmological intention of describing the universe theoretically in its lawlike order, just as it is. In contrast, the *historical-hermeneutic* sciences, which are concerned with the sphere of transitory things and mere opinion, cannot be linked up so smoothly with this tradition—they have nothing to do with cosmology. But they, too, comprise a *scientistic consciousness*, based on the model of science. For even the symbolic meanings of tradition seem capable of being brought together in a cosmos of facts in ideal simultaneity. Much as the cultural sciences may comprehend their facts through understanding and little though they may be concerned with discovering general laws, they nevertheless share with the empirical-analytic sciences the methodological consciousness of describing a structured reality within the horizon of the theoretical attitude. Historicism has become the positivism of the cultural and social sciences.

Positivism has also permeated the self-understanding of the *social sciences*, whether they obey the methodological demands of an empirical-analytic behavioral science or orient themselves to the pattern of normative-analytic sciences, based on presuppositions about maxims of action.[6] In this field of inquiry, which is so close to practice, the concept of value-freedom (or ethical neutrality) has simply reaffirmed the ethos that modern science owes to the beginnings of theoretical thought in Greek philosophy: psychologically an unconditional commitment to theory and epistemologically the severance of knowledge from interest. This is represented in logic by the distinction between descriptive and prescriptive statements, which makes grammatically obligatory the filtering out of merely emotive from cognitive contents.

Yet the very term "value freedom" reminds us that the postulates associated with it no longer correspond to the classical meaning of theory. To dissociate values from facts means counterposing an abstract Ought to pure Being. Values are the nominalistic by-products of a centuries-long critique of the emphatic concept of Being to which theory was once exclusively oriented. The very term "values," which neo-Kantianism brought into philosophical currency, and in relation to which science is supposed to preserve neutrality, renounces the connection between the two that theory originally intended.

Thus, although the sciences share the concept of theory with the major tradition of philosophy, they destroy its classical claim. They borrow two elements from the philosophical heritage: the methodological meaning of the theoretical attitude and the basic ontological assumption of a structure of the world independent of the knower. On the other hand, however, they have abandoned the connection of *theoria* and *kosmos*, of *mimesis* and *bios theoretikos* that was assumed from Plato through Husserl. What was once supposed to comprise the practical efficacy of theory has now fallen prey to methodological prohibitions. The conception of theory as a process of cultivation of the person has become apocryphal. Today it appears to us that the mimetic conformity of the soul to the proportions of the universe, which seemed accessible to contemplation, had only taken theoretical knowledge into the service of the internalization of norms and thus estranged it from its legitimate task.

III

In fact the sciences had to lose the specific significance for life that Husserl would like to regenerate through the renovation of pure theory. I shall reconstruct his critique in three steps. It is directed in the first place against the objectivism of the sciences, for which the world appears objectively as a universe of facts whose lawlike connection can be grasped descriptively. In truth, however, knowledge of the apparently objective world of facts has its transcendental basis in the prescientific world. The possible objects of scientific analysis are constituted a priori in the self-evidence of our primary life-world. In this layer phenomenology discloses the products of a meaning-generative subjectivity. Second, Husserl would like to show that this productive subjectivity disappears under the cover of an objectivistic self-understanding, because the sciences have not radically freed themselves from interests rooted in the primary life-world. Only phenomenology breaks with the naive attitude in favor of a rigorously contemplative one and definitively frees knowledge from interest. Third, Husserl identifies transcendental self-reflection, to which he accords the name of phenomenological description, with theory in the traditional sense. The philosopher owes the theoretical attitude to a transposition that liberates him from the fabric of empirical interests. In this regard theory is "unpractical." But this does not cut it off from practical life. For, according to the traditional concept, it is precisely the consistent abstinence of theory that produces action-orienting culture. Once the theoretical attitude has been adopted, it is capable in turn of being mediated with the practical attitude:

> This occurs in the form of a novel practice . . . , whose
> aim is to elevate mankind to all forms of veridical
> norms through universal scientific reason, to transform
> it into a fundamentally new humanity, capable of
> absolute self-responsibility on the basis of absolute
> theoretical insight.

If we recall the situation of thirty years ago, the prospect of rising barbarism, we can respect this invocation of the therapeutic power of phenomenological description; but it is unfounded. At best, phenomenology grasps transcendental norms in accordance with which consciousness necessarily operates. It describes (in Kantian terms) laws of pure reason, but not norms of a universal legislation derived from practical reason, which a free will could obey. Why, then, does Husserl believe that he can claim practical efficacy for phenomenology as pure theory? He errs because he does not discern the connection of positivism, which he justifiably criticizes, with the ontology from which he unconsciously borrows the traditional concept of theory.

Husserl rightly criticizes the objectivist illusion that deludes the sciences with the image of a reality-in-itself consisting of facts structured in a lawlike manner; it conceals the constitution of these facts, and thereby prevents consciousness of the interlocking of knowledge with interests from the life-world. Because phenomenology brings this to consciousness, it is itself, in Husserl's view, free of such interests. It thus earns the title of pure theory unjustly claimed by the sciences. It is to this freeing of knowledge from interest that Husserl attaches the expectation of practical efficacy. But the error is clear. Theory in the sense of the classical tradition only had an impact on life because it was thought to have discovered in the cosmic order an ideal world structure, including the prototype for the order of the human world. Only as cosmology was *theoria* also capable of orienting human action. Thus Husserl cannot expect self-formative processes to originate in a phenomenology that, as transcendental philosophy, purifies the classical theory of its cosmological contents, conserving something like the theoretical attitude only in an abstract manner. Theory had educational and cultural implications not because it had freed knowledge from interest. To the contrary, it did so because it derived *pseudonormative power* from *the concealment of its actual interest.* While criticizing the objectivist self-understanding of the sciences, Husserl succumbs to another objectivism, which was always attached to the traditional concept of theory.

IV

In the Greek tradition, the same forces that philosophy reduces to powers of the soul still appeared as gods and superhuman powers. Philosophy domesticated them and banished them to the realm of the soul as internalized demons. If from this point of view we regard the drives and affects that enmesh man in the empirical interests of his inconstant and contingent activity, then the attitude of pure theory, which promises *purification* from these very affects, takes on a new meaning: disinterested contemplation then obviously signifies emancipation. The release of knowledge from interest was not supposed to purify theory from the obfuscations of subjectivity but inversely to provide the subject with an ecstatic purification from the passions. What indicates the new stage of emancipation is that catharsis is now no longer attained through mystery cults but established in the will of individuals themselves by means of theory. In the communication structure of the polis, individuation has progressed to the point where the identity of the individual ego as a stable entity can only be developed through identification with abstract laws of cosmic order. Consciousness, emancipated from archaic powers, now anchors itself in the unity of a stable cosmos and the identity of immutable Being.

Thus it was only by means of ontological distinctions that theory originally could take cognizance of a self-subsistent world purged of demons. At the same time, the illusion of pure theory served as a protection against regression to an earlier stage that had been surpassed. Had it been possible to detect that the identity of pure Being was an objectivistic illusion, ego identity would not have been able to take shape on its basis. The repression of interest appertained to this interest itself.

If this interpretation is valid, then the two most influential aspects of the Greek tradition, the theoretical attitude and the basic ontological assumption of a structured, self-subsistent world, appear in a connection that they explicitly prohibit: the connection of knowledge with human interests. Hence we return to Husserl's critique of the objectivism of the sciences. But this connection turns *against* Husserl. Our reason for suspecting the presence of an unacknowledged connection between knowledge and interest is not that the sciences have abandoned the classical concept of theory, but that they have not completely abandoned it. The suspicion of objectivism exists because of the *ontological illusion of pure theory* that the sciences still deceptively share with the philosophical tradition *after casting off its practical content.*

With Husserl we shall designate as objectivistic an attitude that naively correlates theoretical propositions with matters of fact. This attitude presumes that the relations between empirical variables represented in theoretical propositions are self-existent. At the same time, it suppresses the transcendental framework that is the precondition of the meaning of the validity of such propositions. As soon as these statements are understood in relation to the prior frame of reference to which they are affixed, the objectivist illusion dissolves and makes visible a knowledge-constitutive interest.

There are three categories of processes of inquiry for which a specific connection between logical-methodological rules and knowledge-constitutive interests can be demonstrated. This demonstration is the task of a critical philosophy of science that escapes the snares of positivism.[7] The approach of the empirical-analytic sciences incorporates a *technical* cognitive interest; that of the historical-hermeneutic sciences incorporates a *practical* one; and the approach of critically oriented sciences incorporates the *emancipatory* cognitive interest that, as we saw, was at the root of traditional theories. I should like to clarify this thesis by means of a few examples.

V

In the *empirical-analytic sciences* the frame of reference that prejudges the meaning of possible statements establishes rules both for the construction of theories and for their critical testing.[8] Theories comprise hypothetico-deductive connections of propositions, which permit the deduction of lawlike hypotheses with empirical content. The latter can be interpreted as statements about the covariance of observable events; given a set of initial conditions, they make predictions possible. Empirical-analytic knowledge is thus possible predictive knowledge. However, the *meaning* of such predictions, that is their technical exploitability, is established only by the rules according to which we apply theories to reality.

In controlled observation, which often takes the form of an experiment, we generate initial conditions and measure the results of operations carried out under these conditions. Empiricism attempts to ground the objectivist illusion in observations expressed in basic statements. These observations are supposed to be reliable in providing immediate evidence without the admixture of subjectivity. In reality basic statements are not simple representations of facts in themselves, but express the success or failure of our operations. We can say that facts and the relations between them are apprehended descriptively. But this way of talking must not conceal that as such the facts relevant to the empirical sciences are first constituted through an a priori organization of our experience in the behavioral system of instrumental action.

Taken together, these two factors, that is the logical structure of admissible systems of propositions and the type of conditions for corroboration suggest that theories of the empirical sciences disclose reality subject to the constitutive interest in the possible securing and expansion, through information, of feedback-monitored action. This is the cognitive interest in technical control over objectified processes.

The *historical-hermeneutic sciences* gain knowledge in a different methodological framework. Here the meaning of the validity of propositions is not constituted in the frame of reference of technical control. The levels of formalized language and objectified experience have not yet been divorced. For theories are not constructed deductively and experience is not organized with regard to the success of operations. Access to the facts is provided by the understanding of meaning, not observation. The verification of lawlike hypotheses in the empirical-analytic sciences has its counterpart here in the interpretation of texts. Thus the rules of hermeneutics determine the possible meaning of the validity of statements of the cultural sciences.[9]

Historicism has taken the understanding of meaning, in which mental facts are supposed to be given in direct evidence, and grafted onto it the objectivist illusion of pure theory. It appears as though the interpreter transposes himself into the horizon of the world or language from which a text derives its meaning. But here, too, the facts are first constituted in relation to the standards that establish them. Just as positivist self-understanding does not take into account explicitly the connection between measurement operations and feedback control, so it eliminates from consideration the interpreter's pre-understanding. Hermeneutic knowledge is always mediated through this pre-understanding, which is derived from the interpreter's initial situation. The world of traditional meaning discloses itself to the interpreter only to the extent that his own world becomes clarified at the same time. The subject of understanding establishes communication between both worlds. He comprehends the substantive content of tradition by *applying* tradition to himself and his situation.

If, however, methodological rules unite interpretation and application in this way, then this suggests that hermeneutic inquiry discloses reality subject to a constitutive interest in the preservation and expansion of the intersubjectivity of possible action-orienting mutual understanding. The understanding of meaning is directed in its very structure toward the attainment of possible consensus among actors in the framework of a self-understanding derived from tradition. This we shall call the *practical* cognitive interest, in contrast to the technical.

The systematic *sciences of social action*, that is economics, sociology, and political science, have the goal, as do the empirical-analytic sciences, of producing nomological knowledge.[10] A critical social science, however, will not remain satisfied with this. It is concerned with going beyond this goal to determine when theoretical statements grasp invariant regularities of social action as such and when they express ideologically frozen relations of dependence that can in principle be transformed. To the extent that this is the case, the *critique of ideology*, as well, moreover, as *psychoanalysis*, take into account that information about lawlike connections sets off a process of reflection in the consciousness of those whom the laws are about. Thus the level of unreflected consciousness, which is one of the initial conditions of such laws, can be transformed. Of course, to this end a critically mediated knowledge of laws cannot through reflection alone render a law itself inoperative, but it can render it inapplicable.

The methodological framework that determines the meaning of the validity of critical propositions of this category is established by the concept of *self-reflection*. The latter releases the subject from dependence on hypostatized powers. Self-reflection is determined by an emancipatory cognitive interest. Critically oriented sciences share this interest with philosophy.

However, as long as philosophy remains caught in ontology, it is itself subject to an objectivism that disguises the connection of its knowledge with the human interest in autonomy and responsibility (*Mündigkeit*). There is only one way in which it can acquire the power that it vainly claims for itself in virtue of its seeming freedom from presuppositions: by acknowledging its dependence on this interest and turning against its own illusion of pure theory the critique it directs at the objectivism of the sciences.[11]

VI

The concept of knowledge-constitutive human interests already conjoins the two elements whose relation still has to be explained: knowledge and interest. From everyday experience we know that ideas serve often enough to furnish our actions with justifying motives in place of the real ones. What is called rationalization at this level is called ideology at the level of collective action. In both cases the manifest content of statements is falsified by consciousness' unreflected tie to interests, despite its illusion of autonomy. The discipline of trained thought thus correctly aims at excluding such interests. In all the sciences routines have been developed that guard against the subjectivity of opinion, and a new discipline, the sociology of knowledge, has emerged to counter the uncontrolled influence of interests on a deeper level, which derive less from the individual than from the objective situation of social groups. But this accounts for only one side of the problem. Because science must secure the objectivity of its statements against the pressure and seduction of particular interests, it deludes itself about the fundamental interests to which it owes not only its impetus but *the conditions of possible objectivity* themselves.

Orientation toward technical control, toward mutual understanding in the conduct of life, and toward emancipation from seemingly "natural" constraint establish the specific viewpoints from which we can apprehend reality as such in any way whatsoever. By becoming aware of the impossibility of getting beyond these transcendental limits, a part of nature acquires, through us, autonomy in nature. If knowledge could ever outwit its innate human interest, it would be by comprehending that

the mediation of subject and object that philosophical consciousness attributes exclusively to *its own* synthesis is produced originally by interests. The mind can become aware of this natural
basis reflexively. Nevertheless, its power extends into the very
logic of inquiry.

Representations and descriptions are never independent
of standards. And the choice of these standards is based on attitudes that require critical consideration by means of arguments,
because they cannot be either logically deduced or empirically
demonstrated. Fundamental methodological decisions, for example such basic distinctions as those between categorial and
noncategorial being, between analytic and synthetic statements,
or between descriptive and emotive meaning, have the singular
character of being neither arbitrary nor compelling.[12] They prove
appropriate or inappropriate. For their criterion is the metalogical
necessity of interests that we can neither prescribe nor represent,
but with which we must instead *come to terms*. Therefore my
first thesis is this: *The achievements of the transcendental subject
have their basis in the natural history of the human species.*

Taken by itself this thesis could lead to the misunderstanding that reason is an organ of adaptation for men just as
claws and teeth are for animals. True, it does serve this function.
But the human interests that have emerged in man's natural
history, to which we have traced back the three knowledge-constitutive interests, derive both from nature and *from the cultural
break* with nature. Along with the tendency to realize natural
drives they have incorporated the tendency toward release from
the constraint of nature. Even the interest in self-preservation,
natural as it seems, is represented by a social system that com-
pensates for the lacks in man's organic equipment and secures
his historical existence *against* the force of nature threatening
from without. But society is not only a system of self-preservation. An enticing natural force, present in the individual as
libido, has detached itself from the behavioral system of self-
preservation and urges toward utopian fulfillment. These individual demands, which do not initially accord with the
requirement of collective self-preservation, are also absorbed by
the social system. That is why the cognitive processes to which

social life is indissolubly linked function not only as means to the reproduction of life; for in equal measure they themselves determine the definitions of this life. What may appear as naked survival is always in its roots a historical phenomenon. For it is subject to the criterion of what a society intends for itself as the good life. My second thesis is thus that knowledge equally serves as an instrument and transcends mere self-preservation.

The specific viewpoints from which, with transcendental necessity, we apprehend reality ground three categories of possible knowledge: information that expands our power of technical control; interpretations that make possible the orientation of action within common traditions; and analyses that free consciousness from its dependence on hypostatized powers. These viewpoints originate in the interest structure of a species that is linked in its roots to definite means of social organization: work, language, and power. The human species secures its existence in systems of social labor and self-assertion through violence, through tradition-bound social life in ordinary-language communication, and with the aid of ego identities that at every level of individuation reconsolidate the consciousness of the individual in relation to the norms of the group. Accordingly the interests constitutive of knowledge are linked to the functions of an ego that adapts itself to its external conditions through learning processes, is initiated into the communication system of a social life-world by means of self-formative processes, and constructs an identity in the conflict between instinctual aims and social constraints. In turn these achievements become part of the productive forces accumulated by a society, the cultural tradition through which a society interprets itself, and the legitimations that a society accepts or criticizes. My third thesis is thus that knowledge-constitutive interests take form in the medium of work, language, and power.

However, the configuration of knowledge and interest is not the same in all categories. It is true that at this level it is always illusory to suppose an autonomy, free of presuppositions, in which knowing first grasps reality theoretically, only to be taken subsequently into the service of interests alien to it. But the mind can always reflect back upon the interest structure that joins subject and object a priori: this is reserved to self-reflection. If the latter cannot cancel out interest, it can to a certain extent make up for it.

It is no accident that the standards of self-reflection are exempted from the singular state of suspension in which those of all other cognitive processes require critical evaluation. They possess theoretical certainty. The human interest in autonomy and responsibility is not mere fancy, for it can be apprehended a priori. What raises us out of nature is the only thing whose nature we can know: *language*. Through its structure, autonomy and responsibility are posited for us. Our first sentence expresses unequivocally the intention of universal and unconstrained consensus. Taken together, autonomy and responsibility constitute the only Idea the we possess a priori in the sense of the philosophical tradition. Perhaps that is why the language of German Idealism, according to which "reason" contains both will and consciousness as its elements, is not quite obsolete. Reason also means the will to reason. In self-reflection knowledge for the sake of knowledge attains congruence with the interest in autonomy and responsibility. The emancipatory cognitive interest aims at the pursuit of reflection as such. My *fourth thesis* is thus that *in the power of self-reflection, knowledge and interest are one.*

However, only in an emancipated society, whose members' autonomy and responsibility had been realized, would communication have developed into the non-authoritarian and universally practiced dialogue from which both our model of reciprocally constituted ego identity and our idea of true consensus are always implicitly derived. To this extent the truth of statements is based on anticipating the realization of the good life. The ontological illusion of pure theory behind which knowledge-constitutive interests become invisible promotes the fiction that Socratic dialogue is possible everywhere and at any time. From the beginning philosophy has presumed that the autonomy and responsibility posited with the structure of language are not only anticipated but real. It is pure theory, wanting to derive everything from itself, that succumbs to unacknowledged external conditions and becomes ideological. Only when philosophy discovers in the dialectical course of history the traces of violence that deform repeated attempts at dialogue and recurrently close off the path to unconstrained communication does it further the process whose suspension it otherwise legitimates: mankind's evolution toward autonomy and responsibility. My *fifth thesis* is thus that *the unity of knowledge and interest proves itself in a dialectic that takes the historical traces of suppressed dialogue and reconstructs what has been suppressed.*

VII

The sciences have retained one characteristic of philosophy: the illusion of pure theory. This illusion does not determine the practice of scientific research but only its self-understanding. And to the extent that this self-understanding reacts back upon scientific practice, it even has its point.

The glory of the sciences is their unswerving application of their methods without reflecting on knowledge-constitutive interests. From knowing not what they do methodologically, they are that much surer of their discipline, that is of methodical progress within an unproblematic framework. False consciousness has a protective function. For the sciences lack the means of dealing with the risks that appear once the connection of knowledge and human interest has been comprehended on the level of self-reflection. It was possible for fascism to give birth to the freak of a national physics and Stalinism to that of a Soviet Marxist genetics (which deserves to be taken more seriously than the former) only because the illusion of objectivism was lacking. It would have been able to provide immunity against the more dangerous bewitchments of misguided reflection.

But the praise of objectivism has its limits. Husserl's critique was right to attack it, if not with the right means. As soon as the objectivist illusion is turned into an affirmative *Weltanschauung*, methodologically unconscious necessity is perverted to the dubious virtue of a scientistic profession of faith. Objectivism in no way prevents the sciences from intervening in the conduct of life, as Husserl thought it did. They are integrated into it in any case. But they do not of themselves develop their practical efficacy in the direction of a growing rationality of action.

Instead, the positivist self-understanding of the *nomological sciences* lends countenance to the substitution of technology for enlightened action. It directs the utilization of scientific information from an illusory viewpoint, namely that the practical mastery of history can be reduced to technical control of objectified processes. The objectivist self-understanding of the *hermeneutic sciences* is of no lesser consequence. It defends sterilized knowledge against the reflected appropriation of active traditions and locks up history in a museum. Guided by the objectivist attitude of theory as the image of facts, the nomological and hermeneutical sciences reinforce each other with regard to their practical consequences. The latter displace our connection with tradition into the realm of the arbitrary, while the former, on the levelled-off basis of the repression of history, squeeze the conduct of life into the behavioral system of instrumental action. The dimension in which acting subjects could arrive rationally at agreement about goals and purposes is surrendered to the obscure area of mere decision among reified value systems and irrational beliefs.[13] When this dimension, abandoned by all men of good will, is subjected to reflection that relates to history objectivistically, as did the philosophical tradition, then positivism triumphs at the highest level of thought, as with Comte. This happens when critique uncritically abdicates its own connection with the emancipatory knowledge-constitutive interest in favor of pure theory. This sort of high-flown critique projects the undecided process of the evolution of the human species onto the level of a philosophy of history that dogmatically issues instructions for action. *A delusive philosophy of history, however, is only the obverse of deluded decisionism.* Bureaucratically prescribed partisanship goes only too well with contemplatively misunderstood value freedom.

These practical consequences of a restricted, scientistic consciousness of the sciences[14] can be countered by a critique that destroys the illusion of objectivism. Contrary to Husserl's expectations, objectivism is eliminated not through the power of renewed *theoria* but through demonstrating what it conceals:

the connection of knowledge and interest. Philosophy remains true to its classic tradition by renouncing it. The insight that the truth of statements is linked in the last analysis to the intention of the good and true life can be preserved today only on the ruins of ontology. However even this philosophy remains a specialty alongside of the sciences and outside public consciousness as long as the heritage that it has critically abandoned lives on in the positivistic self-understanding of the sciences.

Notes

Preface

1. An interpretive model for analyzing the social context in which positivism arose and today has taken on an ideological function is contained in my essay dedicated to Herbert Marcuse, "Technology and Science as 'Ideology,'" in my *Toward a Rational Society* (Boston: Beacon, 1970), pp. 81–122.

2. Published as an appendix to the present work. See below, pp. 301–317.

3. The second volume of G. Radnitzky's *Contemporary Schools of Metascience* (Göteborg, 1968) deals with the "hermeneutic-dialectical approach." It includes ideas derived from Adorno's and Apel's works and my own and elaborates them against the background of analytic philosophy of science. Since this work appeared after the completion of my manuscript, I can make only this general reference to the many points of overlap.

Part One

1. TRANSLATOR'S NOTE: German and French distinguish between *Erkenntnis* and *connaissance* on the one hand and *Wissen* and *savoir* on the other, the former emphasizing the act, process, form, or faculty of knowing and the latter the passive content of what is known. In English, this distinction is most accurately rendered as that between "cognition" and "knowledge." Nevertheless, English-language epistemology is the theory of "knowledge," and this is how *Erkenntnis* has been translated in the text, as "knowledge," with "cognition" retained to denote an instance of it and in the adjectival form.

2. TRANSLATOR'S NOTE: *Transzendentallogisch* is the adjectival form of *transzendentale Logik*, that is, transcendental logic. In the text, "transcendental-logical" always has this meaning, in other words "of or from the perspective of transcendental logic."

3. TRANSLATOR'S NOTE: *Forschung* means both "inquiry" and "research." It has been translated mostly as the former.

4. TRANSLATOR'S NOTE: *Reflektieren*. The differences between the German and English usage of "to reflect" and "reflection" are a source of difficulty in accurately translating into English the present work or any work that is significantly influenced by German Idealism. In English the word "reflect" tends to mean, aside from "mirror," either "bend back" or "recurve" or the mental operation of reflecting *on* something (albeit the self) that is external to the act of reflection. In German usage, particularly as developed by German Idealism and its dialectic of subject and object, the

word "reflect" expresses the idea that the act in which the subject reflects on something is one in which the object of reflection itself recurves or bends back in a way that reveals its true nature. The process through which consciousness reflects back upon itself, insofar as it reveals the constitution of consciousness and its objects, also dissolves the naive or dogmatic view of objects; thus they themselves are re-flected *through* consciousness. Accordingly, "reflect" can be used transitively in a cognitive context. In this instance, a literal, and conceptually accurate translation would read, "to strengthen science's belief . . . instead of to reflect it."

5. TRANSLATOR'S NOTE: *Identitätsphilosophie.* The philosophy of identity is that which postulates the identity of thought and being, of subject and object. German Idealism attempted to overcome Kant's separation of the subject and the thing-in-itself by asserting that the realm of nature and objects was a mere externalization of an absolute subjectivity.

6. TRANSLATOR'S NOTE: *Bildung* means both formation or shaping and the (humanistic) education, cultivation, and acculturation of a self-conscious subject. *Bildungsprozess* has been translated as "self-formative process" in the sense of a personal or cultural process of growth and development. "Self-formative" does not imply the realization of a plan chosen in advance by the self, but a process in which the self nevertheless participates.

Chapter One

1. See Hegel's "Vorlesungen uber die Geschichte der Philosophie," in Georg W. F. Hegel, *Sämtliche Werke,* ed. Hermann Glockner (Stuttgart: Frommann, 1949–59), 19:555 ff., and the *Enzyklopädie* of 1830, ed. Friedhelm Nicolin and Otto Pöggeler (Hamburg: Felix Meiner, 1959), p. 43 ff.

2. TRANSLATOR'S NOTE: *The* critical philosophy means Kantianism.

3. "Vorlesungen," *loc. cit.,* p. 555 f.

4. TRANSLATOR'S NOTE: In the text "methodical" (*methodisch*) means "relating to or by means of method," while "methodological" (*methodologisch*) means "relating to methodology, the study of method."

5. TRANSLATOR'S NOTE: *Ursprungsphilosophie,* literally "philosophy of the origin," means philosophy that attempts to provide a self-contained deduction of the world and itself from an original principle or ground. It has been translated as "First Philosophy."

6. Theodor W. Adorno, *Zur Metakritik der Erkenntnistheorie,* (Stuttgart: Kohlhammer, 1956), introduction, especially p. 14 ff.

7. *Enzyklopädie,* p. 43 f.

8. *Phänomenologie des Geistes,* ed. Johannes Hoffmeister (Hamburg: Felix Meiner, 1948), p. 64 f.

9. TRANSLATOR'S NOTE: "Organon": an instrument of thought or knowledge; the title given to Aristotle's logical writings.

10. The instrumental view of the cognitive process provides Hegel with the guide to an interpretation of Kant's critique of reason that amazingly anticipates pragmatist conceptions. See especially the "Vorlesungen uber die Geschichte der Philosophie," *loc. cit.,* p. 555. "Knowledge is represented as an instrument . . . : before proceeding toward truth itself, the

nature and form of the instrument is first supposed to be known. It is active; we are supposed to examine whether it is capable of achieving what is demanded: seizing the object. . . . It is as though one could attack the truth with stakes and pikes." The transcendental aesthetic can then be interpreted instrumentally, as follows:

> The matter is conceived as follows. Outside there are things in themselves, but without time and space. Now consciousness comes and in advance contains within itself time and space as the possibility of experience, just as, in order to eat, it has a mouth, teeth, etc. as the conditions of eating. The things that are eaten do not have the mouth and teeth; and what eating does to things, space and time does to them. Just as consciousness puts things between its mouth and teeth, so it does with space and time. (*Ibid.*, p. 563.)

Since "instruments" of organic constitution are used as an example here, this passage already contains points of departure for the pragmatism of an anthropological theory of cognition, expanded to the level of the history of the species. See the epistemological discussion in Konrad Lorenz's paper, "Gestaltwahrnehmung als Quelle wissenschaftlicher Erkenntnis," in his *Gesammelte Abhandlungen* (Munich, 1966), 2:255 ff.

11. *Phänomenologie des Geistes*, p. 64.

12. Karl Popper, *The Open Society and Its Enemies* (Princeton: Princeton University Press, 1963.

13. *Phänomenologie des Geistes*, p. 67 f.

14. TRANSLATOR'S NOTE: *Das erscheinende Wissen* literally means "appearing knowledge," that is, knowledge as it appears or manifests itself. The text refers even more frequently to *das erscheinende Bewußtsein*, "appearing consciousness," which has been translated as "consciousness in its manifestations."

15. *Ibid.*, p. 68.

16. *Ibid.*, p. 70 f.

17. TRANSLATOR'S NOTE: To preserve continuity with the conceptual scheme of Kant and Hegel, *ansichseiend* has been translated as "(being) in itself," meaning self-existent independently of consciousness.

18. *Ibid.*, p. 74.

19. *Ibid.*, p. 68.

20. *Ibid.*, p. 74.

21. Georg Lukács, *Der junge Hegel* (Zurich: Europa, 1948), p. 592 ff. TRANSLATOR'S NOTE: *Wissenschaft* means "science" in the sense of systematic, objective knowledge. While in most cases it is adequately rendered by "science," it has been translated as "scientific knowledge" in contexts dealing with Hegel's philosophy owing to the great difference between Hegel's meaning and the conventional meaning of science.

22. Hegel later endorsed this view at several points: "In the *Phenomenology of Mind* . . . I have presented consciousness in its progressive motion from the first immediate antithesis between itself and its object to absolute knowledge. This course is followed by all forms of the *relation of consciousness to the object* and has the *concept of scientific knowledge* as its result. Thus this concept needs no justification here (disregarding the

fact that it emerges within logic itself), because it has obtained it in the *Phenomenology*. And it is incapable of any justification other than this, its own production by consciousness, in which all its forms are resolved in truth." "Logik," Georg Lasson, ed., in *Sämtliche Werke*, Lasson, ed. (Leipzig: Felix Meiner, 1923), 3:29. See also *ibid.*, 3:53.

23. *Phänomenologie des Geistes*, p. 75.

24. *Ibid.*, p. 74.

25. *Logik*, 3:7.

26. In the *Encyclopedia*, the term is indeed used in this sense. There (paragraphs 413–439) the phenomenology of mind refers to a stage in the development of subjective mind.

27. In Berlin, this preliminary notion, which occupied only a small space in the Heidelberg *Encyclopedia*, was expanded by Hegel to more than 60 paragraphs. In a letter (*Briefe* 3:126), he writes, "This introduction has become that much more difficult for me because it can be situated only prior to and not within philosophy itself." See the introduction to the new edition of the *Enzyklopädie*, *loc. cit.*, p. ix ff.

28. This is the thesis of Hans Friedrich Fulda's penetrating study, *Das Problem einer Einleitung in Hegels Wissenschaft der Logik* (Frankfurt am Main: V. Klostermann, 1965).

Chapter Two

1. *Enzyklopädie*, paragraph 381.

2. MEGA, I, 3:171 f.

3. "As the abstract Idea, revelation (*Offenbaren*) is immediate transition, the *becoming* of nature. As the revelation of mind, which is free, it is the positing of nature as *its* world: a positing (*Setzen*) that, as reflection, at the same time concretely presupposes (*voraussetzen*) and thereby causes the world as independent nature." *Enzyklopädie*, paragraph 384.

4. "If real, corporeal man, standing on the firm round earth and inhaling and exhaling all the forces of nature, posits his real objective essential powers as alien objects through his externalization, the subject is, nevertheless, not the process of positing. . . . The objective being only . . . creates and posits objects because it is posited by objects, because it is natural in its very roots. . . . Thus, in its act of positing, it does not descend from its 'pure activity' into creating the object; instead, its objective product only confirms its objective activity [activity directed at objects]." MEGA, I, 3:160.

5. *Ibid.*

6. Karl Marx and Friedrich Engels, *Werke* (Berlin: Dietz, 1959), 3:5.

7. TRANSLATOR'S NOTE: Here "anthropological" refers to the philosophical theory of man and not to the science of anthropology (ethnology, ethnography, etc.).

8. TRANSLATOR'S NOTE: "Intuition" (*Anschauung*) means here sensation, not a faculty of psychic insight.

9. TRANSLATOR'S NOTE: In certain contexts *Praxis* has been translated as "conduct" or "activity." The use of "praxis" in English has been

avoided even in the context of Marxian theory for two reasons. First, the word *Praxis* does not as such mean anything more in German than "practice" does in English: action as opposed to theory. Marx's use of it is an *interpretation* of the traditional concept of practice. Second, the author is attempting to shed new light both on Marx's conception of *Praxis* and its meaning in general, and it would be misleading to prejudice this attempt terminologically. It is true, of course, that in current English "practical" often means "technically skilled" or "expedient" rather than "relating to human action" (that is symbolic interaction).

10. TRANSLATOR'S NOTE: *Arbeit* means "work" or "labor." In line with the author's linking it to instrumental action, active adaptation, and technology and distinguishing this sphere from that of symbolic interaction, social organization, and cultural tradition, it has been generally translated as "work," which emphasizes its functional character. Nevertheless, in keeping with traditional usage, "labor" has been retained for *Arbeit* in the discussion of Marxian theory.

11. *Das Kapital* (Berlin: Dietz), 1:47.

12. *Ibid.*, p. 185.

13. TRANSLATOR'S NOTE: By "existing for itself," Marx, following Hegel, means "self-conscious."

14. MEGA, I, 3:162.

15. See my essay "Zur Diskussion um Marx und den Marxismus," in *Theorie und Praxis*, 2d ed. (Neuwied: Luchterhand, 1967), p. 261 ff.

16. Jean Paul Sartre, *Critique de la Raison Dialectique* (Paris: Gallimard, 1960).

17. A representative example is the book by the Prague philosopher Karel Kosík, *Die Dialektik des Konkreten* (Frankfurt am Main: Suhrkamp, 1967). See also the works of the philosophical circle surrounding the journal *Praxis*, which has been published in Zagreb since 1965. In this connection see Gajo Petrovic, *Marx in the Midtwentieth Century* (Garden City: Anchor, 1967).

18. *Kapital*, 1:185.

19. MEGA, I, 3:162.

20. "Deutsche Ideologie," in *Werke*, 3:38.

21. "Ökonomisch-philosophische Manuskripte," MEGA, I, 3:121.

22. "Deutsche Ideologie," p. 43.

23. TRANSLATOR'S NOTE: In the text the words "objectify" and "objectivate" have been employed to render two different concepts. To objectify (*vergegenständlichen*) means to make into an object of instrumental action or of natural science separate from and external to the subject—in other words, to constitute in the Kantian sense. To objectivate (chiefly *objektivieren*) means to give form in a symbolic system, that is to make into a vehicle of communicative action. The latter may become external to the subject in the sense that others can participate in it, but it is at the same time that in which the subject exists. See Chapter 7 below.

24. *Ibid.*, p. 44.

25. *Kapital*, 1:47.

26. *Grundrisse der Kritik der Politischen Ökonomie* (Berlin: Dietz, 1953), p. 389.

27. "They are products of human industry: natural material transformed into organs of human will over nature or of man's activity in nature.

They are *organs of the human brain created by the human hand*: objectified cognitive power." (*Grundrisse*, p. 594.)

28. Alfred Schmidt has observed this:

"In the litigation between Kant and Hegel, Marx takes a mediating position that is nevertheless hard to locate. His materialist critique of Hegel's identity of subject and object takes him back to Kant; yet being, while not identical with thought, does not appear as an unknowable 'thing in itself.' " With the concept of transcendental apperception, Kant wanted as it were to show once and for all how a unified world of experience comes into being. Marx, however, while retaining Kant's thesis of the non-identity of subject and object, adheres to the post-Kantian understanding that history cannot be bracketed out, that is that subject and object enter into changing relations with one another, just as the unity of the subjective and objective realized in the products of labor also implies that the proportion between labor and natural material varies considerably.' " See Alfred Schmidt, *Der Begriff der Natur in der Lehre von Marx* (Frankfurt am Main: Europäische Verlagsanstalt, 1962), p. 103. Marx's quotation from *Zur Kritik der politischen Ökonomie* (Berlin, 1958), p. 30.

29. Hegel had already opened up this perspective, although with a polemical intention. See above, p. 320, n. 10.

30. See below, Chapters 5 and 6.

31. In the abovementioned work, Alfred Schmidt refers in this context to a late work of Marx, his marginal glosses to Adolph Wagner's *Lehrbuch der politischen Ökonomie*, quoted in Bela Fogarasi, *Logik* (Berlin, 1955):

> For the doctrinaire professor the relations of man to nature are from the beginning not practical relations, that is based on action, but theoretical relations. . . . Man relates to the objects of the external world as to the means of satisfying his needs. But men do not at all begin by being "in this theoretical relation to the objects of the external world." Like all animals they begin by eating, drinking, etc. That is, they are not in a general relation, but rather are active, appropriate certain objects of the external world through action, and in this way satisfy their needs (that is they begin with production). As this process is repeated, it is impressed on their brains that objects are capable of "satisfying" man's "needs." Men and animals also learn to distinguish "theoretically" from all other objects those external objects that serve to satisfy their needs. At a certain level of subsequent development, after men's needs and the modes of action with which the former are satisfied have in the meantime multiplied and developed further, men attributed names to whole classes of these objects, which they distinguished on the basis of experience from the other objects of the external world. This is a necessary process, since men are in a continuous relation of labor with one another and with individual objects in the process of production, that is in the process of appropriating objects; also, they soon come into conflict with other men about these objects. For this naming only expresses ideationally what repeated action has changed into experience, namely that

for men who already live in particular social relations—this assumption follows necessarily from the existence of language —certain external objects to satisfy their needs.

32. TRANSLATOR'S NOTE: *Erfolgskontrolliertes Handeln* literally means "action controlled (or monitored) by its results (or success)." This concept has been translated as "feedback-controlled action," with the emphasis being on feedback from performance in the environment as part of adaptive processes.

33. *Briefe an Kugelmann* (Berlin, 1952), p. 67, letter of July 11, 1868.

34. *Critique of Pure Reason*, paragraph 16.

35. "Versuch einer neuen Darstellung der Wissenschaftslehre," *Ausgewählte Werke*, ed. Fritz Medicus (Hamburg: Felix Meiner, 1962), 3:109. See Dieter Henrich, *Fichte's ursprüngliche Einsicht* (Frankfurt am Main: V. Klostermann, 1967).

36. The philosopher attains certainty about himself as ego by giving himself up to the act of self-consciousness:

> He comprehends his act as an *action in general*, of which he already has a concept from his previous experience, and as this *particular action* that *returns* into itself, as he observes it in himself. Through this characteristic difference he distinguishes it from the sphere of action in general. What action is can only be observed, and not developed from or communicated through concepts. But what is contained in this observation or intuition is comprehended through its opposition to mere *being*.

"Zweite Einleitung in die Wissenschaftslehre," *Ausgewählte Werke*, 3:45.

37. "History is nothing but the succession of individual generations, of which each exploits the materials, capital, and forces of production transmitted to it by all its predecessors. Thus each generation on the one hand continues its acquired activity under entirely altered circumstances and on the other modifies the old circumstances with an entirely altered activity . . ." "Deutsche Ideologie," 3:45.

38. *Grundrisse*, p. 389.

39. "Deutsche Ideologie," p. 20 f.

40. MEGA, I, 3:123.

Chapter Three

1. *Ibid.*, p. 156.

2. *Ibid.*, p. 122.

3. TRANSLATOR'S NOTE: Published as the preface to the second edition in most English-language editions.

4. "As soon as life has survived a given period of development and gone over from a given stage into another, it also begins to be governed by other laws. . . . With the varying development of the forces of production, conditions and the laws that regulate them change." See *Kapital*, 1:17.

5. *Ibid.*, p. 16.

6. MEGA, I, 3:123.

7. *Grundrisse*, p. 594.

8. *Ibid.*, p. 585.

9. Thus the means of labor undergo various metamorphoses, "of which the last is the *machine* or rather an *automatic system of machinery* (system of machinery: its *automatic state* is only the most perfect and most adequate form of machinery and is what transforms it into a system), set in motion by an automaton, a moving force that moves itself" (*ibid.*, p. 584). In Aristotelian concepts Marx anticipates automation. He discerns that the development of the productive forces to this degree only commences once the sciences together with their technological applications become the primary productive force:

> What enables the machine to perform the same labor earlier performed by the worker is the analysis and application of mechanical and chemical laws arising directly from science. The development of machinery in this direction, however, begins only when large-scale industry has already attained a higher level and the aggregate of the sciences has been taken into the service of capital (*ibid.*, p. 591).

Marx speaks of nothing short of the "transformation of the process of production from a simple labor process into a scientific process that empresses the forces of nature into its service and lets them operate in the service of human needs" (*ibid.*, p. 588).

10. *Ibid.*, p. 592 f.

11. *Ibid.*, p. 374.

12. *Ibid.*

13. *Ibid.*, p. 593.

14. In the introduction to the *Critique of Political Economy* of 1857, which contains the few detailed references to the method of political economy to be found in Marx, the reduction of social practice to one of its two elements, that is to work, is clearly visible (*Zur Kritik der politischen Ökonomie* (Berlin, 1958), 235–270. Marx starts with the premise that work always takes the form of social labor. The individual subject working on natural material, in other words the model of instrumental action, is an abstraction from the labor that is always combined systematically in an interaction framework as the cooperation of different functions of labor:

> The starting point naturally, is individuals producing in society—and therefore the socially determined production of individuals. The individual and isolated hunter or fisher, with whom Smith and Ricardo begin, belongs to the unimaginative fantasies of the 18th-century Robinsonades . . . (*ibid.*, p. 235).

At the same time, social production can be viewed according to the model of instrumental action. Labor intervenes between instinct and its gratification and thus mediates the "process of material exchange" that, at the animal level, takes place as immediate transfer between the organism and its environment. The reproduction of society also follows this cycle, in which objects are produced and appropriated. At this level production and appropriation are mediated once again by the distribution and exchange of goods:

> In production the members of society appropriate (produce, form) natural products for human needs. Distribution determines the proportion in which the individual takes part in these products. Exchange provides him with the particular products into which he transforms the quota allotted him by distribution. Finally, in consumption the products become the objects of enjoyment, of individual appropriation (*ibid.*, p. 242).

Thus production appears as the starting point, consumption the end product, and distribution and exchange the middle. This entire life process is now comprehended by Marx from the perspective of production. The creation of the means of life, production, and the preservation of life, reproduction, are two aspects of the same process:

> As want, or as need, consumption itself is an inner element of productive activity; but the latter is the starting point of realization and thus its self-surpassing element, the act in which the entire process begins again. The individual produces an object and, through its consumption, returns into himself again, but as a productive individual and one who reproduces himself. Consumption thus appears as an aspect of production (*ibid.*, p. 249).

Production is the determinate form of reproduction that distinguishes man's "process of material exchange." This follows from a perspective that comprehends man "from below," that is as a natural being.

Now Marx sees that in social production the appropriation of products also is socially organized. "Through social laws" distribution determines the producer's share in the output of social production. These laws establishing his share take the immediate form of property rights:

> All production is the individual's appropriation of nature within and by means of a particular social form. In this sense it is a tautology to say that property (appropriation) is a condition of production. . . . To say that there can be no production . . . where no property exists is a tautology (*ibid.*, p. 241).

The property relations on which distribution depends are the basis of the organization of social relations. In the relation of distribution to the sphere of production we thus see the relation of the institutional framework to instrumental action, the two elements that Marx does not adequately discriminate in the concept of practice. With his answer to the question, "Is distribution an independent sphere alongside and outside of production?" he implicitly decides the relation between interaction and work.

The immediate answer is obvious: plainly the distribution of income depends on the distribution of positions in the system of social labor. The independent variable is "place in the process of production."

> An individual who participates in production in the form of wage labor takes part in products, the result of production, in the form of wages. The organization of distribution is completely determined by the organization of production (*ibid.*, p. 250).

Nevertheless, the "organization of production" depends on the distribution of the means of production, which means on the "distribution of the members of society among the various forms of production. (Subsumption of individuals under determinate relations of production)" (*ibid.*, p. 252). The relations of production, however, are the organization of obligations and rewards operative in the area of production itself. Consequently, no matter how we look at it, distribution is dependent on the institutional framework, that is on the property order, and not on the form of production as such. The only way Marx salvages production as the independent variable is by terminological equivocation:

> Production, when considered apart from this distribution inherent in it, is an empty abstraction, whereas conversely the distribution of products is immediately given with this distribution, which is originally a constitutive element of production (*ibid.*).

The concept of production is given such a broad meaning that even the relations of production are implied by it. This gives Marx the opportunity of insisting that production also produces the institutional framework in which production takes place: "The relation obtaining between production and this distribution that determines it [sic] is obviously a question concerning production itself" (*ibid.*). Strictly speaking, however, this means only that changes in the institutional framework depend as much on the development of the forces of production as does the process of production on the relations of production:

> If someone were to say that, since production must begin with a certain distribution of the instruments of production, distribution is at least in this sense prior to production and its premise, it must be said in response that production does in fact have its conditions and premises, which form its elements. At the very beginning these may appear "natural" (*ibid.*).

Here Marx is probably thinking of natural qualities of social interaction such as sex, age, and kinship relations.

> Through the process of production itself they are transformed from "natural" into historical conditions and, although they may appear as a natural premise of production for one period, they are its historical result in another. They are continually modified within production itself (*ibid.*).

These definitional attempts to subsume all aspects of social practice under the concept of production cannot conceal that Marx has to take account of social preconditions of production that, unlike the material, instruments, energy, and organization of labor, do not belong immediately to the labor process itself. With good reason, Marx wants to construct the categorial framework in such a way that "pre-economic facts" do not enter into the mechanism of the historical evolution of the species. But the distribution inherent in production, the institutionalized relation of force that establishes the distribution of the instruments of production, is based on a structure of symbolic interaction. Despite all definitional equations, the latter cannot be analyzed into elements of production, want, instrumental action, and immediate consumption.

15. *Zur Kritik der Politischen Ökonomie*, p. 249.

16. See my contribution to the *Festschrift* for Karl Löwith: "Arbeit und Interaktion: Bemerkungen zu Hegels Jenenser Realphilosophie," in *Natur und Geschichte. Karl Löwith zum 70. Geburtstag*, Hermann Braun und Manfred Riedel, eds. (Stuttgart: Kohlhammer, 1967). This essay is reprinted in *Technik und Wissenschaft als 'Ideologie'* (Frankfurt am Main: Suhrkamp, 1968) and will appear in English in *Theory and Practice*, to be published by Beacon Press. See also my postface to *Hegels Politische Schriften* (Frankfurt am Main: Suhrkamp, 1966), p. 343 ff.

17. *Kapital*, 1:77 f.

18. See Theodor Adorno, *Negative Dialektik* (Frankfurt am Main: Suhrkamp, 1967).

Part Two

1. On the critique of formalism in investigations of the foundations of logic and mathematics see Friedrich Kambartel, *Erfahrung und Struktur* (Frankfurt am Main: Suhrkamp, 1968).

2. Today Paul Lorenzen's works on protologic are the most promising attempt to derice the rules of formal logic from the perspective of constitution. See Paul Lorenzen, *Methodisches Denken* (Frankfurt am Main: Suhrkamp, 1968) and Wilhelm Kamlah and Paul Lorenzen, *Logische Propadeutik* (Mannheim, 1967).

Chapter Four

1. See Karl Popper, *The Poverty of Historicism* (Boston: Beacon, 1957).

2. Auguste Comte, *Cours de Philosophie Positive*, 2d ed. (Paris: Baillière, 1864), 4:360 f.

3. Albrecht Wellmer, *Methodologie als Erkenntnistheorie* (Frankfurt am Main: Suhrkamp, 1967).

4. *Discours sur l'Esprit Positif*, Iring Fetscher, ed. (Hamburg: F. Meiner, 1956), p. 82 ff.

5. *Ibid.*, p. 91.

6. TRANSLATOR'S NOTE: "Object domain" means here the universe of whatever counts as a possible object of science or a science.

7. *Ibid.*, p. 27.

8. *Ibid.*, p. 51.

9. *Cours de Philosophie Positive*, 6.

10. *Ibid.*, 6:600 f.

11. *Ibid.*

12. *Ibid.*

13. *Discours*, p. 85 f.

14. *Ibid.*, p. 59 f.

15. *Cours de Philosophie Positive*, 6:618.

16. *Discours*, p. 33 f.
17. *Ibid.*, p. 27; see also *Cours de Philosophie Positive*, 6.
18. *Discours*, p. 91.
19. *Ibid.*, p. 29.
20. *Ibid.*, p. 89.
21. *Erkenntnis und Irrtum* (Leipzig: Barth, 1905), p. 8.
22. *Die Analyse der Empfindungen und das Verhaltnis des Physischen zum Psychischen*, 6th ed. (Jena: G. Fischer, 1911), p. 14.
23. *Ibid.*, p. 299 f.
24. *Ibid.*, p. 19 ff.
25. *Ibid.*, p. 17 f.
26. *Ibid.*, p. 18.
27. *Ibid.*, p. 290 f.
28. *Erkenntnis und Irrtum*, p. 10.
29. *Analyse*, p. 9.
30. *Erkenntnis und Irrtum*, p. 12 f.
31. *Analyse*, p. 257.
32. *Ibid.*, p. 256.
33. *Ibid.*, p. 261. See also p. 258 f.:

Thus the adaptation of thoughts to facts is the goal of all natural-scientific work. Here science merely continues intentionally and consciously what occurs by itself unnoticed in everyday life. As soon as we are capable of self-observation, we find our thoughts already frequently adapted to the facts. Thoughts present us with the elements in groupings similar to the facts of sensation (*sinnliche Tatsachen*). But our limited store of thoughts does not suffice for our continuously growing experience. Almost every new fact brings with it a continuation of adaptation, which is expressed in the process of *judgment*. . . . A judgment is thus always an *addition* to a sense representation for the sake of the more complete depiction of a fact of sensation.

34. *Ibid.*, p. 271.
35. Charles Sanders Peirce, *Collected Papers*, Charles Hartshorne and Paul Weiss, eds. (Cambridge: Harvard U. P., 1931–35), II, 62. The arabic numerals refer here and in all subsequent references to Peirce to paragraphs and not to pages.

Chapter Five

1. "The Logic of 1873," VII, 319.
2. VIII, 12.
3. "The Logic of 1873," VII, 321.
4. "Scientific Method," VII, 54.
5. *Ibid.*, 50.
6. "The Logic of 1873," VII, 326.
7. "Different minds may set out with the most antagonistic views, but the progress of investigation carries them by a force outside of themselves to one and the same conclusion. This activity of thought by which we are

carried, not where we wish, but to a fore-ordained goal, is like the operation of destiny. No modification of the point of view taken, no selection of other facts for study, no natural bent of mind even, can enable a man to escape the predestinate opinion. This great hope is embodied in the conception of truth and reality. The opinion which is fated to be ultimately agreed to by all who investigate, is what we mean by the truth, and the object represented in this opinion is the real. That is the way I would explain reality." ("How to Make Our Ideas Clear," V, 407.)

8. *Ibid.*, 406.

9. "The Logic of 1873," VII, 322.

10. See the seventh of the "Questions Concerning Certain Faculties Claimed for Man," V, 259 ff.

11. VII, 337.

12. ". . . , since it is impossible to know intuitively that a given cognition is not determined by a previous one, the only way in which this can be known is by hypothetic inference from observed facts. But to adduce the cognition by which a given cognition has been determined is to explain the determinations of that cognition. And it is the only way of explaining them. For something entirely out of consciousness which may be supposed to determine it, can, as such, only be known and only adduced in the determinate cognition in question. So, that to suppose that a cognition is determined solely by something absolutely external, is to suppose its determinations incapable of explanation. Now, this is a hypothesis which is warranted under no circumstances, inasmuch as the only possible justification for a hypothesis is that it explains the facts, and to say that they are explained and at the same time to suppose them inexplicable is self-contradictory." ("Concerning Certain Faculties," V, 260.)

13. In a certain way Peirce anticipates Cassirer's philosophy of symbolic forms. In the tradition of Kantianism, Cassirer was the first to make the transition from the transcendental critique of consciousness to the critique of language. The understanding can no longer simply effect the synthesis of phenomena; in the given, only symbols make transparent the trace of what is not given. Thus the content of the world becomes present to the mind through the mind's generating out of itself forms that can represent a reality that is inaccessible to intuition. Reality appears only as symbolically represented reality. Thus for Cassirer symbolic representation is the basic function of transcendental consciousness. Peirce, too, believes "that there is no element whatever of man's consciousness which has not something corresponding to it in the word" (V, 314). The spontaneous activity of semiotic representation is the condition of possible receptivity. The copy theory of realism does not hold for any stage of knowledge, not even for the elementary strata of perception:

> If this be the case, what goes by the name of the association of images is in reality an association of judgments. The association of ideas is said to proceed according to three principles—those of resemblance, of contiguity, and of causality. But it would be equally true to say that signs denote what they do on the three principles of resemblance, contiguity, and causality. There can be no question that anything *is* a sign of whatever is associated with it by resemblance, by contiguity, or by causality: nor can

there be any doubt that any sign recalls the thing signified.
So, then, the association of ideas consists in this, that a judgment
occasions another judgment, of which it is the sign. Now this is
nothing less nor more than inference ("Consequences of
Four Incapacities," V, 307). Unlike Cassirer, however, Peirce
cannot base the process of semiotic mediation on the
transcendental unity of consciousness. What is basic is the process
of inference mediated by signs; only in it is the understanding first
constituted:

> Man makes the word, and the word means nothing which
> the man has not made it mean, and that only to some man.
> But since man can think only by means of words or other
> external symbols, these might turn round and say: "You mean
> nothing which we have not taught you, and then only so far
> as you address some words as the interpretant of your
> thought." In fact, therefore, men and words reciprocally
> educate each other; each increase of a man's information
> involves and is involved by, a corresponding increase of a
> word's information (*ibid.*, V, 313).

14. V, 265.
15. V, 289.
16. "Consequences of Four Incapacities," V, 311.
17. "Berkeley," VIII, 12.
18. *Ibid.*
19. "Consequences of Four Incapacities," V, 290.
20. V, 283; see also V, 73.
21. V, 287.
22. V, 289.
23. *Ibid.*
24. V, 291.
25. *Ibid.*
26. Even Karl-Otto Apel's clear reconstruction of this unusual
attempt to bring the empiricist concept of knowledge into accord with the
semiotic does not solve this difficulty:

> He (Peirce) accepts the model of the causal affection of the senses
> by things of the external world and the idea that we can infer
> from "natural signs" (of "impressions" in consciousness) to the
> existence and quality of things in the external world. But he does
> not identify the affection of the senses, represented in
> "impressions," with knowledge (which in that case would have to
> be conceived primarily as "introspective," "intuitive," and
> unconnected to the employment of signs). Instead, he identifies
> knowledge with hypothetical inferences to things in the external
> world. They result from conditions that can be investigated on a
> purely physical and physiological basis (conditions of nerve stimuli
> in factual encounter with "brute facts") and from the sign
> quality of psychic data, which are not already knowledge
> themselves (that is, so-called "feelings," in which the results of
> nerve stimulation are given purely qualitatively, in the mode of

emotional mood). For Peirce, knowledge is neither being affected by things-in-themselves nor the intuition of given data, but rather the "mediation" of a consistent opinion about the real—that is, the precise "representation" of external "facts." The latter indicate their existence in the encounter of subject and object, which can be investigated physically and physiologically. And, in the confused manifold of emotional data, they deposit the qualitative, expressive signs or images ("icons") of their "suchness." These icons are reduced to the unity of a consistent "proposition" about external fact in hypothetical inference (the "conception" of something as something) through the discovery of a predicate in the form of an interpreting symbol ("interpretant").

See the introduction to Charles Sanders Peirce, *Schriften I*, Karl-Otto Apel, ed. (Frankfurt am Main: Suhrkamp, 1967), p. 47 f.
    27. See the second of Peirce's "Lectures on Pragmatism," V, 41 ff.; Apel, *op. cit.*, p. 48 ff.; and Murray G. Murphey, *The Development of Peirce's Philosophy* (Cambridge: Harvard U. P., 1961), p. 303 ff.
    28. "Berkeley," VIII, 16.
    29. VIII, 14 f.
    30. VIII, 13.
    31. "Consequences of Four Incapacities," V, 311.
    32. *Ibid.*, 312.

Chapter Six

    1. "In deduction, or necessary reasoning, we set out from a hypothetical state of things which we define in certain abstracted respects. Among the characters to which we pay no attention in this mode of argument is whether or not the hypothesis of our premises conforms more or less to the state of things in the outward world. We consider this hypothetical state of things and are led to conclude that, however it may be with the universe in other respects, wherever and whenever the hypothesis may be realized, something else not explicitly supposed in that hypothesis will be true invariably" ("Lectures on Pragmatism," V, 161).
    2. *Ibid.*, 171.
    3. "Scientific Method," VII, 115n. The expression "quasi-experimentation" is intended to preclude too narrow an interpretation of induction: ". . . by quasi-experimentation I mean the entire operation either of producing or of searching out a state of things to which the conditional predictions deduced from hypothesis shall be applicable and of noting how far the prediction is fulfilled" (*ibid.*). The strategy of verification, which requires the rule of inductive inference, also includes the selection of results that are as improbable as possible. A hypothesis is more seriously tested, the greater the possibility of falsification:

> The verification . . . must consist in basing upon the hypothesis predictions as to the results of experiments, especially those of such predictions as appear to be otherwise least likely to be

true, and in instituting experiments in order to ascertain whether they will be true or not (*ibid.*, V, 89).

4. Under the term "abduction" (which he also calls "hypothesis") Peirce subsumes two different processes without clearly distinguishing between them. Sometimes he understands by abduction only the employment of a lawlike hypothesis for the end of causal explanation: here we infer from a result to a case with the aid of a valid rule. This inference leads to an explanatory hypothesis, which can then be tested (see below, p. 336, n. 30). In the section "Deduction, Induction, and Hypothesis" (II, 619 ff.) Peirce elucidates this *explanatory employment* of abductive inference in terms of the example of Napoleon. The application of abduction that is relevant for the reconstruction of the possibility of scientific progress, however, is its *innovative employment*. Starting with a (surprising) result, we search for a rule with whose aid we can infer the case: the rule itself, therefore, is not yet assumed as valid. Thus the representation of abduction as inference from a rule (as major premise) and a result (as minor premise) to the case (as conclusion) is not quite accurate here. For the major premise is what is *arrived at*. The *systematic* discovery of new lawlike hypotheses, however, freed from dependence on chance inspiration, is conceivable only if the unexpected result necessarily leads to a *determinate* negation, that is to a modification of the refuted lawlike hypothesis within the semantic domain it has already marked out.

In addition, Peirce is thinking also of non-inductive generalization. Starting with an empirical regularity given with a case and result, we search for a lawlike hypothesis from which one of the two variables can be derived by means of the other. Then "we have a kind of mixture of induction and hypothesis supporting one another; and of this kind are most of the theories of physics" (II, 640). In this passage Peirce uses the example of the kinetic theory of gas to clarify this procedure and then defines the relation of abduction and induction as follows:

> The great difference between induction and hypothesis is, that the former infers the existence of phenomena such as we have observed in cases which are similar, while hypothesis supposes something of a different kind from what we have directly observed, and frequently something which it would be impossible for us to observe directly. Accordingly, when we stretch an induction quite beyond the limits of our observation, the inference partakes of the nature of hypothesis. It would be absurd to say that we have no inductive warrant for a generalization extending a little beyond the limits of experience . . . Yet, if an induction be pushed very far, we cannot give it much credence unless we find that such an extension explains some fact which we can and do observe.

Thus we see that under abduction Peirce subsumes two different procedures. The first serves the causal explanation of an event and, given a lawlike hypothesis, leads to an explanatory hypothesis. The second, on the contrary, serves the *discovery* of a lawlike hypothesis. This case, which is the interesting one for the logic of inquiry, comprises both the modification of a given lawlike hypothesis that has been refuted by an unexpected result and the non-inductive progression from an inductively obtained formula for uniformities to a lawlike hypothesis that "fits" the formula.

5. "Grounds of Validity," V, 354.

6. *Ibid.*, V, 341.

7. "Concerning Certain Faculties," V, 347.

8. V, 351.

9. "Grounds of Validity," V, 352.

10. Peirce does not hesitate to express this tautology:

As all knowledge comes from synthetic inference, we must equally infer that all human certainty consists merely in our knowing that the processes by which our knowledge has been derived are such as must generally have led to true conclusions. ("Probability of Induction," II, 693).

11. "Scientific Method," VII, 110.

12. "Lectures on Pragmatism," V, 27.

13. "How to Make Our Ideas Clear," V, 398.

14. See "What Pragmatism Is," V, 417.

15. "To develop . . . [the] meaning [of a thought], we have, therefore, simply to determine what habits it produces, for what a thing means is simply what habits it involves. Now, the identity of a habit depends on how it might lead us to act, not merely under such circumstances as are likely to arise, but under such as might possibly occur, no matter how improbable they may be. What the habit is depends on *when* and *how* it causes us to act" (*ibid.*, V, 417).

16. "Lectures on Pragmatism," V, 18.

17. The famous, but not particularly clear formulation of the so-called pragmatist maxim is in "How to Make Our Ideas Clear," written in 1878 (V, 402; see also *ibid.*, V, 398). In his encyclopedia article on pragmatism from 1902, Peirce clarified this maxim (see V, 1 ff.). There a clearer formulation is to be found: "In order to ascertain the meaning of an intellectual conception one should consider what practical consequences might conceivably result by necessity from the truth of that conception; and the sum of these consequences will constitute the entire meaning of the conception" (*ibid.*, V, 9).

18. TRANSLATOR'S NOTE: The Hegelian phrase "the movement of the concept" (*die Bewegung des Begriffs*) refers to the immanent development of thought through the unfolding and incorporation of its inherent contradictions.

19. "A Survey of Pragmaticism," V, 467.

20. "Lectures on Pragmatism," V, 197.

21. "Elements of Logic," II, 710.

22. *Ibid.*, II, 711.

23. *Ibid.*

24. See "Deduction, Induction, Hypothesis," II, 643.

25. This is the basis of Popper's principle of falsifiability. See Karl Popper, *The Logic of Scientific Discovery* (New York: Harper, 1965).

26. "Elements of Logic," II, 713.

27. "What Pragmatism Is," V, 425.

28. "Three Types of Reasoning," V, 170.

29. "What Pragmatism Is," V, 427.

30. Accordingly, the validity of abductive inference can be demonstrated only in the case of simple abduction, that is causal explanation (see above, p. 334 n. 4). Abductive inference from a result to its cause by recourse to a valid rule leads to a causal hypothesis. It can be tested by deriving conditional predictions from the assumed cause (as initial condition) and various other rules. In this way we test the validity of abductive explanations inductively (see II, 642). Thus the methodological justification of induction also can be invoked indirectly for abduction. The explanatory employment of abduction, however, is of no interest in the context of the logic of inquiry. Scientific progress rests on the *innovative* employment of abduction, in which abductive inference leads from an unexpected result that cannot be explained on the basis of valid rules to new theoretical assumptions. This is the case of an experiment with a surprising outcome, which forces us to modify the lawlike hypothesis so that the *actual* initial conditions can be derived from it and the result as the latter's cause. This modification of the refuted lawlike hypothesis, which was the basis of an erroneous prediction, obviously occurs not arbitrarily, as the emanation of an imagination that generates hypotheses, but according to certain rules. But the rules of *this* abduction cannot be reduced to the foundations of induction. If I am correct, they cannot be accounted for at all within the pragmatist system of reference of purposive-rational action. For the characteristic innovative achievement of abduction consists in the elaboration of a negative experience: in other words, in determinate negation. The negative outcome of an experiment compels the reinterpretation of the basic predicates of the theory from which the refuted hypothesis had been derived. In this process, abduction appears to work with the implicit surplus (*Überschuss*) of the predicates' semantic contents over what has been operationally exhausted. These predicates are unproblematic as long as a theory is applied. But if the theory is remolded, they are as it were reopened and rejoined to the horizon of experience within ordinary language. For paradigms containing theoretical approaches originate in the primary experiences of everyday life (cf. Thomas S. Kuhn, *The Structure of Scientific Revolutions* [Chicago: The University of Chicago Press, 1962]). Peirce alluded to this "anthropomorphism" of scientific model building: "I have after long years of the severest examination become fully satisfied that, other things being equal, an anthropomorphic conception, whether it makes the best nucleus for a scientific working hypothesis or not, is far more likely to be approximately true than one that is not anthropomorphic" (V, 47 n.). But if abduction, once evoked by failures of instrumental action, leads back to explicating the prescientific basis of experience stored in ordinary language, it draws its revisory power from a structure of communicative action that is not comprehended by the pragmatist system of reference. This does not affect the fact that the logical connection of abduction with the two other modes of inference is generated only within the behavioral system of instrumental action.

31. "That which any true proposition asserts is *real*, in the sense of being as it is regardless of what you or I may think about it. Let this proposition be a general conditional proposition as to the future, and it is a real general such as is calculated really to influence human conduct; and

such the pragmaticist holds to be the rational purport of every concept" (*ibid.*, V, 432).
32. "The Logic of 1873," VII, 340.
33. "Issues of Pragmatism," V, 457. Peirce had introduced the example of the diamond in this context in 1878 in his famous essay, "How to Make Our Ideas Clear," V, 403 ff.
34. *Ibid.*, V, 457.
35. See V, 402 n. 2 (1893), and "Philosophy of Mind," VII, 512 ff.
36. "Scientific Method," VII, 58.
37. "Why Study Logic?", II, 176 and 178.
38. "The Logic of 1873," VII, 341.
39. *Ibid.*, VII, 344.
40. "Concerning Certain Faculties," V, 233.
41. "Consequences of Four Incapacities," V, 314 and 317.

Chapter Seven

1. TRANSLATOR'S NOTE: There is no univocal translation of *Geisteswissenschaften*: this word has been translated as "humanities," "sciences of man," "social sciences," etc. This is largely because of the connotative richness and complexity of the word *Geist*, meaning mind or spirit, both "objective" and "subjective." Since in the last analysis *Geist* refers to everything that exists by virtue of man's symbol-making capacity, I have translated *Geisteswissenschaften* as "cultural sciences."
2. I shall be dealing mainly with Dilthey's later methodological essays, the "Grundlegung der Geisteswissenschaften" (Foundations of the Cultural Sciences) and the "Aufbau der geschichtlichen Welt in den Geisteswissenschaften" (The Constitution of the Historical World in the Cultural Sciences), reprinted in volume VII of his *Gesammelte Schriften* (Gottingen: Vandenhoeck & Ruprecht, 1913–1967). These works are already influenced by Husserl's *Logische Untersuchungen* and consequently avoid the clear danger of psychologism present in Dilthey's earlier works. In addition I shall draw upon the essays and papers collected in volume V, including the important "Ideen uber eine beschreibende und zergliedernde Psychologie" and the essay on the origins of hermeneutics. Finally, I shall also take account of the first book of the "Einleitung in die Geisteswissenschaften" (Introduction to the Cultural Sciences) in volume I. On Dilthey's logic of the cultural sciences see Hans-Georg Gadamer, *Wahrheit und Methode*, 2d ed. (Tubingen: J. C. B. Mohr, 1965), p. 205 ff., and Georg Misch, *Lebensphilosophie und Phänomenologie* (Stuttgart: B. G. Teubner, 1930).
3. Dilthey, "Der Aufbau," in *Gesammelte Schriften*, 7:79 and 7:81.
4. 5:248.
5. 7:89.
6. TRANSLATOR'S NOTE: That is, in terms of the distinction made above between objectification and objectivation, Dilthey regards the former as a limiting case of the latter.

7. 7:82 f.
8. 5:264.
9. 7:90.
10. 7:118.
11. "The natural sciences subordinate [phenomena] to their constructions by bringing about uniformity among the phenomena that are to be ordered; this they do through abstraction, by means of these constructions. In contrast, the cultural sciences incorporate, primarily by taking the immeasurably expanding historical-social reality, as it is given only in its external manifestations or in effects or as mere product, the objectivated sediment of life, and translating it back into the living mental state in which it arose. Where we have abstraction in the natural sciences, we have here, in contrast, the process of translating back into the fullness of life through a sort of transposition" (5:265).
12. 5:143 f.
13. 5:263.
14. 7:87 f.
15. 7:84.
16. TRANSLATOR'S NOTE: "Objective mind" means symbolic structures objectivated as cultural patterns and products.
17. 7:84 f.
18. 7:86 f.
19. 7:87.
20. See my essay "Marxismus als Kritik" (Marxism as Critique) in *Theorie und Praxis*.
21. 7:148.
22. 7:278.
23. *Ibid.*
24. It has been developed by Heidegger in the form of an existential hermeneutics of being-in-the-world. See his *Sein und Zeit* (Halle: Niemeyer, 1927).
25. 7:74.
26. 7:204.
27. 7:131.
28. 7:131 f. One can already detect in Dilthey the view of linguistic analysis that the factual meaning structures of an individual life-world are sedimented in symbolic structures: "All these characteristics of the self and of objects or persons derived from life relations are elevated to consciousness and expressed in language" (7:133 f.). What is fused in the perceptual-conceptual scheme of a life relation as meaning, value, and goal is separated out in the grammatical forms of the descriptive, evaluative, and prescriptive uses of language.
29. 7:73 f.
30. 7:243. See also 7:72 and 7:229.
31. 7:228.
32. 7:237.
33. 7:232.
34. 7:132 f.
35. 7:146 f.
36. 7:134 f.

37. 5:319. This is, moreover, how Dilthey justifies the superiority of hermeneutics in the sense of the skilled interpretation of linguistic expression: "Therefore the art of understanding has its center in the explication or interpretation of the residues of human existence contained in writing" (ibid.).

38. 7:141.

39. Dilthey comprehends the spirit of generations, epochs, and cultures on the analogy of the meaning or significance of an individual life history. Epochs find their limit in a horizon of life as individuals do in their world. By "horizon of life" he means

> the limitation in whch the men of a period live with regard to their thought, feeling, and willing. It contains a relation of life, life relations, life experience, and thought formation that keeps and binds individuals in a definite sphere concerning modifications of their views, value formation, and purposive action. Here inevitabilities rule over individual human beings (7:177 f.).

Epochs, too, are concentrated in the identity of a *Zeitgeist* that permeates all objectivations of this historical context, just as life histories are concentrated in the identity of a meaning that constitutes the ego: "Like the individual, every cultural system and community has a center within itself, where the view of reality, valuation, and the production of goods are combined into a whole" (7:154). In this sense Dilthey speaks elsewhere of a "centering of ages and epochs in themselves, through which the problem of significance and meaning in history is solved" (7:186).

40. This question is the point of departure of the contemporaneous attempt of Heinrich Rickert to provide a methodologically rigorous version of the dualism of the natural and cultural sciences. He limited the claim of the Kantian critique of reason to the realm of validity of nomological science, in order to make room for the cultural sciences, elevated by Dilthey to the status of epistemological critique. In contrast to Dilthey, Rickert does not take up Hegel's concept of objective mind and the dialectical relations of intersubjectivity. Rather, he comprehends culture, on the analogy of nature, from the perspective of transcendental philosophy. Whereas phenomena are constituted as "nature" under general laws according to categories of the understanding, "culture" is formed through the relation of facts to a system of values. It is to this individualizing value-relation that cultural phenomena owe their unrepeatable historical meaning. Rickert discerns the logical impossibility of the strict idiographic science advocated by Wilhelm Windelband in *Geschichte und Naturwissenschaft* (Freiburg, 1894). He views as a fact the singular activity of the sciences that are based on understanding. For in inevitably general expressions, which are oriented toward the repeatable, they grasp the meaning of historical events, which is unrepeatable. But his solution cannot satisfactorily explain this fact.

Rickert's tacit premise is a vitalistic one, namely the irrationality of a reality that enters experience uncurtailed only on the nonlinguistic level and is decomposed into alternative views by the transcendentally mediated intervention of the knowing mind. Reality must then be viewed either in the form of lawlike continuity or heterogeneous individuals, and these complementary aspects remain separate. The selection of appropriate theoretical systems of reference confronts us with a complete alternative. Statements of one system cannot be transformed into statements of the other. The unity of reality, once sundered in transcendental perspective, is provided only by the term "heterogeneous continuum." Unity is merely extrapolated and does not correspond to any synthesis of the finite understanding. But how can the very reality that is comprehended subject to universal laws as nature be individualized through relation to values, if the categories of value themselves have the logical status of generality? Rickert postulates that values do not have the same status as class concepts. He asserts that cultural phenomena are not subsumed by the values that constitute them in the same way that elements are under the extension of a class. (See "Die vier Arten des Allgemeinen in der Geschichte," appendix to the fifth edition of Die Grenzen der naturwissenschaftlichen Begriffsbildung [Tubingen: Mohr, 1929], p. 739 ff., especially p. 749 f.) This claim, however, cannot be fulfilled within the transcendental logic in which it is asserted. Rickert has to merely circumscribe the concept of historical totality because he mistrusts the dialectical means that could grasp it. A logic of the cultural sciences based on premises of the transcendental critique of consciousness cannot extricate itself from the dialectic of the general and the particular described by Hegel. This dialectic leads beyond Hegel to the concept of the cultural phenomenon as something historically individuated that requires identification precisely as the non-identical entity that it is.

Rickert's philosophy of value itself subsists on the same ambivalence, which comes from not having completed the transition from Kant to Hegel. Rickert constructs the concept of culture primarily on the foundations of transcendental idealism. Like the category of nature, "culture" has transcendental meaning as the totality of phenomena in a system of prevailing values. It says nothing about objects, but determines the conditions of the possible apprehension of objects. This has its counterpart in the optimistic assumption that a value system must be derivable a priori from practical reason. (This position was taken by Rickert in his first study, Kulturwissenschaft und Naturwissenschaft [Freiburg, 1899].) But Rickert had to abandon it immediately. (His modified position is to be found in the systematic elaboration of the theory in Die Grenzen der naturwissenschaftlichen Begriffsbildung, loc. cit.) The material profusion of so-called values could be deciphered only from the real context of cultures, in which the value-oriented action of historical subjects had been objectivated, even if the validity of values is independent of this genesis. But once this must be conceded, the quasi-Kantian concept of culture succumbs to the transcendental-empirical ambiguity that had unfolded dialectically in Hegel's concept of objective mind. The cultural sciences encounter their objects as already constituted. The cultural meanings of empirically valid value systems have arisen from value-oriented action. In the empirical form of historically congealed and transmitted values, therefore, the transcendentally mediated activity of subjects engaged in value-oriented action is absorbed and preserved. With history, a new dimension is incorporated into the object domain of science. In it, part of transcendental consciousness is externalized via the minds of acting subjects: that is a meaning is objectivated that, in any individual case, can claim validity only in a transcendentally elaborated

fabric of values. Because Rickert does not want to abandon the principles of transcendental philosophy, they crumble in his hands despite his intentions.
    41. 7:141.
    42. 7:143.
    43. 7:145.

Chapter Eight

    1. Dilthey's complete works, 7:207 ff.
    2. 7:206.
    3. 7:205.
    4. 7:206.
    5. 1:225.
    6. 7:206.
    7. Ibid.
    8. Helmuth Plessner, Lachen und Weinen (Bern, 1961). See also his "Über Hermeneutik des nichtsprachlichen Ausdrucks," a lecture at the 8th German Congress for Philosophy at Heidelberg, 1966.
    9. 7:206.
    10. Jürgen Habermas, "Zur Logik der Sozialwissenschaften," supplement no. 5 to Philosophische Rundschau (Tubingen: J. C. B. Mohr, 1967), p. 124 ff.
    11. 7:226.
    12. Ibid.
    13. 7:227.
    14. 7:153.
    15. 5:330.
    16. 7:136.
    17. 7:207.
    18. 7:210.
    19. 7:217.
    20. 5:320.
    21. 1:38 f.
    22. 7:138.
    23. Ibid.
    24. 7:137.
    25. This regression to objectivism has been excellently analyzed by Gadamer; however, I do not think that it can be understood in terms of a dichotomy between science and vitalism. See Gadamer, op. cit., p. 218 ff.
    26. 7:213 f.
    27. 7:204.
    28. 5:317.
    29. 7:219.
    30. 7:213.
    31. Ibid.
    32. 7:146.
    33. 1:49 and 1:51 f.
    34. 5:258.

35. See my "Zur Logik der Sozialwissenschaften," *loc. cit.*, especially chapter III, p. 95 ff.
36. 7:188.

Part Three

Chapter Nine

1. TRANSLATOR'S NOTE: *Mündigkeit* literally means majority in the sense of full legal age. Kant introduced it as a historical category of enlightenment in his essay *What Is Enlightenment?* I have translated it with the phrase "autonomy and responsibility."
2. Immanuel Kant, "Kritik der Urteilskraft," in *Werke*, Wilhelm Weischedel, ed. (Wiesbaden: Insel, 1958), 5:280 ff.
3. Kant, "Grundlegung zur Metaphysik der Sitten," *Werke*, 4:42 n. Kant later makes the distinction between empirical and pure interest more precise in *ibid.*, 4:97 n.
4. Kant, "Metaphysik der Sitten," *Werke*, 4:317.
5. 4:101.
6. *Ibid.*, 4:98.
7. *Ibid.*
8. *Ibid.*, 4:99.
9. "Kritik der praktischen Vernunft," *Werke*, 4:249.
10. *Ibid.*, 4:250.
11. 4:252.
12. "Kritik der reinen Vernunft," *Werke*, 2:677.
13. "Kritik der praktischen Vernunft," 4:251.
14. Fichte, "Zweite Einleitung in die Wissenschaftslehre," *loc. cit.*, 3:43 f.
15. "Erste Einleitung in die Wissenschaftslehre," *Ausgewählte Werke*, 3:17.
16. *Ibid.*
17. *Ibid.*
18. "Kritik der reinen Vernunft," 2:440 f.
19. *Ibid.*, 2:450.
20. Fichte, *loc. cit.*, 3:17 f.
21. "Zweite Einleitung," 3:56.
22. "Erste Einleitung," 3:18.

Chapter Ten

1. Karl-Otto Apel, *Analytic Philosophy of Language and the Geisteswissenschaften*, translated by Harald Holstelitie (Dordrecht: D. Reidel, 1967), and "Szientifik, Hermeneutik, Ideologiekritik," in *Man and World* I, 1968, p. 37 ff.
2. The Standard Edition of the Complete Psychological Works of Sigmund Freud, translated from the German under the general editorship of James Strachey, in collaboration with Anna Freud, assisted by Alix

Strachey and Alan Tyson (London: The Hogarth Press, 1967). All subsequent quotations and references are from this edition.

3. *Gesammelte Schriften*, 7:261.

4. *Ibid.*

5. *Ibid.*

6. *Ibid.*, 3:260.

7. "New Introductory Lectures on Psychoanalysis," 22:57.

8. "The Claims of Psychoanalysis to Scientific Interest," 13:176 (translation altered).

9. See *The Psychopathology of Everyday Life*. See "The Interpretation of Dreams," vols. 4 and 5; "On Dreams," vol. 5.

10. "On Dreams," 5:642. As early as the preface to his pioneering work on "The Interpretation of Dreams," Freud writes,

> For psychological investigation shows that the dream is the first member of a class of abnormal psychical phenomena of which further members, such as hysterical phobias, obsessions and delusions, are bound for practical reasons to be a matter of concern to physicians. . . . Dreams can make no such claim to practical importance; but their theoretical value as a paradigm is on the other hand proportionately greater. Anyone who has failed to explain the origin of dream-images can scarcely hope to understand phobias, obsessions, or delusions. . . . (4:xxiii)

11. 5:514.

12. "New Introductory Lectures," 22:13 f.

13. *Ibid.*, 22:27 f. For his earlier views see "The Interpretation of Dreams."

14. "New Introductory Lectures," 22:14 f.

15. *Ibid.*, 22:9.

16. Whereas today censorship prohibits undesirable books, and confiscates and destroys editions, at an earlier time other methods of making books innocuous prevailed:

> One way would be for the offending passages to be thickly crossed through so that they were illegible. In that case they could not be transcribed, and the next copyist of the book would produce a text which was unexceptionable but which had gaps in certain passages, and so might be unintelligible in them. Another way, however, if the authorities were not satisfied with this, but wanted also to conceal any indication that the text had been mutilated, would be for them to proceed to distort the text. Single words would be left out or replaced by others, and new sentences interpolated. Best of all, the whole passage would be erased and a new one which said exactly the opposite put in its place. The next transcriber could then produce a text that aroused no suspicion but which was falsified. It no longer contained what the author wanted to say; and it is highly probable that the corrections had not been made in the direction of truth.
>
> If the analogy is not pursued too strictly, we may say that repression has the same relation to the other methods of defence

as omission has to distortion of the text, and we may discover in the different forms of this falsification parallels to the variety of ways in which the ego is altered. ("Analysis Terminable and Interminable," 23:236 f.)

17. "The Interpretation of Dreams," 5:567.

18. Ibid., 5:598.

19. "New Introductory Lectures," 22:28.

20. See especially " 'Wild' Psychoanalysis," vol. 11; "Remembering, Repeating, and Working-Through," vol. 12; "Lines of Advance in Psycho-Analytic Therapy," vol. 17; "Constructions in Analysis," vol. 23; "Analysis Terminable and Interminable," ibid.

21. "Introductory Lectures on Psychoanalysis," 16:435.

22. "Freud's Psychoanalytic Procedure," 7:252 f.

23. " 'Wild' Psychoanalysis," 11:225.

24. "Constructions in Analysis," 23:265.

25. "An Outline of Psycho-Analysis," 23:178.

26. "The Dynamics of Transference," 12:108.

27. "Remembering, Repeating, Working-Through," 12.

28. "Lines of Advance in Psycho-Analytic Therapy," 17:161.

29. Ibid., 17:163.

30. "Some Additional Notes on Dream-Interpretation as a Whole," 19:133.

31. TRANSLATOR'S NOTE: The official translation of Freud's concepts das Ich and das Es as the ego and the id was a serious mistake that both reflects and has contributed to the scientistic self-misunderstanding of metapsychology. Das Ich means the I and das Es the it. That is, they refer to the antithesis between reflexive, personal subjectivity and reified, impersonal objectivity. Freud's famous statement of the goal of psychoanalysis, "Wo Es war, soll Ich werden," should read in English, "Where it was, I shall become," or perhaps, "Where it-ness was, I-ness shall come into being." The choice of scientific Latin to render these terms in English reifies the I into an object by making it into an "ego," which is not the word used to express reflexivity, self-consciousness, and agency in English. As an "ego," the I is already an it, and the qualitative distinction between I and it is not visible in comparing the terms ego and id. At the same time, this scientistic terminology obscures the connection between the models of reflection of psychoanalysis and German Idealism. All this notwithstanding, the weight of recent tradition has made it seem advisable to retain "ego" and "id" in this translation.

32. "Analysis Terminable and Interminable," 23:247 f.

33. Ibid., 23:248.

34. 13:186 f.

35. The self-scrutiny acquired through training analysis is necessary not only to preserve the superiority of the analyst, who enters into interactions, keeps a certain distance within them, and transforms interaction patterns in a planned manner during the course of analysis. More important is the fact that the patient can only work himself up to the level of self-reflection at which the physician encounters him. Self-reflection is not a solitary movement; it is tied to the intersubjectivity of linguistic communication with an other. In the end, self-consciousness is constituted only on

the basis of mutual recognition. When the physician lets the patient free himself from the transference situation and releases him as an autonomous ego, the subjects must define themselves in relation to one another in such a way that the former patient knows that the identity of his ego is only possible through the identity of an other who recognizes him and whose identity in turn is dependent on his recognition.

36. "The Ego and the Id," vol. 19; "Inhibitions, Symptoms, and Anxiety," vol. 20; "New Introductory Lectures on Psychoanalysis," vol. 22, and "An Outline of Psychoanalysis," vol. 23.

37. "New Introductory Lectures," 22:68.

38. "An Outline of Psychoanalysis," 23:162.

39. "Negation," 19:238.

40. TRANSLATOR'S NOTE: Antriebspotential: Antrieb means drive, motive force, impetus, impulse. I have used "impulse" instead of "drive" in order to avoid objectivistic and deterministic implications.

41. TRANSLATOR'S NOTE: The word "surplus" stands for the German "überschiessend," literally "overshooting," and, in this context, "going beyond limits." "Surplus" eliminates the dynamic character of "überschiessend."

42. "Inhibitions, Symptoms, and Anxiety," 20:145.

43. Ibid., 20:97 f.

44. "The Ego and the Id," 19:20.

45. In Sprachzerstörung und -Rekonstruktion (Frankfurt am Main: Suhrkamp, 1970), Alfred Lorenzer has elaborated very clearly this concept of repression as a deformation of ordinary language into a private language in terms of Freud's own example of little Hans' phobia of horses.

46. "New Introductory Lectures," 22:68 f.

47. Starting with his study of melancholia, Freud conceives internalization as the mechanism through which an abandoned love object "is re-established internally." Thus an identification can be preserved even if the object cathexis must be dissolved. The model for internalization is the internal establishment of the abandoned parental objects, which, combined with the normal passing of the Oedipal situation, "institutes" the super-ego.

48. "The Ego and the Id," 19:52 f.

49. "An Outline of Psychoanalysis," 23:181 f.

Chapter Eleven

1. "An Autobiographical Study," 20.

2. "What else can it be?" ("Some Elementary Lessons in Psychoanalysis," 23:282).

3. "New Introductory Lectures," 22:159.

4. "Some Elementary Lessons," 23:282.

5. "An Outline of Psychoanalysis," 23:196.

6. "An Outline of Psychoanalysis," 23:182.

7. The three parts that Freud sent to Fliess in October 1895 were first published in 1950 as an appendix to the collection of letters Aus den Anfängen der Psychoanalyse, translated as Origins of Psychoanalysis (New York: Basic Books). See Ernest Jones, The Life and Work of Sigmund Freud (New York: Basic Books, 1953), 1:379 ff.

8. See Jones, *loc. cit.*, p. 385.
9. "The Interpretation of Dreams," 5:536.
10. *Ibid.*, 5:537.
11. *Ibid.*, 5:598.
12. *Ibid.*, 5:598 f.
13. "An Autobiographical Study," 20:22.
14. "Remembering, Repeating, and Working-Through," 12:155 f.
15. "Recommendations to Physicians Practising Psychoanalysis," 12:114.
16. "Analysis Terminable and Interminable," 23:225.
17. "New Introductory Lectures," 22:22.
18. Or quasi-action: selection is a substitute for the actual manipulation of the initial conditions.
19. Alfred Lorenzer, *Kritik des psychoanalytischen Symbolbegriffs* and *Sprachzerstörung und -Rekonstruktion* (both published in Frankfurt am Main in 1970 by Suhrkamp Verlag).
20. Alasdair McIntyre's separation of motive and cause in *The Unconscious* (London: Routledge, 1958) makes this relationship unrecognizable.
21. TRANSLATOR'S NOTE: "*Vorgriff*," here translated as "anticipation," means an interpretive concept or model that pre-structures that to which it is applied.
22. See Arthur Danto, *Analytical Philosophy of History* (Cambridge: Cambridge Univ. Press, 1965), p. 143 ff. TRANSLATOR'S NOTE: The German *Geschichte*, like the French *histoire*, means both "history" and "story."
23. See Chapter 8 above.
24. "Lines of Advance in Psycho-Analytic Therapy," 17:167.
25. "Constructions in Analysis," 23:262 f.
26. "Remarks on the Theory and Practice of Dream-Interpretation," 19:115.
27. See McIntyre, *op. cit.*, p. 112 ff.
28. "Constructions in Analysis," 23:262.
29. "In short, we conduct ourselves on the model of a familiar figure in one of Nestroy's farces—the manservant who has a single answer on his lips to every question or objection: 'It will all become clear in the course of future developments.' " (*Ibid.*, 23:265.)
30. "Introductory Lectures on Psychoanalysis," 16:436.
31. See Danto, *op. cit.*, chapters X, XI (p. 201 ff.).

Chapter Twelve

1. "New Introductory Lectures," 22:179.
2. TRANSLATOR'S NOTE: The German "*Kultur*" means both culture and civilization.
3. "An Outline of Psychoanalysis," 17:195.
4. "Civilization and Its Discontents," 21:144.
5. "Introductory Lectures on Psychoanalysis," 16:312.
6. "The Claims of Psychoanalysis to Scientific Interest," 13:186.

7. *Ibid.*
8. "Civilization and Its Discontents," 21:89 ff.
9. "The Future of an Illusion," 21:5 f.
10. *Ibid.*, 21:6.
11. *Ibid.*, 21:10.
12. *Ibid.*, 21:31.
13. *Ibid.*, 21:12.
14. See above, p. 52 ff.
15. "The Future of an Illusion," 21:46.
16. Freud developed this idea with reference to the taboo on killing. See *ibid.*, 21:40 ff.
17. *Ibid.*, 21:9. See also "New Introductory Lectures," 22.
18. On this see Theodor W. Adorno, "Weltgeist und Naturgeschichte," in *Negative Dialektik*, p. 293 f.
19. Even Herbert Marcuse's excellent interpretation of the social theory implicit in Freud's works does not completely avoid this danger. See his *Eros and Civilization* (Boston: Beacon, 1955).
20. "The Future of an Illusion," 21:55 f. Freud distinguished between need and interest. Need dispositions are components of the "id." We speak of interests when motivations are linked to ego functions. Paradoxically expressed, interests are ego needs. Taking this distinction as our starting point, we can correlate the knowledge-constitutive interests with ego functions. Reality-testing is based on a cognitive capacity that develops in the behavioral system of instrumental action and in intelligent adaptation to external conditions of life. The technical cognitive interest in expanding the power of technical control over objectified processes corresponds to this operational learning of feedback-controlled behavioral rules. Censorship of instincts, in contrast, presupposes a cognitive capacity that takes form in interaction structures by means of identification and internalization. The practical cognitive interest in securing the intersubjectivity of mutual understanding corresponds to this moral learning of social roles. Finally, the synthesis of id and super-ego, that is the integration of unconscious elements into the ego, takes place through a cognitive capacity that arises in pathological contexts of specifically distorted communication. The emancipatory cognitive interest in the undoing of repression and false consciousness corresponds to this self-reflective learning process. However, in so correlating the knowledge-constitutive interests with ego functions in the framework of the structural model, we must remain aware that this very model of ego, id, and super-ego is derived from experiences of reflection and is thus situated at the meta-theoretical level. As long as this is clear, an interpretation of knowledge-constitutive interests in concepts of metapsychology cannot support the reductive psychologization of the connection of knowledge and interest. On the other hand, not much is gained by such an interpretation. For the further analysis of the knowledge-constitutive interests entails abandoning metapsychology and indeed the whole level of the logic of inquiry and returning to the objective structure of the history of the human species. Here again it becomes clear that epistemology can be elaborated only as social theory.
21. Friedrich Nietzsche, *Werke*, 2d ed., ed. by Karl Schlechta (Munich: Hanser, 160), 3:486.

22. *Ibid.*, 1:1021.
23. *Ibid.*, 3:343.
24. *Ibid.*, 1:1044.
25. *Ibid.*, 3:862.
26. *Ibid.*, 1:217.
27. *Ibid.*, 1:231.
28. *Ibid.*, 1:232.
29. *Ibid.*, 1:281.
30. *Ibid.*, 3:814. (Gadamer's foundation of philosophical hermeneutics still unavowedly obeys this intention. See the foreword to the second edition of Gadamer, *op. cit.*)
31. Nietzsche, 3:442.
32. *Ibid.*, 3:440.
33. *Ibid.*, 3:526.
34. *Ibid.*, 3:440.
35. *Ibid.*, 3:726.
36. *Ibid.*, 3:903.
37. *Ibid.*, 3:560.
38. *Ibid.*, 3:499.
39. *Ibid.*, 3:446.
40. *Ibid.*, 1:471.
41. *Ibid.*, 3:790 f.

Appendix

1. Friedrich W. J. von Schelling, *Werke*, edited by Manfred Schröter (Munich: Beck, 1958–59), 3:299.
2. Bruno Snell, "Theorie und Praxis," in *Die Entdeckung des Geistes*, 3d ed. (Hamburg: Claassen, 1955), p. 401 ff.; Georg Picht, "Der Sinn der Unterscheidung von Theorie und Praxis in der griechischen Philosophie," in *Evangelische Ethik* (1964), 8:321 ff.
3. "Traditionelle und kritische Theorie," in *Zeitschrift für Sozialforschung*, 6:245 ff. Reprinted in Max Horkheimer, *Kritische Theorie*, edited by Alfred Schmidt (Frankfurt am Main: Fischer, 1968), pp. 137–191.
4. The appendix was the basis of my inaugural lecture at the University of Frankfurt am Main on June 28, 1965. Bibliographical notes are restricted to a few references.
5. *Die Krisis der europäischen Wissenschaften und die transzendentale Phänomenologie* in *Gesammelte Werke* (The Hague: Martinus Nijhoff, 1950), vol. 6.
6. See Gérard Gäfgen, *Theorie der wirtschaftlichen Entscheidung* (Tübingen: Mohr, 1963).
7. This path has been marked out by Karl-Otto Apel. See Chapter 10, n. 1, above.
8. See Popper's *The Logic of Scientific Discovery*, and my paper "Analytische Wissenschaftstheorie," in *Zeugnisse* (Frankfurt am Main: Europäische Verlagsanstalt, 1963), p. 473 ff.
9. I concur with the analyses in Part II of Hans-Georg Gadamer, *Wahrheit und Methode*.

10. Ernst Topitsch, editor, *Logik der Sozialwissenschaften* (Cologne: 1965).

11. Theodor W. Adorno, *Zur Metakritik der Erkenntnistheorie.*

12. Morton White, *Toward Reunion in Philosophy* (Cambridge: Harvard University Press, 1956).

13. See my essay "Dogmatismus, Vernunft und Entscheidung" (Dogmatism, Reason, and Decision) in *Theorie und Praxis.*

14. In *One-Dimensional Man* (Boston: Beacon, 1964) Herbert Marcuse has analyzed the dangers of the reduction of reason to technical rationality and the reduction of society to the dimension of technical control. In another context, Helmut Schelsky has made the same diagnosis:

> With a scientific civilization that man himself creates according to plan, a new peril has entered the world: the danger that man will develop himself only in external actions of altering the environment, and keep and deal with everything, himself and other human beings, at this object level of constructive action. This new self-alienation of man, which can rob him of his own and others' identity . . . is the danger of the creator losing himself in his work, the constructor in his construction. Man may recoil from completely transcending himself toward self-produced objectivity, toward constructed being; yet he works incessantly at extending this process of scientific self-objectification.

See Schelsky's *Einsamkeit und Freiheit* (Hamburg: 1963), p. 299.

Index